diabetic LIVING® HEALTHY MAKEOVERS for Diabetes™

Houghton Mifflin Harcourt

Boston New York
2017

Library of Congress Cataloging-in-Publication Data is available.

ISBN: 978-0-544-80064-9 (paperback);
978-0-544-80031-1 (ebk)

Meredith Corporation
Diabetic Living® Healthy Makeovers for Diabetes™

Editorial Director: Doug Kouma

Creative Director: Michelle Bilyeu

Contributing Project Manager: Shelli McConnell,
Purple Pear Publishing, Inc.

Design and Layout: Wendy Musgrave

Copy Editor: Gretchen Kauffman

Cover Art Director: Nikki Sanders

Cover Photographer: Blaine Moats

Cover Food Stylist: Jennifer Peterson

Diabetic Living® Test Kitchen Director: Lynn Blanchard

Diabetic Living® Test Kitchen Chef: Carla Christian, RD, LD

Houghton Mifflin Harcourt

Editorial Director: Cindy Kitchel

Executive Editor: Anne Ficklen

Editorial Associate: Molly Aronica

Managing Editor: Marina Padakis Lowry

Production Editor: Helen Seachrist

Art Director: Tai Blanche

Production Director: Tom Hyland

Printed in the United States of America
DOW 10 9 8 7 6 5 4 3 2 1
4500635170

Keep enjoying the foods you love by making them healthier.

A diagnosis of diabetes or prediabetes means changes in your life, but it doesn't mean you have to give up all your favorite foods. Instead, it means approaching cooking and eating in a more thoughtful way.

This book will show you easy ways to transition your cooking with recipes that cut carbohydrates without sacrificing flavor and satisfaction by suggesting more-healthful ingredients and demonstrating diabetes-smart cooking techniques. Portion control is part of the equation, too, so we give you an easy guide for filling your plate *(page 150)*.

You will find dishes that your whole family will enjoy—everything from breakfasts to desserts. We've lightened your favorites *(page 166)* and created healthful versions of restaurant classics *(page 206)*. Plus, we've included new recipes with tricks to add big flavor without salt or extra fat.

Discover how easy it is to eat well and feel great by making over your cooking.

The *Diabetic Living*® Editors

27

90

240

TABLE OF
Contents
Healthy Makeovers for Diabetes™

Remake
YOUR PANTRY

Fill your pantry and refrigerator with the ingredients you'll need to prepare the best-quality meals for you and your family. Stock the shelves with whole grain pastas, grains (such as bulgur, brown rice, and quinoa), and cereals. Look for reduced-fat, reduced-sodium versions of foods like evaporated milk, yogurt, tomatoes, and broth. Keep quick-thaw items like fish and vegetables in the freezer. And use dried herbs, salt-free seasonings, citrus, and vinegars to brighten flavors without salt.

Integral to many breakfast dishes, milk is a good source of calcium and protein. Fat-free milk saves you 45 calories per cup compared with 2 percent milk.

MILK

Minimally processed hot cereals typically have little, if any, added sweeteners. These include steel-cut oats and muesli which are rich in heart-healthy whole grains.

HOT CEREAL

Bran cereal typically packs 10–14 grams of fiber per ½-cup serving, a good start to meeting your daily fiber quota. Opt for bran cereal that contains oat fiber and/or psyllium, which may help lower LDL (bad) cholesterol.

BRAN CEREAL

Egg whites sold in refrigerated cartons lend hunger-satisfying protein to your breakfast without the cholesterol found in whole eggs, so you can enjoy them often.

EGG WHITES

Pantry Picks:
Breakfast

Simplify your morning by keeping healthful choices like these on hand. Build your breakfast by balancing protein and quality carbohydrates to stay energized throughout the morning.

Healthier Swaps

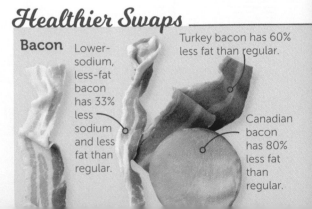

Bacon Lower-sodium, less-fat bacon has 33% less sodium and less fat than regular.

Turkey bacon has 60% less fat than regular.

Canadian bacon has 80% less fat than regular.

NATURAL PEANUT BUTTER

Natural peanut butter has a layer of oil at the top that's stirred in before using. It's generally unsweetened and contains healthful fats, but not the cholesterol-raising hydrogenated oils in conventional peanut butter.

HASH BROWNS

Shredded hash brown potatoes supply heart-healthy potassium and the antioxidant vitamin C. Use them in breakfast casseroles, omelets, and potato pancakes.

GREEK YOGURT

Plain fat-free Greek yogurt is an excellent source of protein and provides beneficial bacteria, or probiotics. Preliminary studies suggest some probiotics found in yogurt may boost the body's production of a hormone that reduces hunger.

FROZEN FRUIT

Frozen fruits such as berries, mango chunks, and sliced peaches are picked at their nutritional peak, so vitamins A and C and other nutrients are locked in. Frozen fruit also delivers heart-protective antioxidants.

Egg

1 egg

¼ cup egg substitute has 50% fewer calories than a whole egg.

Two egg whites have no cholesterol.

Cream Cheese

Reduced-fat cream cheese has 215 fewer calories than regular.

Low-sodium black beans shine in salads, wraps, and Mexican dishes. A ½-cup serving packs 7 grams fiber, which may help lower LDL (bad) cholesterol.

BLACK BEANS

Whole wheat sandwich thins are filling and average only 90–100 calories and 20–22 grams carbohydrate per serving, making them a smart sandwich base.

WHOLE WHEAT SANDWICH THINS

Whole wheat tortillas vary in nutrition based on size and brand. Keep them diabetes-friendly by selecting smaller tortillas that are high in fiber, low in fat (no more than 3 grams fat per serving), and free of trans fat.

WHOLE WHEAT TORTILLAS

With lettuce, darker leaves hint at higher nutrient content. For example, 1 cup shredded romaine packs 80 percent of daily needs for vitamin A (beta-carotene) compared with 7 percent in 1 cup iceberg lettuce.

LETTUCE

Pantry Picks:
Lunch

Make lunch a no-brainer with nutritious staples like these. Use them to make salads, sandwiches, and other quick noontime favorites.

Healthier Swaps

Turkey Deli Meat Lower-sodium turkey deli meat has 25% less sodium than regular.

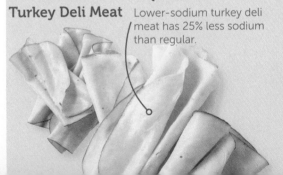

Salad dressing doesn't have to be fat-free. In fact, a bit of fat boosts the body's ability to absorb antioxidants from vegetables. Choose dressing with less than 240 milligrams sodium per serving.

SALAD DRESSING ❯

Tomatoes have heart-healthy potassium and the antioxidant lycopene. A study found women who ate two raw romas daily for a month had a significant boost in HDL (good) cholesterol.

TOMATOES ❯

Start meals with reduced-sodium vegetable soup. Eating a broth-base soup first at mealtime helps fill you up so you eat fewer higher-calorie foods.

VEGETABLE SOUP ❯

Skinless, boneless chicken breast is low in fat and high in hunger-busting protein. Cook and shred plain chicken breasts to use in soups, salads, and wraps.

CHICKEN BREAST ❯

Salsa is a tasty, low-calorie topping for more than Mexican fare. Choose one with less than 140 milligrams sodium per serving.

SALSA ❯

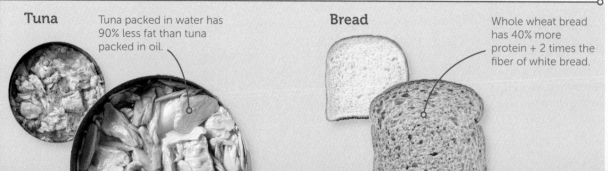

Tuna

Tuna packed in water has 90% less fat than tuna packed in oil.

Bread

Whole wheat bread has 40% more protein + 2 times the fiber of white bread.

11

Spinach is rich in antioxidant vitamins A (beta-carotene) and C. Because spinach ranks sixth on the Environmental Working Group's list of most highly pesticide-contaminated produce items, choose organic when you can.

SPINACH

Extra virgin olive oil is overwhelmingly higher in polyphenols (a type of antioxidant) compared to refined olive oil. Newer research suggests these polyphenols may contribute more to olive oil's cardiovascular benefits than the monounsaturated fat in olive oil.

OLIVE OIL

Tofu is a low-fat, protein-rich alternative to meat. Extra-firm tofu is best at mimicking the texture of meat in recipes.

TOFU

Pasta sauce made from tomatoes is an excellent source of lycopene, which may help protect against diabetic retinopathy and cardiovascular disease. Look for lower-sugar pasta sauce to top any number of healthful dishes, including baked chicken and fish.

PASTA SAUCE

Brown rice is a heart-healthy whole grain. It's as quick and convenient as refined white rice when you choose instant, frozen, and shelf-stable microwavable options.

BROWN RICE

Pantry Picks:
Dinner

Have healthful options like these on hand for creating family-appealing dinners even when time is tight.

Healthier Swaps

Ground Beef

1 lb. extra-lean ground beef (95% lean) has about 500 fewer calories than regular (80% lean).

LENTILS

Lentils may be small, but they're packed with fiber and plant protein. In one large study, eating just one daily serving of legumes, such as lentils, was linked to a 40 percent lower risk of heart attack.

BROTH

Reduced-sodium and unsalted broths and stocks make quick soup starters and also provide a low-fat, low-calorie substitute for the oil typically used to sauté vegetables.

FROZEN SALMON

Wild-caught frozen salmon fillets are rich in heart-healthy omega-3 fats and an excellent source of hunger-satisfying protein. Buy plain fillets and season them yourself (try a squeeze of fresh lemon juice) to avoid excess sodium.

BROCCOLI

Broccoli has just 6 grams of carbohydrate and 30 calories per 1-cup serving, and it's packed with vitamin C and other protective antioxidants. Both the florets and stalks can be used in soups, salads, and many other dishes.

FROZEN VEGGIES

Frozen mixed vegetables, available in many combinations, are an easy, colorful way to boost the fiber, vitamin, and antioxidant content of meals.

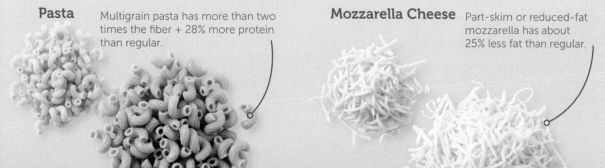

Pasta Multigrain pasta has more than two times the fiber + 28% more protein than regular.

Mozzarella Cheese Part-skim or reduced-fat mozzarella has about 25% less fat than regular.

Apples are rich in health-protective antioxidants. Studies indicate that people who eat an apple a day have a significantly lower risk of dying from cardiovascular disease.

APPLES

Sweet peppers are perfect for crunching. And they're a super source of vitamin C, a powerful antioxidant that helps protect blood vessels from the free-radical damage that contributes to atherosclerosis.

SWEET PEPPERS

Reduced-fat cheese is a good compromise between higher-calorie regular cheese and rubbery fat-free cheese. Plus, newer research suggests certain fats unique to dairy foods may help reduce risk of obesity and diabetes—so enjoy a little dairy fat.

REDUCED-FAT CHEESE

Pantry Picks:
Snacks

Good snacks should give you quick energy and staying power. Keep healthful choices on hand that contain protein or fiber and are low in refined sugar.

Simple Snack Ideas

Strawberries and Yogurt
¾ cup sliced strawberries + 5 oz. plain fat-free Greek yogurt

Low-fat cottage cheese is a protein-rich snack that pairs well with fruit and raw vegetables. If sodium is an issue for you, buy the low-sodium version.

COTTAGE CHEESE

Nuts, when eaten regularly, may help lower total and LDL (bad) cholesterol levels, as well as reduce heart disease risk. When nuts are consumed with carbohydrate-rich foods, they may help check the rise in blood sugar.

NUTS

Popcorn is a whole grain snack. Make your own microwave popcorn by drizzling a bit of olive oil on ¼ cup popcorn kernels. Place them in a small brown paper bag, fold the top down a couple times, lay the bag on its side, and microwave on high about 2 minutes.

POPCORN

Dry-roasted soybeans are a lower-calorie alternative to nuts. They give you the crunch you crave along with about 14 grams protein per ¼ cup.

DRY-ROASTED SOY BEANS

Dark chocolate is rich in flavanols, which may help lower blood pressure, improve the function of the inner lining of arteries, reduce inflammation, and lower cholesterol.

DARK CHOCOLATE

Carrots and Curds

¾ cup raw carrot chips +
½ cup small-curd low-fat cottage cheese

PB Apples

1 small apple
+ 2 Tbsp. PB2 powdered peanut butter prepared with water

15

Make Over YOUR MORNINGS

Make your morning kick-start a priority with low-fat, low-carb, and high-protein choices that will nourish and sustain you and your family. You'll find recipes featuring foods high in complex carbohydrates, fiber, or protein that can help rev your metabolism without slowing you down. Whether you need something fast or have time to sit down and enjoy a hot breakfast, remember to eat the most important meal of the day!

Out-of-Hand
BREAKFAST

Sometimes you don't have the time to sit down for breakfast. Treat yourself right with a nutritious and tasty option that you can eat on the go.

Apple-Cran-Oat Breakfast Cookies

SERVINGS 20 (1 cookie each)
CARB. PER SERVING 34 g
PREP 25 minutes   BAKE 15 minutes
COOL 5 minutes

- 2$\frac{1}{2}$ cups regular rolled oats
- 1 cup almond meal
- $\frac{1}{2}$ cup whole wheat flour
- $\frac{1}{4}$ cup nonfat dry milk powder
- 1 tsp. baking soda
- 1 tsp. ground cinnamon
- $\frac{1}{4}$ tsp. salt
- 1 orange
- 1 cup packed brown sugar*
- 2 eggs, lightly beaten
- 1 6-oz. carton plain fat-free Greek yogurt
- 1$\frac{1}{2}$ tsp. vanilla
- 1$\frac{1}{2}$ cups chopped apple
- 1$\frac{1}{2}$ cups coarsely chopped fresh cranberries
- $\frac{2}{3}$ cup powdered sugar*

1. Preheat oven to 350°F. Line two cookie sheets with parchment paper.
2. In a large bowl combine the first seven ingredients (through salt). Remove 2 tsp. zest and squeeze 1 Tbsp. juice from the orange. In another bowl stir together the zest, brown sugar, eggs, yogurt, and 1 tsp. of the vanilla until well mixed. Stir egg mixture into oat mixture until evenly moistened. Fold in apple and cranberries.
3. Drop $\frac{1}{4}$-cup mounds of dough onto prepared cookie sheets. Pat each into a flattened circle (approximately $\frac{1}{2}$ inch thick). Bake about 15 minutes or until set and baked through. Cool 5 minutes on cookie sheets. Transfer to wire racks; cool completely.
4. For icing, whisk together powdered sugar, the orange juice, and the remaining $\frac{1}{2}$ tsp. vanilla. If needed, stir in enough additional orange juice, $\frac{1}{2}$ tsp. at a time, to make icing drizzling consistency. Drizzle icing over cookies. Let stand until icing is set.

*SUGAR SUBSTITUTES We do not recommend using sugar substitutes for this recipe.
TO STORE Layer cookies between sheets of waxed paper in an airtight container; cover. Store in the refrigerator up to 3 days or freeze up to 3 months. Let stand at room temperature 30 minutes before serving.

PER SERVING: 201 cal., 5 g total fat (1 g sat. fat), 19 mg chol., 111 mg sodium, 34 g carb. (4 g fiber, 17 g sugars), 7 g pro.

INGREDIENT MAKEOVER

Greek yogurt replaces vegetable oil in these cookies, cutting fat and bumping up protein and calcium.

19

INGREDIENT MAKEOVER

Bagel thins allow you to enjoy breakfast sandwiches with more fiber and fewer carbs than regular bagels.

Mango-Bacon Breakfast Sandwiches

SERVINGS 4 (1 sandwich each)
CARB. PER SERVING 32 g
PREP 20 minutes   CHILL up to 3 days
COOK 3 minutes

- 8 slices lower-sodium, less-fat bacon
- 1 green onion
- 1 medium mango, halved, seeded, peeled, and thinly sliced
- 4 whole wheat bagel thins, split
- 4 ³/₄-oz. slices reduced-fat Monterey Jack cheese with jalapeño peppers or Colby and Monterey Jack cheese
- Nonstick cooking spray

1. In a medium skillet cook bacon according to package directions until crisp. Drain on paper towels. Cut bacon slices crosswise in half.

2. Thinly slice the green onion, keeping white and green parts separate; reserve the white part for another use. Top bagel thin bottoms with bacon slices, mango, green onion, and cheese. Add bagel thin tops. Tightly wrap individual sandwiches with plastic wrap. Chill up to 3 days.

3. Unwrap sandwiches. Lightly coat an unheated panini press, covered indoor electric grill, or large nonstick skillet with cooking spray. Heat over medium heat or according to manufacturer's directions. Lightly coat outsides of sandwiches with cooking spray.

4. Place sandwiches, in batches if necessary, on panini press, grill, or skillet. For press or grill, close lid; grill 2 to 3 minutes or until toasted. (If using skillet, place a heavy saucepan or skillet on sandwiches. Cook 2 to 4 minutes or until toasted, turning once.)

PER SERVING: 258 cal., 9 g total fat (4 g sat. fat), 18 mg chol., 482 mg sodium, 32 g carb. (6 g fiber, 10 g sugars), 16 g pro.

Bacon-and-Egg Muffins

SERVINGS 12 (1 muffin each)
CARB. PER SERVING 17 g
PREP 30 minutes BAKE 15 minutes
COOL 5 minutes

- 4 slices lower-sodium, less-fat bacon, cut into thirds
- 5 eggs
- 2 Tbsp. water
- Dash black pepper
- Nonstick cooking spray
- 1 cup all-purpose flour
- 1/2 cup yellow cornmeal
- 2 Tbsp. sugar*
- 2 tsp. baking powder
- 1/4 tsp. salt
- 1 cup low-fat milk (1%)
- 3 Tbsp. vegetable oil or melted butter
- 3 Tbsp. unsweetened applesauce
- 1/2 cup shredded reduced-fat cheddar cheese (2 oz.)

1. Preheat oven to 400°F. In a large skillet cook bacon just until it begins to crisp. Drain, reserving drippings. Return 2 tsp. of the drippings to the skillet. For scrambled eggs, in a small bowl beat three of the eggs, the water, and pepper. Cook egg mixture in hot skillet over medium heat, without stirring, until mixture begins to set on bottom and around edges. With a large spatula, lift and fold the partially cooked egg mixture so the uncooked portion flows underneath. Continue cooking over medium heat until egg mixture is cooked through but is still glossy and moist. Transfer to a small bowl.
2. Coat twelve 2^1/2-inch muffin cups with cooking spray. In a medium bowl stir together the next five ingredients (through salt). Make a well in the center of the flour mixture. In a separate bowl whisk together the remaining two eggs, the milk, oil, and applesauce. Add egg mixture all at once to flour mixture. Stir just until moistened (batter

should be lumpy). Fold in scrambled eggs and cheese. Spoon batter into muffin cups (cups will be full). Place one bacon piece on each muffin.
3. Bake 15 to 17 minutes or until light brown and a toothpick inserted in centers comes out clean. Cool in cups on a wire rack 5 minutes. Run a small metal spatula or table knife around edges of muffins to loosen and remove from cups. Serve warm.
*SUGAR SUBSTITUTE Choose Splenda Sugar Blend. Follow package directions to use product amount equivalent to 2 Tbsp. sugar.
SERVING SUGGESTION Make sure you get enough protein to get you through the morning. Pair these warm and delicious muffins with a glass of kefir or a small bowl of fat-free Greek yogurt.

PER SERVING: 159 cal., 7 g total fat (2 g sat. fat), 83 mg chol., 231 mg sodium, 17 g carb. (1 g fiber, 4 g sugars), 7 g pro

PER SERVING: Same as above, except 156 g cal. 16 g carb (3 g sugars).

INGREDIENT MAKEOVER

Reduce fat in baked goods by substituting **unsweetened applesauce** for some of the vegetable oil.

Lemon-Strawberry Chia Seed Muffins

SERVINGS 12 (1 muffin each)
CARB. PER SERVING 24 g or 19 g
PREP 20 minutes   BAKE 15 minutes
COOL 5 minutes

- $1/4$ cup water
- 2 Tbsp. chia seeds, ground
- $3/4$ cup low-fat (1%) milk
- $1/4$ cup canola oil
- $1/4$ cup plain fat-free Greek yogurt
- 1 cup all-purpose flour
- 1 cup regular rolled oats
- $1/2$ cup sugar*
- 1 Tbsp. baking powder
- 1 Tbsp. lemon zest
- $1/4$ tsp. salt
- $1/2$ cup chopped strawberries

1. Preheat oven to 375°F. Coat twelve $2^1/2$-inch muffin cups with *nonstick cooking spray.* In a bowl combine the water and chia seeds. Whisk in milk, oil, and yogurt.

2. In a bowl combine the next six ingredients (through salt). Make a well in the center of flour mixture. Add chia mixture all at once to flour mixture; stir just until moistened (batter should be lumpy). Fold in strawberries.

3. Spoon batter into the prepared muffin cups, filling each cup about three-fourths full.

4. Bake 15 to 20 minutes or until a toothpick inserted near centers of muffins comes out clean. Cool in muffin cups on a wire rack 5 minutes. Remove from cups. Serve warm.

*SUGAR SUBSTITUTE Choose Splenda Sugar Blend. Follow package directions to use product amount equivalent to $1/2$ cup sugar.

PER SERVING: 157 cal., 6 g total fat (1 g sat. fat), 1 mg chol., 180 mg sodium, 24 g carb. (2 g fiber, 10 g sugars), 3 g pro.

PER SERVING WITH SUBSTITUTE: Same as above, except 144 cal., 19 g carb. (5 sugars).

Make Over Your Mornings

INGREDIENT MAKEOVER

Ground **chia seeds** mixed with water create a gelled mixture that is a great egg replacer in baked goods, cutting fat and cholesterol.

TEST KITCHEN TIP

Use a blender or spice grinder to grind the chia seeds.

Zucchini-Chocolate Chip Scones

SERVINGS 6 (1 scone each)
CARB. PER SERVING 29 g or 28 g
PREP 25 minutes   BAKE 13 minutes

- $3/4$ cup all-purpose flour
- $1/2$ cup whole wheat flour
- $1 1/2$ Tbsp. sugar*
- $3/4$ tsp. baking powder
- $1/4$ tsp. ground cinnamon
- $1/8$ tsp. ground nutmeg
- $1/8$ tsp. baking soda
- $1/8$ tsp. salt
- 2 Tbsp. butter, cut up
- $1/4$ cup refrigerated or frozen egg product, thawed, or 1 egg, lightly beaten
- $1/4$ cup buttermilk or sour milk**
- $1/2$ cup shredded zucchini
- $1/4$ cup miniature semisweet chocolate pieces

1. Preheat oven to 400°F. In a large bowl stir together the first eight ingredients (through salt). Using a pastry blender, cut in butter until mixture resembles coarse crumbs. Make a well in center of flour mixture.
2. In another bowl combine egg and buttermilk; stir in zucchini and chocolate pieces. Add buttermilk mixture all at once to flour mixture. Using a fork, stir just until moistened.
3. Turn dough out onto a lightly floured surface. Knead dough by folding and gently pressing it 10 to 12 strokes or until nearly smooth. Pat dough into a 6-inch circle. Cut dough circle into six wedges.
4. Place dough wedges 2 inches apart on an ungreased baking sheet. Bake 13 to 15 minutes or until edges are light brown. Remove scones from baking sheet; serve warm.
*SUGAR SUBSTITUTE Choose Splenda Sugar Blend. Follow package directions to use product amount equivalent to $1 1/2$ Tbsp. sugar

**TIP For sour milk, place $3/4$ tsp. lemon juice or vinegar in a glass measuring cup. Add enough fat-free milk to make $1/4$ cup total liquid; stir. Let the mixture stand 5 minutes before using.
TO STORE Cool scones on a wire rack. Place scones in a freezer container or plastic freezer bag. Freeze up to 1 month. To serve, let frozen scones stand at room temperature 30 minutes. Place scones on a baking sheet; bake in a 350°F oven 8 to 10 minutes or until warm.

PER SERVING: 195 cal., 7 g total fat (4 g sat. fat), 11 mg chol., 201 mg sodium, 29 g carb. (2 g fiber, 9 g sugars), 5 g pro.

PER SERVING WITH SUBSTITUTE: Same as above, except 190 cal., 28 g carb. (8 sugars).

INGREDIENT MAKEOVER

Egg product is the go-to substitute for whole eggs when you want to eliminate the fat and cholesterol found in whole eggs without sacrificing quality.

Multigrain sandwich thins have more fiber and less fat than the plain English muffins typically used in breakfast sandwiches.

Mediterranean Breakfast Sandwiches

SERVINGS 2 (1 sandwich each)
CARB. PER SERVING 25 g
START TO FINISH 20 minutes

2 multigrain sandwich thins
2 tsp. olive oil
1 1/2 tsp. snipped fresh rosemary or 1/4 tsp. dried rosemary, crushed
2 eggs
1 cup fresh baby spinach
1 small tomato, cut into 4 thin slices
2 Tbsp. reduced-fat feta cheese
Dash kosher salt
Freshly ground black pepper

1. Preheat oven to 375°F. Split sandwich thins; brush cut sides with 1 tsp. of the olive oil. Place on baking sheet; toast in oven about 5 minutes or until edges are light brown and crisp.
2. Meanwhile, in a large skillet heat the remaining 1 tsp. olive oil and the rosemary over medium-high heat. Break eggs, one at a time, into skillet. Cook about 1 minute or until whites are set but yolks are still runny. Break yolks with spatula. Flip eggs; cook until done. Remove from heat.
3. Top two sandwich thin halves with spinach, tomato slices, eggs, and feta cheese. Sprinkle with the salt and pepper. Top with remaining thin halves.

PER SERVING: 242 cal., 12 g total fat (3 g sat. fat), 214 mg chol., 501 mg sodium, 25 g carb. (6 g fiber, 3 g sugars), 13 g pro.

Mixed-Berry Smoothies

SERVINGS 2 ($1^{1}/_{4}$ cups each)
CARB. PER SERVING 33 g
START TO FINISH 5 minutes

2 cups frozen mixed berries or
  1 cup frozen blueberries plus
  1 cup frozen strawberries
1 6-oz. carton blueberry fat-free
  yogurt with artificial sweetener
$^{1}/_{2}$ cup light cranberry-raspberry
  juice
$^{1}/_{3}$ cup nonfat dry milk powder

1. In a blender combine all ingredients. Cover and blend until smooth, scraping down sides of blender as needed. Pour into two glasses or insulated to-go cups. Serve immediately. If desired, top with fresh blueberries.

PER SERVING: 161 cal., 0 g total fat, 4 mg chol., 116 mg sodium, 33 g carb. (5 g fiber, 15 g sugars), 8 g pro.

INGREDIENT MAKEOVER

Use **yogurt with artificial sweetener** and **light cranberry-raspberry juice** to significantly reduce the calories, carbs, and sugars typically found in smoothies.

Make-Ahead
BREAKFAST

Make your morning less rushed. Spend a little time prepping the night before and wake up to a hearty and healthful meal.

Overnight Chia-Almond Pancakes with Berry Syrup

SERVINGS 8 (2 pancakes + 2 Tbsp. syrup + $1^1/2$ tsp. almonds each)
CARB. PER SERVING 37 g or 36 g
PREP 20 minutes CHILL 24 hours
COOK 6 minutes

- $1^1/4$ cups white whole wheat flour
- 1 cup all-purpose flour
- 2 Tbsp. chia seeds, ground
- 1 Tbsp. sugar*
- 1 Tbsp. baking powder
- $1/2$ tsp. salt
- $2^1/4$ cups unsweetened original soy milk
- 2 eggs, lightly beaten
- $1/4$ cup canola oil
- $1/2$ tsp. almond extract
- 1 recipe Berry Syrup
- $1/4$ cup slivered almonds, toasted

1. In a large bowl stir together the first six ingredients (through salt). In another bowl combine soy milk, eggs, oil, and almond extract. Cover and chill bowls separately up to 24 hours.

2. To make pancakes, add soy milk mixture all at once to flour mixture. Stir just until moistened (batter should be slightly lumpy).

3. For each pancake, pour about $1/4$ cup batter onto a hot, lightly greased griddle or heavy skillet; spread batter. (If batter is too thick, thin with a little additional soy milk.) Cook over medium heat 3 to 4 minutes per side or until pancakes are lightly golden. Turn over when surfaces are bubbly and edges are slightly dry.

4. To serve, drizzle pancakes with Berry Syrup and sprinkle with almonds.
BERRY SYRUP In a small saucepan melt $1/3$ cup low-sugar strawberry preserves over medium-low heat. In a bowl whisk together $1/3$ cup orange juice and $1/2$ tsp. cornstarch until smooth; add all at once to preserves. Cook and stir over medium-low heat until thickened and bubbly. Cook and stir 1 minute more. Stir in $1/2$ cup chopped strawberries.
*SUGAR SUBSTITUTE Choose Splenda Sugar Blend. Follow package directions to use product amount equivalent to 1 Tbsp. sugar.

TO FREEZE Layer cooked pancakes between sheets of wax paper. Place in an airtight container; cove. Freeze up to 1 month. To reheat, microwave one frozen pancake wrapped in waxed paper 30 to 40 seconds or until heated (or remove from wax paper and toast frozen pancake in a toaster 2 to 3 minutes or until heated).

PER SERVING: 287 cal., 12 g total fat (1 g sat. fat), 47 mg chol., 370 mg sodium, 37 g carb. (4 g fiber, 7 g sugars), 9 g pro.

PER SERVING WITH SUBSTITUTE: Same as above, except 285 cal., 36 g carb. (6 g sugars)

INGREDIENT MAKEOVER

Chia seeds add fiber and help keep you feeling full longer.

For a dairy-free alternative, use **soy milk**, which is naturally cholesterol free.

Pumpkin-Spiced Breakfast Bread Pudding

SERVINGS 8 ($^3/_4$ cup each)
CARB. PER SERVING 36 g or 31 g
PREP 20 minutes   CHILL 2 hours
BAKE 30 minutes   STAND 10 minutes

   Nonstick cooking spray
12   oz. baguette-style French
     bread, cut into 1-inch cubes
     and dried*
$1^1/_2$ cups fat-free milk
1   cup refrigerated or frozen
     egg product, thawed, or
     4 eggs, beaten
1   cup canned pumpkin
$^1/_3$ cup packed brown sugar**
1   tsp. pumpkin pie spice
4   oz. reduced-fat cream cheese
     (Neufchâtel), cut into small
     cubes
$^1/_2$ cup coarsely chopped pecans,
     toasted
1   tsp. powdered sugar**

1. Coat a 2-quart rectangular baking dish with cooking spray. Arrange bread cubes in prepared dish.

2. In a large bowl combine the next five ingredients (through pumpkin pie spice). Slowly pour egg mixture over bread cubes; press lightly with the back of a large spoon to moisten. Dot with cream cheese cubes. Cover with plastic wrap and chill 2 to 24 hours.

3. Let bread pudding stand at room temperature 30 minutes. Preheat oven to 350°F. Uncover dish. Bake 30 to 35 minutes or until center is puffed, golden, and registers 160°F near the center of the bread pudding. Remove from oven. Let stand on a wire rack 10 minutes. Sprinkle with pecans and powdered sugar.

*TIP To dry bread cubes, preheat oven to 300°F. Place bread cubes in an ungreased 15×10-inch baking pan. Bake 12 to 15 minutes or until crisp, stirring once or twice.

**SUGAR SUBSTITUTES Choose Splenda Brown Sugar Blend. Follow package directions to use product amount equivalent to $^1/_3$ cup brown sugar. We do not recommend using sugar substitute for the powdered sugar.

PER SERVING: 262 cal., 8 g total fat (2 g sat. fat), 11 mg chol., 354 mg sodium, 36 g carb. (2 g fiber, 14 g sugars), 9 g pro.

PER SERVING WITH SUBSTITUTE: Same as above, except 247 cal., 31 g carb. (9 g sugars), 351 mg sodium

INGREDIENT MAKEOVER

Fat-free milk and **egg product** are lower-fat alternatives to whole eggs and whole milk.

Reduced-fat cream cheese in a small amount adds creaminess.

Mexican Breakfast Burritos

SERVINGS 6 (1 burrito each)
CARB. PER SERVING 30 g
PREP 20 minutes   COOK 8 minutes
CHILL up to 3 days

- 2 green onions
- $\frac{3}{4}$ cup chopped green sweet pepper or poblano pepper
- 1 Tbsp. canola oil
- 2 cloves garlic, minced
- $\frac{1}{2}$ tsp. ground cumin
- $\frac{1}{8}$ to $\frac{1}{4}$ tsp. cayenne pepper
- 1 cup canned reduced-sodium black beans, rinsed and drained
- 6 eggs, lightly beaten
- $\frac{1}{2}$ cup shredded reduced-fat Mexican-style four-cheese blend
- $\frac{1}{3}$ cup salsa
- 2 Tbsp. snipped fresh cilantro
- 6 8-inch low-carb whole wheat or multi-grain tortillas

1. Thinly slice green onions, keeping the white and green parts separate. In a large nonstick skillet cook white parts of green onions and the sweet pepper in hot oil over medium heat 5 minutes, stirring occasionally. Add green parts of onions, the garlic, cumin, and cayenne pepper. Cook and stir 1 minute more. Stir in black beans.
2. Add eggs to bean mixture in skillet. Cook, without stirring, over medium-low heat, until mixture begins to set on the bottom and around the edges. Using a spatula or a large spoon, lift and fold the partially cooked egg mixture so the uncooked portion flows underneath. Continue cooking over medium heat 2 to 3 minutes or until egg mixture is cooked through but is still glossy and moist. Immediately remove from heat.
3. Add cheese, salsa, and cilantro to egg mixture. Stir gently to combine. Spoon egg mixture evenly onto tortillas just below the center. Fold bottom edge of each tortilla up and over filling. Fold in opposite sides; roll up.
4. To refrigerate, wrap each burrito tightly with plastic wrap. Refrigerate up to 3 days. (To freeze, wrap each burrito tightly with plastic wrap; wrap again with foil. Place in an airtight container; freeze up to 1 month.)
5. To serve, unwrap individual burrito; place on plate. Microwave, uncovered, on 50% power (medium) 3 to 4 minutes or until heated, turning once. (To serve frozen burritos, unwrap individual burrito; place on plate. Microwave, uncovered, on 30% power (medium-low) 8 to 10 minutes or until heated, turning twice.)
6. Cut burrito in half or wrap burrito halfway with foil to take on the go. If desired, serve with additional salsa.

PER SERVING: 265 cal., 11 g total fat (3 g sat. fat), 192 mg chol., 447 mg sodium, 30 g carb. (6 g fiber, 3 g sugars), 15 g pro.

INGREDIENT MAKEOVER

Sweet peppers and **beans** add volume to the burrito filling, so you use half as many eggs.

Refrigerator Maple-Date Muffins with Quinoa

SERVINGS 12 (4 mini muffins each)
CARB. PER SERVING 24 g
PREP 30 minutes   CHILL up to 3 days
BAKE 12 minutes

$\frac{1}{2}$ cup water
$\frac{1}{4}$ cup quinoa
4 pitted dates, chopped
$1\frac{1}{2}$ cups all-purpose flour
$\frac{1}{2}$ cup regular rolled oats
$1\frac{1}{2}$ tsp. baking powder
1 tsp. apple pie spice
$\frac{1}{4}$ tsp. baking soda
$\frac{1}{4}$ tsp. salt
$\frac{1}{2}$ cup buttermilk
$\frac{1}{3}$ cup unsweetened applesauce
$\frac{1}{3}$ cup canola oil
$\frac{1}{4}$ cup refrigerated or frozen
    egg product, thawed,
    or 1 egg, beaten
$\frac{1}{4}$ cup pure maple syrup

1. In a small saucepan bring water and quinoa to boiling; reduce heat. Cover and simmer 15 minutes or until tender and liquid is absorbed, adding dates the last 2 minutes of cooking. Remove from heat. Transfer to a bowl.
2. Meanwhile, in a large bowl stir together the next six ingredients (through salt). Add the remaining ingredients to the quinoa. Add quinoa mixture all at once to flour mixture, stirring just until moistened. Cover tightly with plastic wrap. Refrigerate up to 3 days (or bake immediately).
3. To bake, preheat oven to 375°F. Grease as many $1\frac{3}{4}$-inch muffin cups as desired. Spoon batter into the prepared muffin cups, filling each two-thirds full. Bake about 12 minutes or until a toothpick inserted near the centers comes out clean. If desired, lightly brush each muffin with additional maple syrup. Remove from muffin cups; serve warm.

STANDARD-SIZE MUFFINS: Prepare as directed spoon batter into desired number of $2\frac{1}{2}$-inch muffin cups. Bake 18 to 20 minutes or until a toothpick inserted near centers comes out clean. Makes 12 muffins (1 muffin each).

PER SERVING: 171 cal., 7 g total fat (1 g sat. fat), 1 mg chol., 157 mg sodium, 24 g carb. (1 g fiber, 7 g sugars), 3 g pro.

Make Over Your Mornings

INGREDIENT MAKEOVER

Quinoa adds fiber and protein.

Dates and **maple syrup** provide natural sweetness.

Unsweetened applesauce replaces some of the oil.

Egg product instead of whole eggs reduces fat and cholesterol.

Cajun Breakfast Strata

SERVINGS 6 (1 cup each)
CARB. PER SERVING 30 g
PREP 30 minutes CHILL 2 hours
BAKE 55 minutes STAND 10 minutes

$3/4$ cup chopped red or orange
sweet pepper
$1/2$ cup chopped onion
$1/2$ cup thinly sliced celery
1 Tbsp. canola oil
3 cups trimmed and torn fresh
collard greens or kale
2 cloves garlic, minced
$1/2$ tsp. black pepper
$1/8$ tsp. cayenne pepper
1 14.5-oz. can no-salt-added
diced tomatoes, drained
8 oz. whole grain baguette-style
bread, cubed
6 oz. smoked turkey sausage
or smoked andouille chicken
sausage, thinly sliced
$1^{3}/4$ cups fat-free milk
$1^{1}/2$ cups refrigerated or frozen
egg product, thawed, or
6 eggs, beaten

1. In a large skillet cook sweet pepper,
onion, and celery in hot oil over
medium heat 4 minutes, stirring
occasionally. Add next four ingredients
(through cayenne pepper). Cook 3 to
5 minutes more or until vegetables are
just tender, stirring occasionally. Stir in
drained tomatoes.
2. Lightly grease a 2-quart rectangular
baking dish. Arrange half the bread
cubes in an even layer in prepared dish.
Top with half the sausage and half the
tomato mixture. Repeat layers.
3. In a bowl whisk together milk and
eggs. Slowly pour over the layered
mixture in dish. Press down lightly with
the back of a large spoon. Cover and
chill 2 hours or up to 24 hours.

4. Preheat oven to 350°F. Bake,
uncovered, 55 to 60 minutes or until
160°F in center. Let stand on a wire
rack 10 minutes before serving.

PER SERVING: 247 cal., 7 g total fat
(1 g sat. fat), 16 mg chol., 592 mg sodium,
30 g carb. (4 g fiber, 10 g sugars), 17 g pro.

INGREDIENT MAKEOVER

Use **black pepper** and **cayenne
pepper** to add flavor without salt.

**Turkey sausage, fat-free milk,
and egg product** reduce fat and
cholesterol when compared to
their full-fat versions.

FIBER BOOST

Fresh berries have fiber to help keep you feeling full longer and are loaded with healthful antioxidants and flavonoids.

Daybreak
KICK-START

Certain foods work to boost your metabolism. Eat them to start your day, then enjoy well-selected midmorning snacks to keep body cranking.

Easy Berry Puff Pancake

SERVINGS 2 ($^1/_2$ pancake each)
CARB. PER SERVING 29 g
PREP 15 minutes BAKE 10 minutes

    1   egg
    1   egg white
 $^1/_4$ cup flour
 $^1/_4$ cup fat-free milk
    1   Tbsp. sugar*
    1   tsp. almond extract
    1   tsp. lemon zest
 $1^1/_2$ tsp. butter
    2   Tbsp. sliced almonds
 $^2/_3$ cup fresh blackberries and/or raspberries
    2   tsp. powdered sugar*

1. Preheat oven to 425°F. In a bowl combine the first seven ingredients (through lemon zest). Beat on high 2 minutes.

2. Grease the inside of a 9-inch cast-iron skillet or a dark 9-inch round cake pan with $^1/_2$ tsp. of the butter. Place the remaining 1 tsp. butter in the prepared skillet; place in the hot oven about 2 minutes or until butter is melted and starts to sizzle.

3. Pour batter into the hot skillet; quickly sprinkle with almonds. Bake 10 to 12 minutes or until pancake puffs in center and browns and crisps on edges. Immediately remove pancake from skillet and place on a cooling rack. Cool slightly. Top with berries. Sift powdered sugar over all.

*SUGAR SUBSTITUTES We do not recommend using sugar substitutes for this recipe.

PER SERVING: 226 cal., 9 g total fat (3 g sat. fat), 101 mg chol., 102 mg sodium, 29 g carb. (4 g fiber, 13 g sugars), 10 g pro.

SMART SNACKING

To help slow the rise in your blood sugar and satisfy hunger longer, pair a protein-rich food with a nutritious complex-carbohydrate choice. Keep snacks between 100 and 200 calories. Try these smart choices to keep your metabolism revved:

+ $^1/_2$ pear
  1 oz. light cheese

+ 1 cup kohlrabi sticks
  $^1/_2$ cup shelled edamame

+ 1 mini box raisins
  2 Tbsp. roasted pumpkin seeds

+ $^1/_2$ cup dehydrated apples
  1 oz. pistachios

+ $^1/_4$ cup hummus
  $^1/_2$ cup vegetable sticks

+ 6 oz. Greek yogurt
  $^3/_4$ cup berries

POWER PROTEIN

Whole eggs are satisfying and contain all 9 essential amino acids, which help our bodies utilize protein.

Spanish Eggs

SERVINGS 4 (1 egg + 1 cup tomato mixture each)
CARB. PER SERVING 12 g
START TO FINISH 30 minutes

$^1/_2$ cup chopped onion
 1 small fresh Anaheim chile pepper, stemmed, seeded, and chopped (tip, *page 69*)
 1 clove garlic, minced
 1 Tbsp. olive oil
 2 14.5-oz. cans no-salt-added fire-roasted diced tomatoes
 1 small zucchini, halved lengthwise and thinly sliced (1$^1/_4$ cups)
$^1/_2$ tsp. salt
 2 Tbsp. snipped fresh cilantro
 4 eggs
Crumbled queso fresco (optional)
Corn tortillas, warmed (optional)

1. In a large skillet cook onion, chile, and garlic in hot oil over medium heat about 5 minutes or until tender. Add undrained tomatoes, zucchini, and salt; cook about 5 minutes more or until zucchini is just tender. Stir in snipped cilantro.

2. Break one of the eggs into a measuring cup. Carefully slide egg into the tomato mixture. Repeat with the remaining three eggs, allowing each egg an equal amount of space in the tomato mixture. Cover and simmer over medium-low heat 3 to 5 minutes or until whites are completely set and yolks begin to thicken but are not hard. If desired, sprinkle with queso fresco and additional fresh cilantro and/or serve with corn tortillas.

PER SERVING: 168 cal., 8 g total fat (2 g sat. fat), 186 mg chol., 390 mg sodium, 12 g carb. (3 g fiber, 7 g sugars), 9 g pro.

Pink Power Smoothies

SERVINGS 4 (about 1 cup each)
CARB. PER SERVING 18 g
START TO FINISH 20 minutes

- 1½ cups small cauliflower florets
- 2 cups cubed watermelon (seeds and rinds removed)
- 1½ cups frozen unsweetened whole strawberries
- 1 6-oz. carton strawberry Greek yogurt
- 2 Tbsp. strawberry preserves (optional)

1. In a small saucepan cook cauliflower in enough boiling water to cover about 10 minutes or until very tender; drain. Rinse with cold water to cool quickly; drain.

2. In a blender combine cooked cauliflower and the remaining ingredients. Cover and blend until very smooth, stopping and scraping sides of blender as needed. Serve immediately.

TO MAKE AHEAD Prepare smoothies as directed. Transfer to an airtight freezer container; cover. Store in the refrigerator up to 3 days or freeze up to 6 months. If frozen, thaw in the refrigerator before serving. Stir well before serving.

PER SERVING: 87 cal., 0 g total fat, 0 mg chol., 29 mg sodium, 18 g carb. (2 g fiber, 13 g sugars), 5 g pro.

MORNING FUEL

Lean protein from **Greek yogurt** and fiber from **cauliflower, watermelon,** and **strawberries** help fill you up and give you an energy boost.

Egg White Scramble with Spinach and Cherry Tomato

SERVINGS 4 (^{2}/$_3$ cup eggs + ^{1}/$_2$ cup spinach mixture each)

CARB. PER SERVING 7 g

START TO FINISH 25 minutes

- 12 egg whites, 10 egg whites and 1 whole egg, or 1^1/$_2$ cups refrigerated or frozen egg product, thawed
- ^{1}/$_2$ cup milk or half-and-half
- ^{1}/$_2$ tsp. salt
- ^{1}/$_4$ tsp. black pepper
- 1 Tbsp. olive oil
- 1 clove garlic, minced
- 2 cups packed fresh baby spinach
- 2 cups cherry tomatoes, halved
- ^{1}/$_4$ cup finely shredded Parmesan cheese

1. In a bowl combine egg whites, milk, salt, and pepper. Beat with a whisk until well mixed.

2. In a large nonstick skillet heat oil over medium-high heat. Add garlic; cook and stir 30 seconds. Add spinach and tomatoes; cook and stir about 1 minute or until spinach is wilted and tomatoes are softened. Remove mixture from skillet; keep warm.

3. Pour egg white mixture into skillet. Cook over medium heat, without stirring, until mixture begins to set on the bottom and around the edges. Lift and fold the partially cooked egg white mixture so the uncooked portion flows underneath. Continue cooking 2 to 3 minutes or until egg white mixture is cooked through but is still glossy and moist. Remove from heat. Serve with spinach mixture and sprinkle with cheese.

PER SERVING: 142 cal., 6 g total fat (2 g sat. fat), 6 mg chol., 581 mg sodium, 7 g carb. (2 g fiber, 5 g sugars), 15 g pro.

Oat-Walnut Granola and Yogurt

SERVINGS 10 ($^1/_3$ cup granola + $^1/_2$ cup yogurt each)

CARB. PER SERVING 35 g

PREP 15 minutes   BAKE 30 minutes

  Nonstick cooking spray
  2 cups regular rolled oats
  1 cup bran cereal flakes
  $^3/_4$ cup puffed kamut cereal or puffed wheat cereal
  $^1/_3$ cup chopped walnuts
  $^1/_3$ cup sugar-free or light pancake syrup
  2 Tbsp. canola oil
  $^1/_2$ tsp. ground cinnamon
  $^1/_8$ tsp. salt
  5 cups plain low-fat yogurt

1. Preheat oven to 325°F. Coat a 15x10-inch baking pan with cooking spray. In a bowl combine oats, bran flakes, puffed kamut, and nuts. In a bowl combine syrup, oil, cinnamon, and salt. Pour over oat mixture, toss.

2. Spread oat mixture evenly in prepared pan. Bake, uncovered, 30 to 35 minutes or until oats are lightly browned, stirring twice. Immediately turn out onto a large piece of foil; cool.

3. For each serving, top $^1/_2$ cup yogurt with $^1/_3$ cup granola.

TO STORE Place granola in an airtight container; cover. Store at room temperature up to 2 weeks.

PER SERVING: 269 cal., 9 g total fat (2 g sat. fat), 7 mg chol., 157 mg sodium, 35 g carb. (4 g fiber, 10 g sugars), 13 g pro.

LASTING ENERGY

Combine high-fiber **whole grains** with protein-rich **yogurt** for an energy-filled morning.

Salmon-Artichoke Omelets

SERVINGS 4 (1 filled omelet each)
CARB. PER SERVING 10 g
PREP 20 minutes   COOK 18 minutes

- 1 large red sweet pepper, cut into thin bite-size strips
- 1 Tbsp. olive oil
- 1 14-oz. can quartered artichoke hearts, rinsed, drained, and coarsely chopped
- 2 cloves garlic, minced
- $1/2$ cup sliced green onions
- 2 oz. hot-smoked salmon, skinned, flaked, and bones removed if necessary
- 2 cups refrigerated or frozen egg product, thawed, or 6 eggs and 3 egg whites
- $1/4$ cup water
- $1/8$ tsp. black pepper
- 4 tsp. finely shredded Parmesan cheese

1. For filling, in a large skillet cook sweet pepper in hot oil over medium heat about 5 minutes or until just tender, stirring occasionally. Add artichokes and garlic; cook and stir 30 seconds more. Remove from heat. Stir in the $1/2$ cup green onions and the salmon. Remove from heat.

2. In a bowl combine eggs, water, and black pepper. Using a fork, beat until combined but not frothy. Generously coat a small nonstick skillet with flared sides with *nonstick cooking spray*; heat over medium-high heat.

3. Add one-fourth of the egg mixture to skillet; reduce heat to medium. Immediately begin stirring the eggs gently but continuously with a wooden spoon or heatproof spatula until mixture resembles small pieces of cooked egg surrounded by liquid egg. Stop stirring. Cook 30 to 60 seconds more or until egg is set and shiny.

4. Spoon one-fourth of the filling (about $3/4$ cup) over one side of the eggs. With a spatula, lift and fold the opposite side of eggs over filling. Transfer omelet to a plate; sprinkle with 1 tsp. of the Parmesan cheese. Cover with foil to keep warm. Repeat with remaining egg mixture and filling to make three more omelets. If desired, sprinkle with additional sliced green onions. Serve immediately.

PER SERVING: 150 cal., 5 g total fat (1 g sat. fat), 4 mg chol., 560 mg sodium, 10 g carb. (2 g fiber, 4 g sugars), 16 g pro.

HEALTHY FATS

Salmon is the best food source of heart-healthy omega-3 fatty acids. The protein and healthful fats in salmon give you energy to last until lunch.

Savory Egg and Sweet Potato Scramble

SERVINGS 4 (1¹/₄ cups each)
CARB. PER SERVING 20 g
START TO FINISH 35 minutes

8 eggs
¹/₃ cup milk
¹/₂ tsp. ground cumin
¹/₄ tsp. salt
¹/₄ tsp. black pepper
1 Tbsp. butter
1 lb. sweet potatoes (2 medium), peeled, quartered lengthwise, and thinly sliced
2 Tbsp. sliced green onion
2 cups fresh baby spinach
Fresh Italian parsley
Hot pepper sauce (optional)

1. In a bowl whisk together the first five ingredients (through pepper.)

2. In a large skillet melt butter over medium heat. Add sweet potatoes and green onion. Cook about 8 minutes or just until potatoes are tender and lightly browned, stirring occasionally. Add spinach. Cook and stir about 1 minute or until slightly wilted.

3. Pour egg mixture over potato mixture in skillet. Cook over medium heat, without stirring, until egg mixture begins to set on bottom and around edges. Lift and fold the partially cooked egg mixture so the uncooked portion flows underneath. Continue cooking 2 to 3 minutes or until egg mixture is cooked through but is still glossy and moist. Remove from heat.

4. Sprinkle with parsley. If desired, serve with hot pepper sauce.

PER SERVING: 258 cal., 13 g total fat (5 g sat. fat), 381 mg chol., 390 mg sodium, 20 g carb. (3 g fiber, 5 g sugars), 15 g pro.

TEST KITCHEN TIP

Egg product (2 cups) can be used for whole eggs if you want to trim fat and cholesterol in this dish.

QUALITY CARBS

The sugars in **sweet potatoes** are released slowly, providing a steady source of energy throughout the morning, and their high fiber content helps you feel full longer.

SWAP IN FLAVOR
for Fat

Fat in a recipe usually adds taste and moisture, but more fat doesn't mean better. Instead, choose low-fat cooking techniques that add a pop of flavor to enhance meals. Crispy-coated "fried" foods can be produced in your oven. Simple steamed or poached dishes get a boost with the addition of brightly flavored ingredients like citrus and chiles.

Healthy
COOKING

Cook in the most healthful ways possible with these methods.
Each helps cut fat while boosting natural flavors.

Steaming

Steaming is a moist-heat cooking method that is used for delicate foods such as vegetables and seafood. Because vegetables are not submerged in water, steaming preserves their nutrients and bright color.

**Ginger-Basil
Steamed Vegetables**
SERVINGS 6 (1 cup each)
CARB. PER SERVING 7 g
PREP 15 minutes   COOK 10 minutes

- 4   cups cauliflower florets
- 1   1-inch piece peeled fresh
    ginger, halved
- 1   medium red sweet pepper,
    seeded and cut into strips
- 2   cups snow pea pods, trimmed
- 4   green onions, cut into 2-inch
    pieces
- 2   Tbsp. snipped fresh basil
- 1   Tbsp. olive oil
- 1   Tbsp. lime juice
- $\frac{1}{4}$ tsp. salt
- $\frac{1}{4}$ tsp. black pepper
- $\frac{1}{8}$ tsp. crushed red pepper

1. Place a steamer basket in an extra-large skillet or Dutch oven. Add water to just below the bottom of the basket. Bring water to boiling. Add cauliflower and ginger to steamer basket. Cover and reduce heat. Steam about 5 minutes or until crisp-tender. Add red sweet pepper, pea pods, and green onions to basket; stir gently to combine. Cover and steam 5 to 7 minutes more or until vegetables are crisp-tender. Remove and discard ginger.

2. Transfer vegetables to a serving bowl. Add remaining ingredients. Toss to combine.

PER SERVING: 54 cal., 3 g total fat (0 g sat. fat), 0 mg chol., 119 mg sodium, 7 g carb. (2 g fiber, 3 g sugars), 2 g pro.

STEAMING POINTERS

Add water
Place a steamer basket in a pot. It should extend to the edges of the pot. Add water up to the bottom of the basket but not through the holes.

Add veggies
Bring water to boiling, then add the veggies and cover the pot. Lift the lid carefully so the steam doesn't burn you.

Steaming in Paper

An entire meal steams in one paper packet while it bakes in the oven.

Salmon in Parchment

SERVINGS 4 (1 packet each)
CARB. PER SERVING 13 g
PREP 30 minutes **BAKE** 25 minutes

- 1 lb. fresh or frozen skinless salmon or halibut fillets, $3/4$ to 1 inch thick
- 4 cups sliced carrots,* trimmed fresh green beans,* sliced zucchini or yellow summer squash, sliced fresh mushrooms, and/or sliced red, yellow, or green sweet peppers
- $1/2$ cup sliced green onions
- 1 Tbsp. snipped fresh oregano or 1 tsp. dried oregano, crushed
- 2 tsp. orange zest
- 4 cloves garlic, halved
- $1/4$ tsp. salt
- $1/4$ tsp. black pepper
- 4 tsp. olive oil
- Salt and black pepper
- 1 medium orange, halved and thinly sliced
- 4 sprigs fresh oregano (optional)

1. Thaw fish, if frozen. Preheat oven to 350°F. Rinse fish; pat dry with paper towels. If necessary, cut into four serving-size pieces. Cut four 14-inch squares of parchment paper. In a bowl combine the next seven ingredients (through $1/4$ tsp. black pepper).

2. Divide vegetable mixture among pieces of parchment, placing vegetables on one side of each square. Place a piece of fish on top of each vegetable portion. Drizzle each fish piece with 1 tsp. of the oil. Sprinkle lightly with additional salt and black pepper; top with orange slices. Fold parchment over fish and vegetables; fold in the open sides several times to secure, curving the edge into a circular pattern. Place parchment packets in a single layer in a 15×10-inch baking pan.

3. Bake 25 to 30 minutes or until fish flakes easily. Cut an X in the top of each parchment packet to check doneness; open carefully to avoid steam. To serve, transfer packets to serving plates. If desired, garnish with fresh oregano sprigs.

*TIP If using carrots and/or green beans, precook them. In a covered medium saucepan cook carrots and/or green beans in a small amount of boiling water 2 minutes; drain.

PER SERVING: 262 cal., 12 g total fat (2 g sat. fat), 62 mg chol., 359 mg sodium, 13 g carb. (4 g fiber, 8 g sugars), 25 g pro.

Assemble

Fold parchment in half to mark the center. Arrange veggies in middle of one side of parchment. Top vegetable mixture with fish, drizzle with olive oil, and sprinkle with salt and pepper. Top each fish piece with an orange slice.

Half-moon crimp

Fold parchment over fish. Begin at the bottom, folding and pleating the parchment toward the fish. Continue to fold and pleat, moving toward the top and making a half-moon shape.

Test doneness

You'll have to cut open packets to check for doneness. Check after 25 minutes if the fish is $3/4$ inch thick. If the fish is closer to 1 inch thick, check at 30 minutes.

Oven Frying

Baking applies dry heat that circulates around food. It requires minimal fat to make crumb-coated foods browned and crisp.

Baked Chicken Tenders

SERVINGS 4 (3 tenders each)
CARB. PER SERVING 13 g
PREP 20 minutes BAKE 15 minutes

Nonstick cooking spray
1 to 1¼ lb. skinless, boneless chicken breast halves
Salt
2 egg whites, lightly beaten
1 Tbsp. water
1 tsp. lemon zest
²⁄₃ cup fine dry bread crumbs
¼ cup finely shredded Parmesan cheese (1 oz.)

1. Preheat oven to 400°F. Lightly coat a large baking sheet with cooking spray; set aside. Cut chicken lengthwise into 12 strips. Sprinkle lightly with salt.
2. In a shallow dish combine egg whites, the water, and lemon peel. In another shallow dish stir together bread crumbs and cheese. Dip chicken strips into egg white mixture, then into crumb mixture, turning to coat. Arrange strips on the prepared baking sheet. Lightly coat with additional cooking spray.

3. Bake about 15 minutes or until chicken is done (165°F), turning once halfway through baking.

PER SERVING: 218 cal., 5 g total fat (2 g sat. fat), 86 mg chol., 410 mg sodium, 13 g carb. (1 g fiber, 1 g sugars), 30 g pro.

Take Your Pick

Use other dry coatings to vary the flavor and texture of Baked Chicken Tenders and other oven-fried foods. Make sure they are evenly crushed for best coverage.

Crushed reduced-fat 100% whole grain thin wheat crackers

PER SERVING: 252 cal., 7 g fat (2 g sat. fat), 86 mg chol., 459 mg sodium, 15 g carb. (1 g fiber, 3 g sugars), 31 g pro.

Crushed multigrain tortilla chips

PER SERVING: 255 cal., 9 g fat (2 g sat. fat), 86 mg chol., 388 mg sodium, 11 g carb. (1 g fiber, 0 g sugars), 30 g pro.

Crushed cornflakes

PER SERVING: 218 cal., 5 g fat (2 g sat. fat), 86 mg chol., 410 mg sodium, 13 g carb. (1 g fiber, 1 g sugars), 30 g pro.

COVER
RECIPE

Oven-Fried Pork Chops

SERVINGS 4 (1 chop each)
CARB. PER SERVING 6 g
PREP 20 minutes BAKE 20 minutes

- $3/4$ cup cornflakes
- $1/4$ cup sliced almonds
- $1/2$ tsp. dried Italian seasoning
- $1/4$ tsp. salt
- 2 Tbsp. refrigerated egg product
- 1 Tbsp. fat-free milk
- $1/8$ tsp. black pepper
- 4 boneless pork loin chops, cut $1/2$ to $3/4$ inch thick ($1^{1}/2$ to $1^{3}/4$ lb. total)
- 1 recipe Strawberry Salsa (optional)

1. Preheat oven to 425°F. Line a 15×10-inch baking pan with foil; set pan aside. In a food processor combine cornflakes, almonds, Italian seasoning, and salt. Cover and process until coarsely ground. Place mixture in a shallow dish. In another shallow dish combine egg, milk, and pepper. Trim fat from chops. Dip chops into egg mixture, then into crumb mixture, turning to coat. Place chops in the prepared baking pan. Coat chops with *nonstick cooking spray.*

2. Bake, uncovered, 12 to 15 minutes or until just pink in center (145°F). If desired, serve with Strawberry Salsa.

PER SERVING: 269 cal., 8 g total fat (2 g sat. fat), 111 mg chol., 347 mg sodium, 6 g carb. (1 g fiber, 1 g sugars), 43 g pro.

STRAWBERRY SALSA Combine 2 cups strawberries, chopped; 1 avocado, seeded, peeled, and chopped; $1/2$ cup chopped cucumber; 1 tsp. lime zest; 2 Tbsp. each lime juice and honey; 1 Tbsp. chopped jalapeño chile pepper (tip, *page 69)*; and $1/4$ tsp. black pepper.

MEAT PREPPING POINTERS

Trim the fat
Use a paring knife to trim off any visible fat from the edges of the chop.

Dredge and coat
Coat chops completely in the egg mixture and press into the coating. Make sure chops are coated completely and evenly.

Take Your Pick

Try fish or chicken breast instead of pork, and if you wish, substitute 1 cup herb-seasoned stuffing mix, finely crushed for the first four ingredients.

Oven-Fried Fish
Substitute 1 lb. fresh or frozen skinless fish fillets (such as cod), $1/2$ to $3/4$ inch thick, for the pork chops. Thaw fish, if frozen. Rinse fish; pat dry with paper towels. Prepare as directed, except bake for 4 to 6 minutes per $1/2$-inch thickness or until fish flakes easily.

Oven-Fried Chicken Breasts
Prepare as directed, except substitute four 5-oz. skinless, boneless chicken breast halves for the pork chops. If portions are not $3/4$ inch thick, use the flat side of a meat mallet to lightly pound them to an even $3/4$-inch thickness. Bake about 20 minutes or until chicken is no longer pink (165°F).

49

Stir-Frying

Stir-frying is a Chinese cooking method in which foods are cooked at a high temperature and constantly stirred until cooked through. Stir-frying is perfect for lean meats, seafood, and vegetables.

Sweet and Spicy Edamame-Beef Stir-Fry

SERVINGS 4 ($^3/_4$ cup beef mixture + $^1/_2$ cup rice each)

CARB. PER SERVING 38 g

PREP 20 minutes COOK 10 minutes

- 8 oz. boneless beef sirloin steak
- 3 Tbsp. hoisin sauce
- 2 Tbsp. rice vinegar
- 1 tsp. red chili paste
- 4 tsp. vegetable oil
- 2 tsp. finely chopped fresh ginger
- 2 cups fresh broccoli florets
- 1 cup red and/or yellow sweet pepper strips
- 1 cup frozen shelled edamame
- 2 cups hot cooked brown or white rice

Snipped fresh basil, cilantro, or parsley (optional)

1. If desired, partially freeze beef for easier slicing. Trim fat from meat. Thinly slice meat across the grain into bite-size strips. For sauce, stir together hoisin sauce, vinegar, and chili paste.

2. In a nonstick wok or large skillet heat 2 tsp. of the oil over medium-high heat. Add ginger; cook and stir 15 seconds. Add broccoli and sweet pepper strips; cook and stir about 4 minutes or until crisp-tender. Remove vegetables from wok.

3. Add the remaining 2 tsp. oil to wok. Add beef and edamame; cook and stir about 2 minutes or until beef is desired doneness. Return vegetables to wok.

4. Add sauce to beef mixture, tossing to coat. Heat through. If desired, toss rice with basil. Serve beef mixture over rice.

PER SERVING: 340 cal., 11 g total fat (2 g sat. fat), 24 mg chol., 262 mg sodium, 38 g carb. (6 g fiber, 8 g sugars), 22 g pro.

Take Your Pick

The rice aisle can be confusing. Ideally, you have the time to cook whole grain rice for every meal, but when that's not the case, there are alternatives.

Whole Grain Brown Rice
Whole grain rice is the most nutritious. It contains all portions of the grain, and cooking whole grain rice gives you the most control over nutrition and texture. Allow 45 minutes for cooking.

Instant Brown Rice
Instant rice is whole grain rice that has been precooked and dehydrated. Some texture and nutrients are lost in the process, but cooking time is only 10 minutes. Texture won't be as firm as whole.

Ready-to-Eat Brown Rice
This fully cooked and packaged rice can be heated in seconds. Check labels to determine which products have the best nutritional values.

Brussels Sprouts and Noodle Stir-Fry

SERVINGS 8 (^{3}/4 cup each)
CARB. PER SERVING 15 g
START TO FINISH 30 minutes

- 3 oz. dried whole wheat or multigrain spaghetti, broken
- 2 Tbsp. olive oil
- 1 cup thinly sliced red onion
- 3 cloves garlic, minced
- 12 oz. fresh Brussels sprouts, trimmed and thinly sliced
- 1 Tbsp. grated fresh ginger
- ^{1}/4 to ^{1}/2 tsp. crushed red pepper
- ^{1}/2 cup reduced-sodium chicken broth
- 2 Tbsp. reduced-sodium soy sauce
- ^{1}/2 cup shredded carrot
- ^{1}/3 cup snipped fresh cilantro
- 3 Tbsp. slivered almonds, toasted

1. Cook spaghetti according to package directions; drain. Return spaghetti to pan; cover and keep warm.
2. In a large skillet heat oil over medium-high heat. Add onion and garlic; cook and stir 1 minute. Add Brussels sprouts, ginger, and crushed red pepper; cook and stir 1 minute. Add broth and soy sauce; cook about 2 minutes or until liquid is nearly evaporated, stirring occasionally. Add spaghetti, carrot, and cilantro. Sprinkle with almonds.

PER SERVING: 115 cal., 5 g total fat (1 g sat. fat), 0 mg chol., 196 mg sodium, 15 g carb. (3 g fiber, 2 g sugars), 4 g pro.

STIR-FRY POINTERS

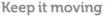

Quick cuts
For fast and even cooking, it's important to cut the meat and vegetables into similar-size pieces. Partially freeze the meat to make it easier to thinly slice.

Keep it moving
Because stir-frying uses such high heat to cook quickly, constant stirring is needed to keep the food from burning.

Grand finale
Have all ingredients ready to add to the wok when needed. Finish with the sauce, stirring to coat.

Poaching

Poaching gently simmers foods in a small amount of liquid. This technique is best for delicate foods such as fish and eggs. Poached foods absorb big flavor but little fat.

Escarole and Poached Egg Salad

SERVINGS 4 (2$\frac{1}{2}$ cups salad + 1 egg + 1 slice toast each)
CARB. PER SERVING 23 g
START TO FINISH 20 minutes

- 8 cups torn escarole or arugula
- 1 large tomato, halved and cut into wedges
- $\frac{1}{2}$ cup frozen peas, thawed
  Vegetable oil
- 4 eggs
- 1 recipe Red Wine Vinaigrette
- $\frac{1}{4}$ cup finely shredded Parmesan cheese (1 oz.)
- 4 slices whole grain country-style bread, toasted

1. Divide escarole and tomato among four salad bowls. Divide peas among the salad bowls.
2. For poached eggs, line a plate with paper towels. Fill a large skillet with 2 inches of water.* Bring water to boiling; reduce heat to simmering (bubbles should begin to break the surface of the water). Break one of the eggs into a cup and slip egg into the simmering water. Repeat with the remaining three eggs, allowing each egg an equal amount of space in the skillet. Simmer eggs, uncovered, 3 to 5 minutes or until whites are completely set and yolks begin to thicken but are not hard. Using a slotted spoon, carefully transfer eggs to the prepared plate to dry.
3. Place an egg on top of each salad. Drizzle with Red Wine Vinaigrette. Sprinkle with Parmesan cheese. Serve with toast.

RED WINE VINAIGRETTE In a screw-top jar combine 2 Tbsp. red wine vinegar; 4 tsp. olive oil; 1 tsp. snipped fresh oregano or $\frac{1}{2}$ tsp. dried oregano, crushed; $\frac{1}{2}$ tsp. Dijon-style mustard; $\frac{1}{4}$ tsp. cracked black pepper; and $\frac{1}{8}$ tsp. salt. Cover and shake well to combine.

*TIP If desired, add 1 teaspoon white vinegar to the water. This will help the egg stay together while cooking and will produce less-stringy pieces of egg white.

PER SERVING: 272 cal., 13 g total fat (3 g sat. fat), 215 mg chol., 432 mg sodium, 23 g carb. (8 g fiber, 4 g sugars), 17 g pro.

POACHING EGGS

Slip them in
Break one egg at a time into a custard cup. Hold the lip of the cup close to the simmering water and slip the egg in.

Drain well
When the eggs are cooked, use a slotted spoon to remove them from the skillet so the liquid drains away.

Citrus Salad with Poached Cod

SERVINGS 4 (3 oz. cooked fish + $1^{1}/_{3}$ cups salad each)
CARB. PER SERVING 9 g
START TO FINISH 25 minutes

- 1 lb. fresh or frozen skinless cod, haddock, or salmon fillets, about 1 inch thick
- 3 limes
- 5 Cara Cara oranges and/or regular oranges
- $1/_{2}$ cup water
- 2 Tbsp. olive oil
- 1 tsp. sugar
- $1/_{4}$ tsp. salt
- $1/_{8}$ tsp. black pepper
- 4 cups arugula, fresh baby spinach, and/or watercress, trimmed

1. Thaw fish, if frozen. Rinse fish and pat dry with paper towels. Remove 1 tsp. zest and squeeze 3 Tbsp. juice from one of the limes. Squeeze $1/_{2}$ to $2/_{3}$ cup juice from two of the oranges. In a bowl combine lime juice and orange juice. Set aside $1/_{4}$ cup of the juices to use in dressing.

2. Pour remaining juices into a large nonstick skillet; add lime zest and the water. Bring to boiling. Add fish; reduce heat to medium. Simmer, covered, 8 to 12 minutes or until fish flakes easily.

3. Meanwhile, for dressing, in a bowl whisk together the reserved $1/_{4}$ cup juices and the next four ingredients (through pepper).

4. Peel and thinly slice the remaining two limes and three oranges. Arrange the citrus slices on serving plates. Top with arugula mixture and fish. Drizzle dressing over salads.

PER SERVING: 188 cal., 8 g total fat (1 g sat. fat), 49 mg chol., 213 mg sodium, 9 g carb. (1 g fiber, 5 g sugars), 21 g pro.

POACHING FISH

Small pond
Don't drown the cod. You want enough poaching liquid to simmer without boiling away but not so much that it covers the fish.

Let it flake
You'll know the fish is done when it starts to flake when tested with a fork. Start checking at the minimum cooking time to avoid overcooking.

Peeling citrus
For pretty slices, use a paring knife to cut off ends, then cut from top to bottom to remove skin and bitter white pith.

Grilling

With the help of a grill pan, you can bring grilling indoors. A grill pan is designed so any fat that cooks out of the food drains away and collects between the ridges of the pan.

Jerk Chicken and Pineapple Slaw

SERVINGS 4 (1 chicken breast half + 1^1/$_2$ cups slaw each)
CARB. PER SERVING 19 g or 18 g
PREP 20 minutes   COOK 8 minutes

3   heads baby bok choy, trimmed and thinly sliced (4 cups)
2   cups shredded red cabbage
^{1}/$_2$ of a fresh pineapple, peeled, cored, and chopped (2 cups)
2   Tbsp. cider vinegar
1   Tbsp. canola oil
4   tsp. packed brown sugar*
^{1}/$_4$ tsp. salt
2   tsp. all-purpose flour
2   tsp. Jamaican jerk seasoning
4   skinless, boneless chicken breast halves (1 to 1^1/$_4$ lb. total)

1. For pineapple slaw, in an extra-large bowl combine bok choy, cabbage, and pineapple. Stir together vinegar, oil, 2 tsp. of the brown sugar, and the salt. Drizzle over bok choy mixture; toss to coat. Refrigerate until needed.
2. In a large resealable plastic bag combine the remaining 2 tsp. brown sugar, the flour, and jerk seasoning. Add chicken to bag. Close bag; shake to coat.
3. Grease a grill pan. Grill chicken in pan over medium heat 8 to 12 minutes or until no longer pink (165°F), turning once.** Transfer chicken to a cutting board; slice chicken. Serve chicken with pineapple slaw.
*SUGAR SUBSTITUTE Choose Splenda Brown Sugar Blend. Follow package directions to use product amount equivalent to 4 tsp. brown sugar.
**TIP If you don't have a grill pan, place the chicken on the ungreased rack of a broiler pan. Broil 4 to 5 inches from the heat 8 to 12 minutes or until no longer pink (165°F), turning once.

PER SERVING: 251 cal., 7 g total fat (1 g sat. fat), 83 mg chol., 414 mg sodium, 20 g carb. (3 g fiber, 14 g sugars), 28 g pro.

PER SERVING WITH SUBSTITUTE: Save as above, except 243 cal., 412 mg sodium, 18 g carb. (12 g sugars)

GRILL-PAN POINTERS

Prep the pan
Evenly grease the cold grill pan by wiping oil on ridges with a paper towel. To get a good sear and grill marks, preheat the pan.

Flip time
The chicken is ready to flip when one side is seared and brown grill marks appear.

Checking doneness
Chicken breast meat needs to cook to 165°F. Because it is a thin cut, insert the instant-read thermometer into the sides of the halves.

Apricot-Chipotle Grilled Pork Tenderloin and Zucchini

SERVINGS 4 (3 oz. pork + $^1/_2$ of a zucchini each)
CARB. PER SERVING 12 g
PREP 25 minutes   GRILL 20 minutes
STAND 3 minutes

- 1 1-lb. pork tenderloin
- 3 green onions
- 2 Tbsp. apricot preserves or jam
- 2 Tbsp. reduced-sodium soy sauce
- 2 tsp. finely chopped canned chipotle pepper in adobo sauce (tip, *page 69*)
- 2 medium zucchini (about 8 oz. each)
- 1 Tbsp. olive oil
- $^1/_4$ tsp. salt
- $^1/_4$ tsp. black pepper
- 2 Tbsp. snipped fresh cilantro or parsley

1. Trim pork. Thinly slice green onions, keeping white parts separate from green tops. Reserve green tops for later. In a bowl combine white parts of green onions, the apricot preserves, soy sauce, and chipotle pepper. Microwave 30 to 60 seconds or until heated. Set aside 2 Tbsp.

2. Trim ends off zucchini. Cut zucchini in half lengthwise. Brush zucchini with olive oil and sprinkle with salt and pepper.

3. Prepare grill for indirect heat using a drip pan. Place pork on a greased rack over drip pan. Grill, covered, over indirect medium heat 20 to 25 minutes or until done (145°F), brushing with 2 Tbsp. of the apricot sauce the last 5 minutes of grilling. Add zucchini halves to grill with pork; grill over direct medium heat 8 to 10 minutes or until tender, turning once. Remove pork and zucchini from grill; tent pork with foil and let stand 3 minutes before slicing.

4. Slice pork. Cut each zucchini piece in half crosswise. Combine reserved green onion tops and the cilantro. Serve pork with zucchini pieces. Top with cilantro mixture and remaining apricot sauce.

PER SERVING: 210 cal., 6 g total fat
(1 g sat. fat), 74 mg chol., 507 mg sodium,
12 g carb. (2 g fiber, 8 g sugars), 26 g pro.

PORK PREPPING POINTERS

Quick trim
Using a sharp knife, carefully trim fat and silverskin from the pork tenderloin.

Tent it
Tenting pork with foil keeps the sauce on the pork from sticking to the foil while pork rests and juices redistribute in the meat.

One BIG Batch

Oven-roasting vegetables draws out their natural sweetness and gives them a robust flavor. Make one batch and let them be the flavor workhorses in four different entrées.

Basic Roasted Vegetables

SERVINGS 20 ($^1/_2$ cup each)
CARB. PER SERVING 14 g
PREP 40 minutes
ROAST 1 hour 15 minutes

Nonstick cooking spray
1$^3/_4$ lb. potatoes or sweet potatoes, peeled (if desired) and cut into 1-inch pieces (5 cups)
2 large onions, coarsely chopped (2 cups), or 2 medium leeks, cut into 1-inch pieces (1 cup)
1 lb. carrots, cut into 1-inch pieces (3 cups)
12 oz. parsnips and/or turnips, cut into 1-inch pieces (2 cups)
1 lb. button or cremini mushrooms, halved (quarter large mushrooms) (7 cups)
1 lb. red sweet peppers, cut into 1-inch pieces (3$^1/_2$ cups)
1 lb. yellow sweet peppers, cut into 1-inch pieces (3$^1/_2$ cups)
2 heads garlic, separated into cloves and peeled
$^1/_2$ cup olive oil
2 tsp. kosher salt
2 tsp. black pepper

1. Preheat oven to 400°F. Line four 15×10-inch baking pans (tip, *below*) with foil. Coat foil with cooking spray. Place potatoes and onions in one prepared pan. Place carrots and parsnips in second prepared pan. Place mushrooms in third prepared pan. Place peppers and garlic in remaining prepared pan. Drizzle olive oil evenly over vegetables in all pans; toss lightly to coat. Sprinkle all vegetables with salt and black pepper.

2. Place pans with the potatoes and onions, and the carrots and parsnips in the oven. Roast, uncovered, 45 to 50 minutes or until tender and browned on the edges, stirring once. Remove pans from oven; let cool on wire racks.

3. Place pan with the peppers and garlic in the oven. Roast 15 minutes. Add pan with the mushrooms to the oven. Roast about 15 minutes more or until vegetables are tender, stirring once. Remove pans from oven; let cool on wire racks.

4. Place cooled vegetables in airtight containers; cover. Store in the refrigerator up to 5 days and use in recipes as desired.

PER SERVING: 112 cal., 6 g total fat (1 g sat. fat), 0 mg chol., 128 mg sodium, 14 g carb. (3 g fiber, 4 g sugars), 2 g pro.

TEST KITCHEN TIPS

If you don't have four 15×10-inch pans, you can prepare the vegetables in batches and reuse pans as needed.

Divide vegetables into the correct portion size for the recipes in this section and store them in separate containers. You will have about 10 cups of freshly roasted vegetables, but they will settle to 9 cups after refrigeration.

Turkey and Roasted
Vegetable Enchilada Casserole

Turkey and Vegetable Enchilada Casserole

SERVINGS 6 ($^{1}/_{6}$ casserole each)
CARB. PER SERVING 30 g
PREP 30 minutes **BAKE** 40 minutes
STAND 10 minutes

- 1 recipe Easy Enchilada Sauce
- 12 6-inch corn tortillas
- 3 cups shredded cooked turkey or chicken
- 2 cups Basic Roasted Vegetables *(page 63)*
- $^{1}/_{2}$ cup sliced green onions
- $^{1}/_{2}$ cup crumbled queso fresco or shredded Monterey jack cheese (2 oz.)
- $^{1}/_{4}$ cup snipped fresh cilantro

1. Preheat oven to 350°F. In a 2-quart baking dish or gratin dish spread $^{1}/_{2}$ cup Easy Enchilada Sauce. Tear 6 corn tortillas into four to six pieces each; arrange over sauce in dish. Spoon half of the turkey, half of the vegetables, and half of the green onions over tortillas. Spoon half of the remaining sauce over top. Repeat layers. Sprinkle with queso fresco. Cover with foil.

2. Bake 30 minutes. Uncover; bake about 10 minutes more or until bubbly. Let stand 10 minutes before serving. Sprinkle with cilantro.

EASY ENCHILADA SAUCE In a medium saucepan heat 1 Tbsp. canola oil over medium heat. Whisk in 1 Tbsp. all-purpose flour. Cook and stir 1 minute. Stir in 1 Tbsp. chili powder and 1 tsp. dried oregano, crushed. Cook and stir 30 seconds. Whisk in one 15-oz. can no-salt-added tomato sauce, $^{3}/_{4}$ cup water, and $^{3}/_{4}$ tsp. salt. Bring to boiling; reduce heat. Simmer, uncovered, 8 to 10 minutes or until desired thickness, stirring occasionally.

PER SERVING: 329 cal., 12 g total fat (3 g sat. fat), 77 mg chol., 582 mg sodium, 30 g carb. (6 g fiber, 6 g sugars), 26 g pro.

Vegetables for Roasting	Preparation	Approx Roasting Time at 450°F
Asparagus	Snap off woody bases. Leave spears whole or cut into 1-inch pieces.	10 to 15 minutes
Baby beets or regular beets	Scrub and peel beets. Trim stem and root ends. If desired, halve or quarter baby beets. Cut regular beets into 1-inch pieces.	30 to 40 minutes (Cover the beets if they start to burn.)
Brussels sprouts	Trim stems and remove any wilted leaves. Cut large sprouts in half.	30 to 40 minutes
Cauliflower	Remove core. Cut into florets.	10 to 15 minutes
Fennel	Trim stalks and cut a thin slice from bottom of bulb. Cut into wedges.	30 to 40 minutes
New potatoes, regular potatoes, or sweet potatoes	Peeling is not necessary, but scrub well. Quarter whole tiny new potatoes. Cut larger potatoes and sweet potatoes into bite-size pieces.	40 to 45 minutes
Onions	Remove papery outer layer. Cut into thin wedges.	30 to 45 minutes
Parsnips	Trim and peel parsnips. Cut into bite-size pieces or thin strips.	40 to 45 minutes
Sweet peppers	Cut into $^{1}/_{2}$-inch-wide strips.	10 to 15 minutes
Zucchini, pattypan, or yellow summer squash	Baby zucchini, pattypan, or summer squash can be roasted whole. For larger squash, cut into bite-size pieces or slices.	10 to 15 minutes

Roasted Vegetable Pasta Salad

SERVINGS 6 (1 cup each)
CARB. PER SERVING 42 g
PREP 15 minutes **STAND** 10 minutes

- ½ cup dried tomatoes (not oil-packed), sliced
- 1 cup dried gemelli or other small shape whole grain pasta (4 oz.)
- 2 cups Basic Roasted Vegetables (*page 63*)
- 3 cups baby or torn fresh arugula or baby spinach
- 1 15-oz. can cannellini (white kidney) beans, rinsed and drained
- 5 Tbsp. white balsamic vinegar or white wine vinegar
- 2 Tbsp. olive oil
- 3 cloves garlic, minced
- ½ tsp. black pepper
- ¼ tsp. salt

1. Place dried tomatoes in a bowl. Cover with boiling water; let stand 10 minutes. Cook pasta according to package directions; drain. Rinse pasta under cold water; drain well. Drain tomatoes.

2. In a large bowl combine pasta, tomatoes, Roasted Vegetables, arugula, and beans. Whisk together the remaining ingredients. Add to pasta mixture; gently toss to coat.

PER SERVING: 281 cal., 9 g total fat (1 g sat. fat), 0 mg chol., 347 mg sodium, 42 g carb. (6 g fiber, 11 g sugars), 9 g pro.

Braised Chicken Thighs and Vegetables with Polenta

SERVINGS 8 (2 thighs + $^1/_2$ cup polenta + $^1/_3$ cup vegetables each)
CARB. PER SERVING 27 g
PREP 15 minutes   **COOK** 25 minutes

$^1/_2$ tsp. dried oregano, crushed
$^1/_2$ tsp. ground cumin
$^1/_4$ tsp. salt
$^1/_4$ tsp. turmeric
$^1/_8$ tsp. cayenne pepper
16   skinless, boneless chicken thighs (about 3 lb. total)
 1   Tbsp. vegetable oil
$^2/_3$ cup reduced-sodium chicken broth
 1   recipe Polenta
 3   cups Basic Roasted Vegetables (*page 63*)
 3   cups torn fresh kale

1. Stir together the first five ingredients (through cayenne pepper). Sprinkle chicken with spice mixture. In an extra-large nonstick skillet cook chicken in hot oil over medium-high heat 5 to 8 minutes or until browned, turning once. Add broth to skillet. Bring to boiling; reduce heat. Simmer, covered, about 15 minutes or until chicken is done (at least 170°F). Transfer chicken to a platter; keep warm.

2. Meanwhile, make Polenta. Add Roasted Vegetables and kale to skillet. Bring to boiling; reduce heat. Simmer, uncovered, over medium heat about 5 minutes or until liquid is slightly reduced and vegetables are hot. Serve chicken and vegetables with Polenta.

POLENTA In a medium saucepan bring 3 cups water to boiling. In a bowl combine 1 cup cornmeal and $^1/_2$ tsp. salt; stir in 1 cup cold water. Slowly add cornmeal mixture to boiling water in saucepan, stirring constantly. Cook and stir until mixture returns to boiling. Cook, uncovered, over low heat about 5 minutes or until thick and cornmeal is tender, stirring occasionally. Stir in $^1/_4$ cup fat-free milk.

PER SERVING: 383 cal., 13 g total fat (3 g sat. fat), 160 mg chol., 507 mg sodium, 27 g carb. (4 g fiber, 4 g sugars), 37 g pro.

Sausage and Vegetable Galettes

SERVINGS 6 (1 galette each)
CARB. PER SERVING 39 g
PREP 30 minutes BAKE 15 minutes

- 6 2-oz. frozen cracked wheat roll dough portions, thawed
- 2 cups Basic Roasted Vegetables *(page 63)*
- 1 tsp. dried Italian seasoning, crushed
- 6 oz. fully cooked smoked chicken sausage with apple, halved lengthwise and sliced
- 3/4 cup shredded smoked mozzarella cheese (3 oz.)
- Milk (optional)
- 1/4 cup shredded fresh basil

1. Preheat oven to 375°F. Line a large baking sheet with parchment paper.

2. On a lightly floured surface roll each dough portion into a 5- to 6-inch circle. Spoon vegetables onto centers of dough circles, leaving a 1-inch border. Sprinkle with Italian seasoning. Top with chicken sausage and cheese. Fold edges of dough up over edge of filling, pleating as needed. If desired, brush edges of dough with milk. Carefully transfer galettes to prepared baking sheet.

3. Bake 15 to 18 minutes or until crust is golden and cheese is melted. Top with basil.

PER SERVING: 304 cal., 11 g total fat (3 g sat. fat), 29 mg chol., 522 mg sodium, 39 g carb. (3 g fiber, 10 g sugars), 14 g pro.

Flavor
BURST

With just the right ingredient, you can add a pop of flavor to a dish and never know the fat is missing.

Chile Peppers

Many varieties of chile peppers exist. No matter the level of hotness, all heighten the flavor of recipes. Choose from fresh peppers or other forms such as dried and crushed or ground.

Pork Tenderloin with Cucumber-Mango Salad

SERVINGS 4 (3 slices cooked pork + about $^1/_2$ cup salad each)
CARB. PER SERVING 18 g or 15 g
PREP 10 minutes   ROAST 25 minutes
STAND 3 minutes

- 2 Tbsp. packed brown sugar*
- 2 tsp. five-spice powder
- $^1/_2$ tsp. salt
- 2 12-oz. pork tenderloins
- 4 green onions
- 1 cup chopped, peeled mango
- 2 cups thinly sliced English cucumber
- 1 fresh jalapeño chile pepper, stemmed, seeded, and sliced (tip, *right*) (optional)

1. Preheat oven to 425°F. Line a shallow roasting pan with foil. In a bowl combine brown sugar, five-spice powder, and salt; set 1 tsp. of the brown sugar mixture aside. Sprinkle the remaining brown sugar mixture over pork tenderloins; rub in with your fingers. Place tenderloins in prepared roasting pan.

2. Roast about 25 minutes or until done (145°F). Cover with foil; let stand 3 minutes before slicing.

3. Meanwhile, for cucumber-mango salad, slice the green portions of the green onions into thin strips; chop the white portions. In a bowl combine all of the green onions, the mango, cucumber, jalapeño pepper (if desired), and the reserved brown sugar mixture. Slice pork and serve with salad.

*SUGAR SUBSTITUTE Choose Splenda Brown Sugar Blend. Follow package directions to use product amount equivalent to 2 Tbsp. brown sugar.

PER SERVING: 266 cal., 6 g total fat (2 g sat. fat), 105 mg chol., 365 mg sodium, 18 g carb. (2 g fiber, 15 g sugars), 35 g pro.

PER SERVING WITH SUGAR SUBSTITUTE: Same as above, except 255 cal., 363 mg sodium, 15 g carb. (11 g sugars).

FRESH CHILES

Chile peppers contain oils that can irritate your skin and eyes. Wear plastic or rubber gloves when working with them.

Take Your Pick

Fresh chiles range in hotness from mild and fruity to tear-inducing intensity. Most of the heat comes from the seeds and membrane, so remove those for less kick. Pickled chiles are still zippy but add a briny tang. Crushed red chile peppers can be sprinkled on top, but ground cayenne pepper adds the most character when mixed into a dish.

Fresh Jalapeño Pepper

Pickled Jalapeño Peppers

Crushed Red Pepper

Cayenne Pepper

Vinegar

Vinegar adds an acidic bite to recipes and brightens the other flavors in a dish. Use it to enhance a bottled salad dressing or splash it lightly over food just before serving.

Balsamic Chicken and Vegetables

SERVINGS 4 (4 oz. chicken + $^2/_3$ cup vegetables each)
CARB. PER SERVING 12 g
START TO FINISH 30 minutes

- $^1/_4$ cup Italian salad dressing
- 2 Tbsp. balsamic vinegar
- 1 Tbsp. honey
- $^1/_8$ to $^1/_4$ tsp. crushed red pepper
- 2 Tbsp. olive oil
- 1 lb. chicken breast tenderloins
- 10 oz. fresh asparagus, trimmed and cut into 2-inch pieces, or one 10-oz. pkg. frozen cut asparagus, thawed and well drained
- 1 cup purchased shredded carrot
- $^1/_3$ cup chopped, seeded tomato

1. In a bowl stir together the first four ingredients (through crushed red pepper).
2. In a large skillet heat oil over medium-high heat. Add chicken; cook 5 to 6 minutes or until chicken is tender and no longer pink (165°F), turning once halfway through cooking. Add half of the dressing mixture to skillet; turn chicken to coat. Transfer chicken to a platter; cover and keep warm.
3. Add asparagus and carrot to skillet. Cook and stir 3 to 4 minutes or until asparagus is crisp-tender; transfer to platter.
4. Stir remaining dressing mixture; add to skillet. Cook and stir 1 minute, scraping up browned bits from bottom of skillet. Drizzle dressing mixture over chicken and vegetables. Sprinkle with tomato.

PER SERVING: 269 cal., 12 g total fat (2 g sat. fat), 66 mg chol., 323 mg sodium, 12 g carb. (2 g fiber, 0 g sugars), 27 g pro.

BALSAMIC VINEGAR

Balsamic vinegar is made when white grape pressings are boiled down to dark syrup, then aged. It is deeply flavored, dark, and almost sweet. Boiling balsamic vinegar reduces it to an intense glaze.

Take Your Pick

Beyond basic white or cider varieties, vinegar flavors vary considerably from robust and almost sweet to light and delicate. It all depends on what is used for the base. These three are best in dressings and marinades, but not for reductions as balsamic is used in Balsamic Chicken and Vegetables.

Wine Vinegar
White and champagne vinegars have a light flavor. They are colorless, so the true colors of fresh ingredients shine.

Red Wine Vinegar
Red wine vinegar has a more pronounced flavor than white. Use it in dark-hued recipes.

Rice Vinegar
Made from fermented rice, not rice wine, this vinegar has a mild flavor and subtle sweetness.

Citrus

Get a triple play out of citrus in this recipe. Zest has intense flavor from the oils in the skin. Juice is used as a foundation for a vinaigrette. And whole sections offer juicy bites as part of a salad.

Orange Pistachio-Stuffed Grilled Scallops

SERVINGS 4 (3 scallops + 1 cup arugula mixture each)
CARB. PER SERVING 21 g
PREP 30 minutes **GRILL** 11 minutes

- 12 fresh or frozen large sea scallops (1 to 1¼ lb. total)
- 1 small fennel bulb
- 2 oranges
- 3 Tbsp. olive oil
- 2 Tbsp. snipped fresh Italian parsley
- 1 Tbsp. finely chopped pistachio nuts
- 1 Tbsp. sherry vinegar or white balsamic vinegar
- 2 tsp. honey
- Salt and black pepper
- Olive oil
- 4 cups arugula

1. Thaw scallops, if frozen. Rinse scallops; pat dry with paper towels. Make a horizontal cut through the center of each scallop, cutting almost to, but not through, the opposite side. Chill scallops until needed.

2. Cut off and discard fennel stalks, reserving the wispy leaves. Remove any wilted outer layers from bulb; cut a thin slice from the base. Cut bulb lengthwise into quarters; cut core out of each quarter. Snip enough of the leaves to measure 2 Tbsp.

3. Finely shred 1 tsp. zest from one of the oranges. Working over a bowl to catch the juice, use a small sharp knife to peel and section oranges. Reserve 1 Tbsp. of the juice.

4. For gremolata, in a bowl combine the 2 Tbsp. fennel leaves, the 1 tsp. orange peel, 1 Tbsp. of the oil, the parsley, and the 1 Tbsp. pistachios. For vinaigrette, in a screw-top jar combine the 1 Tbsp. orange juice, the remaining 2 Tbsp. oil, the vinegar, and honey. Cover and shake well. Season to taste with salt and pepper.

5. Lightly grease a large grill pan. Stuff scallops with gremolata and secure with toothpicks if necessary. Reserve any remaining gremolata. Lightly brush scallops with additional oil and sprinkle with salt and pepper. Place scallops in the prepared grill pan.

6. Place grill pan with scallops and the fennel on the rack of a grill over medium-high heat. Grill, covered, 11 to 14 minutes or until scallops are opaque and fennel is tender and lightly charred, turning once halfway through grilling. Remove any toothpicks from scallops. Cut fennel into slices.

7. To serve, divide arugula among plates. Top with scallops, fennel, and orange sections; sprinkle with any remaining gremolata. Drizzle with vinaigrette and, if desired, sprinkle with additional pistachios.

PER SERVING: 275 cal., 12 g total fat (2 g sat. fat), 37 mg chol., 291 mg sodium, 21 g carb. (4 g fiber, 13 g sugars), 21 g pro.

ORANGES

Fresh orange sections, juice, and zest give dishes a boost, enhancing flavor while allowing you to cut back on salt.

Take Your Pick

Navel oranges are considered the best for eating out of hand. Cara Cara oranges, a navel variety, have a distinct pink color and are sweeter than most navels. Tangerines are slightly smaller than navels and have a looser peel.

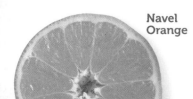
Navel Orange

Cara Cara Orange

Tangerine

Herbs

Fresh herbs are endlessly useful to add big flavor in dressings and marinades, to toss into dishes, or for a simple garnish. Snip them with kitchen scissors for easy preparation.

Beef and Bean Linguine with Mint-Walnut Gremolata

SERVINGS 2 (1^1/$_2$ cups pasta mixture + 2 Tbsp. gremolata each)
CARB. PER SERVING 33 g
PREP 15 minutes   COOK 16 minutes

- 2 Tbsp. snipped fresh mint or basil
- 1 Tbsp. chopped toasted walnuts
- 1 Tbsp. snipped fresh Italian parsley
- 1 tsp. lemon zest
- 2 oz. dried whole grain linguine
- 6 oz. fresh green beans, trimmed (1^1/$_2$ cups)
- 2 tsp. olive oil
- 6 oz. beef top loin steak (strip steak) or beef sirloin steak, trimmed and cut into thin bite-size strips
- ^{1}/$_8$ tsp. salt
- ^{1}/$_8$ tsp. black pepper
  Olive oil nonstick cooking spray
- ^{1}/$_2$ cup thin bite-size red sweet pepper strips
- ^{1}/$_4$ cup chopped onion
- 1 large clove garlic, thinly sliced
- 2 Tbsp. coarsely shredded Parmesan cheese
  Crushed red pepper (optional)

1. For gremolata, in a bowl combine mint, walnuts, parsley, and lemon zest.
2. Cook linguine according to package directions, adding the green beans for the entire cooking time. Drain and return to the pot. Add olive oil; toss to coat. Cover to keep warm.
3. Meanwhile, in a bowl toss steak strips with the salt and black pepper. Coat an unheated medium nonstick skillet with cooking spray; heat skillet over medium-high heat. Add steak strips, sweet pepper, onion, and garlic. Cook 3 to 4 minutes or until steak is pink only in center of strips, stirring occasionally.
4. Add steak mixture and Parmesan to the pasta mixture; toss to combine. Top with gremolata. If desired, sprinkle with crushed red pepper.

PER SERVING: 354 cal., 13 g total fat (3 g sat. fat), 45 mg chol., 291 mg sodium, 33 g carb. (7 g fiber, 6 g sugars), 28 g pro.

GREMOLATA

Gremolata is a beautiful condiment that adds fresh, bright, and flavorful notes when sprinkled on dishes just before serving. A combination of fresh herbs is the key with the bonus of lemon zest, and sometimes garlic, to make the herbs stand out.

Take Your Pick

Mix and match these herbs to top beef, pork, lamb, and poultry. Fresh herbs last longer if placed in a glass of water, like flowers, loosely covered with a plastic bag, and refrigerated. Don't refrigerate basil; it will blacken.

Basil

Mint

Thyme

Oregano

Swap in Flavor for Fat

Cheese

Incorporate crumbled or shredded strong-flavored cheese into sauces or simply sprinkle it over dishes right before serving. With its pungent qualities, a little goes a long way.

Chicken with Roquefort Sauce

SERVINGS 2 (1 chicken breast half + $^1/_2$ of a pear + 3 Tbsp. sauce each)
CARB. PER SERVING 16 g
PREP 15 minutes   **GRILL** 12 minutes

- $^1/_4$ cup plain fat-free yogurt
- 2 Tbsp. chopped red onion
- 1 Tbsp. crumbled Roquefort or other blue cheese
- $1^1/_2$ tsp. snipped fresh chives
  Dash white pepper
- 1 firm yet ripe small pear, halved lengthwise, cored, and stemmed
  Lemon juice
- 2 4-oz. skinless, boneless chicken breast halves
- $^1/_8$ tsp. salt
- $^1/_8$ tsp. black pepper

1. For sauce, in a bowl stir together the first five ingredients (through white pepper). Cover and refrigerate until ready to serve. Brush the cut sides of pear halves with lemon juice. Sprinkle chicken with salt and black pepper.

2. Grill chicken, covered, over medium heat 12 to 15 minutes or until done (165°F), turning once. Place pear halves, cut sides down, on grill rack next to chicken the last 5 minutes of grilling. Serve the chicken and pears with sauce. If desired, sprinkle with additional chives.

*TO BROIL Preheat broiler. Place chicken on the unheated rack of a broiler pan. Broil 4 to 5 inches from the heat 12 to 15 minutes or until done (165°F), turning once. Place pear halves, cut sides down, on broiler rack next to chicken the last 5 minutes of broiling.

PER SERVING: 214 cal., 3 g total fat (1 g sat. fat), 69 mg chol., 214 mg sodium, 16 g carb. (2 g fiber, 11 g sugars), 29 g pro.

ROQUEFORT

Roquefort is a rich-flavored French blue cheese made from sheep's milk. It is sharp, tangy, and salty while still being rich and creamy. Because it is moist, breaking it into little pieces is easy. Use small amounts for making sauces and sprinkling over finished dishes.

Take Your Pick

A small amount of an intensely flavored cheese, such as aged cheddar, Roquefort (or other blue cheese), high-quality Parmesan, or feta, makes a big impact in adding flavor to a dish. It can be part of a sauce, stuffing, or sprinkled over the top just before serving.

White Cheddar Cheese

Blue Cheese

Parmesan Cheese

Feta Cheese

77

Unload THE CARBS

Breads, pasta, and crusts are filled with carbohydrates. But how do you avoid these common bases for so many meal options? Unload empty carbs with fresh and surprising choices that are delicious and more nutrient-packed. Transform cauliflower into pizza crust, zucchini into long "noodles," and cabbage leaves into sandwich wraps.

New NOODLES

Replace carb-heavy pasta with noodles made from vegetables like zucchini, sweet potatoes, and broccoli.

Long Spirals

These classic veggie noodles are easy to make with one of the many specialized tools available. Choose from a speedy counter model or an easy-to-store handheld gadget.

Triple Veggie Pasta

SERVINGS 4 ($1^1/_2$ cups each)
CARB. PER SERVING 12 g
START TO FINISH 30 minutes

- 1 medium zucchini, trimmed
- 1 medium straight-neck yellow summer squash, trimmed
- 1 large carrot (1-inch diameter), peeled and trimmed
- 1 cup light Alfredo pasta sauce
- 1 Tbsp. basil pesto
- $^1/_8$ to $^1/_4$ tsp. crushed red pepper
- 1 Tbsp. olive oil
- 1 cup sliced fresh cremini mushrooms
- 2 cups cooked chicken breast strips
- $^1/_2$ cup halved grape or cherry tomatoes
- $^1/_2$ cup frozen peas
- Small fresh basil leaves or snipped fresh basil

1. Using a spiral vegetable slicer fitted with the small blade, cut zucchini and yellow squash into long strands (you should have about 7 cups lightly packed strands). Keeping squash and carrot separate, cut carrot into long strands (you should have about 1 cup lightly packed strands). If desired, cut through the strands with kitchen scissors to make them easier to serve.

2. In a bowl stir together Alfredo sauce, pesto, and red pepper.

3. In an extra-large skillet heat oil over medium heat. Add mushrooms; cook and stir 4 minutes. Add carrot; cook and stir 1 minute. Add squash; cook and toss with tongs 2 minutes. Stir in Alfredo mixture, chicken, tomatoes, and peas; heat. Sprinkle with basil.

PER SERVING: 269 cal., 13 g total fat (5 g sat. fat), 86 mg chol., 456 mg sodium, 12 g carb. (3 g fiber, 6 g sugars), 26 g pro.

NOODLE NOTE

Make noodles in a hurry with a few quick cranks on a spiral vegetable slicer, or spiralizer. Straight zucchini and summer squash work best—avoid squash with crooks or curves, which are hard to feed through the spiralizer. Fatter carrots work better for creating long noodles.

Sweet potatoes should be long, narrow, and straight. For easier slicing, cook peeled potatoes in enough boiling water to cover 5 minutes. Let cool before slicing.

As you cut vegetable strands in the spiral slicer, use kitchen scissors to snip them into shorter lengths for easy eating.

Sweet Potato, Chicken, and Spinach in Browned Butter

SERVINGS 5 (1$\frac{1}{4}$ cups each)
CARB. PER SERVING 17 g
START TO FINISH 30 minutes

- 2 medium sweet potatoes (about 1 lb. total), peeled
- $\frac{1}{4}$ cup butter
- 1 to 2 Tbsp. snipped fresh sage or rosemary
- 4 cups fresh baby spinach
- $\frac{3}{4}$ cup sliced tart green apple
- $\frac{1}{4}$ tsp. salt
- 2 cups cooked chicken breast strips
- $\frac{1}{2}$ to $\frac{2}{3}$ cup reduced-sodium chicken broth
- 2 Tbsp. finely shredded Parmesan cheese
- 1 Tbsp. coarsely chopped walnuts, toasted (optional)

1. In a large saucepan cook sweet potatoes in enough boiling water to cover 5 minutes. Remove from pan, reserving cooking water. Cool potatoes until easy to handle. Using a spiral vegetable slicer fitted with the large blade, cut potatoes into long strands (you should have about 4 cups lightly packed strands). Return cooking water to boiling. Add sweet potato strands; cook 2 minutes. Drain.

2. Meanwhile, in an extra-large skillet cook butter and sage over medium-low heat about 15 minutes or until butter turns golden brown. Add spinach, apple, and salt; cook and stir over medium heat 1 minute. Gently stir in sweet potato, chicken, and enough of the broth to moisten; heat. Sprinkle with Parmesan and, if desired, walnuts.

PER SERVING: 260 cal., 12 g total fat (7 g sat. fat), 73 mg chol., 389 mg sodium, 17 g carb. (3 g fiber, 5 g sugars), 21 g pro.

Garlicky Zucchini Noodles

SERVINGS 6 (1 cup each)
CARB. PER SERVING 9 g
START TO FINISH 20 minutes

- 2 medium zucchini (about 10 oz. each), trimmed
- 3 Tbsp. walnut oil or olive oil
- 6 cloves garlic, smashed, peeled, and halved lengthwise
- 1/2 cup walnut pieces
- 1/2 tsp. kosher salt
- 1/4 tsp. crushed red pepper
- 4 thin slices prosciutto or pancetta, torn
- 1 cup thinly sliced tart green apple
- 4 oz. soft goat cheese (chèvre), broken into pieces

1. Using a spiral vegetable slicer fitted with the small blade, cut zucchini into long strands (or using a vegetable peeler, cut lengthwise into thin ribbons). If desired, cut through the strands with kitchen scissors to make them easier to serve.

2. In an extra-large skillet heat 2 Tbsp. of the oil over medium-high heat. Add garlic; cook and stir about 2 minutes or until softened and starting to brown. Add zucchini; cook and toss with tongs 1 minute. Transfer to a serving bowl. Add walnuts to skillet; cook and stir 1 to 2 minutes or until toasted. Add to bowl with zucchini. Sprinkle with salt and crushed red pepper.

3. Add the remaining 1 Tbsp. oil to skillet. Add prosciutto; cook about 1 minute or until browned and crisp, turning once. Add to bowl with zucchini mixture. Add apple slices; toss gently to combine. Top with goat cheese.

PER SERVING: 217 cal., 18 g total fat (4 g sat. fat), 13 mg chol., 405 mg sodium, 9 g carb. (2 g fiber, 5 g sugars), 8 g pro.

83

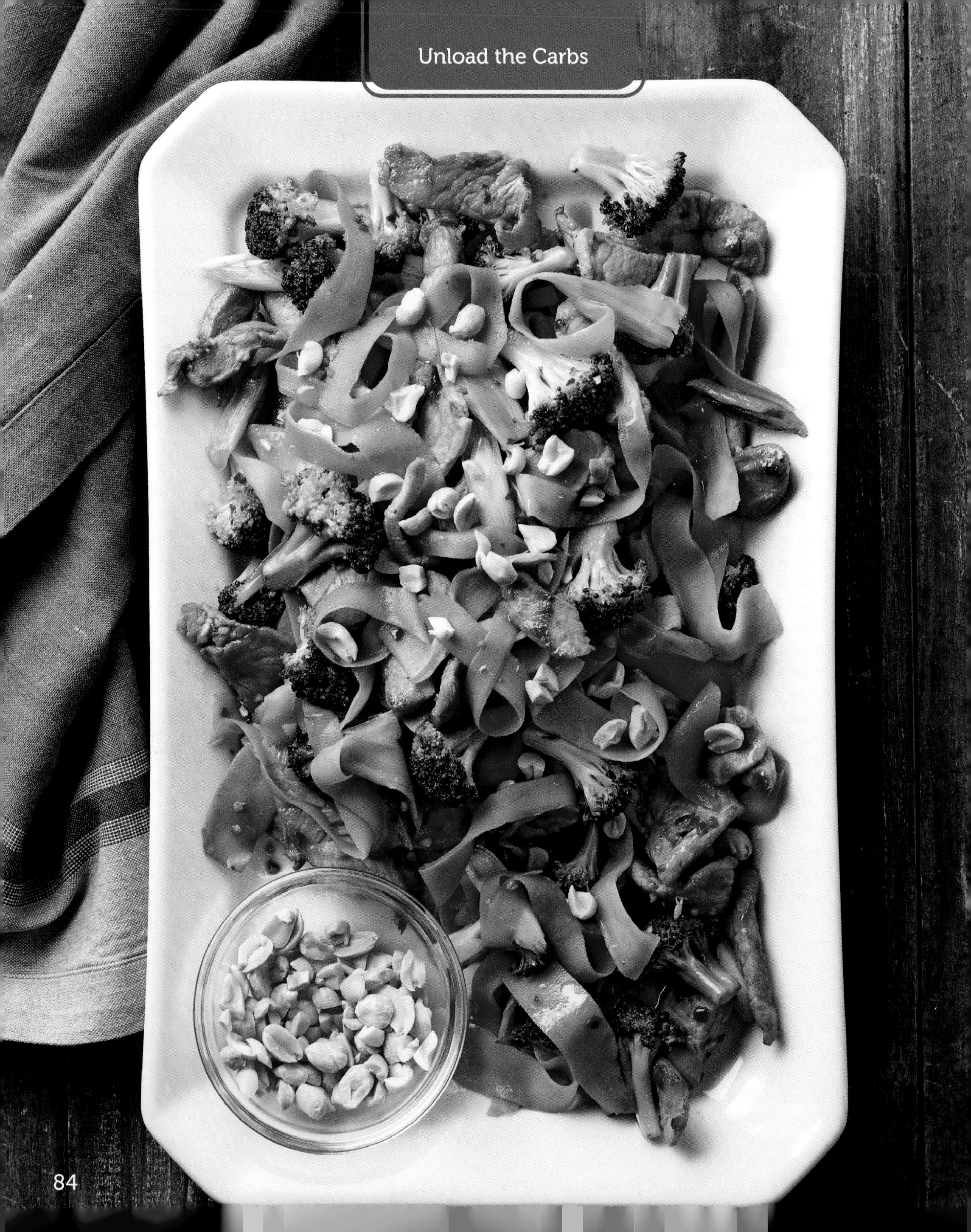

Flat Ribbons

Any long vegetable or stalk can be turned into fresh, pastalike ribbons. All you need is a basic straight-blade vegetable peeler.

Pork and Broccoli Noodle Stir-Fry

SERVINGS 6 (1 cup each)
CARB. PER SERVING 11 g
START TO FINISH 35 minutes

- 3 Tbsp. reduced-sodium soy sauce
- 2 Tbsp. rice vinegar
- 1 Tbsp. packed brown sugar*
- 1/4 tsp. crushed red pepper
- 2 large heads broccoli with stems
- 3 medium carrots, peeled
- 1 Tbsp. vegetable oil
- 2 cloves garlic, minced
- 4 green onions, cut into 1-inch pieces
- 1 lb. lean boneless pork, cut into thin bite-size strips
- 1/4 cup chopped toasted peanuts or walnuts

1. For sauce, stir together the first four ingredients (through red pepper).
2. Cut the florets off broccoli stems, cutting as close to the stems as possible. Set aside 2 cups of the florets (wrap and refrigerate remaining florets for another use). Peel broccoli stems and trim the ends off so they are evenly flat. Using a vegetable peeler, peel the broccoli stems and carrots into ribbons.
3. Pour oil into a wok or extra-large skillet. Preheat over medium-high heat. Add garlic; cook and stir 15 seconds. Add broccoli ribbons and florets, carrots, and green onions; cook and stir 4 to 5 minutes or until vegetables are crisp-tender. Remove from wok.
4. Add half of the pork to hot wok (if needed, add another 2 tsp. vegetable oil); cook and stir about 2 minutes or until no longer pink. Remove from wok. Repeat with remaining pork. Return all pork and vegetables to wok. Stir sauce; add to center of wok. Cook and stir until pork-vegetable mixture is coated and heated through. Top with peanuts.

*SUGAR SUBSTITUTE We do not recommend using a sugar substitute in this recipe.

PER SERVING: 208 cal., 10 g total fat (2 g sat. fat), 44 mg chol., 364 mg sodium, 11 g carb. (3 g fiber, 6 g sugars), 19 g pro.

NOODLE NOTE

For all noodles, start at one end and peel in a uniform strip to the other end.

To make broccoli noodles, look for broccoli heads with straight, full stems. Because the stalks are not uniform, these shapes will be fun and informal.

Choose medium-size carrots for making noodles. If desired, remove the thin outer skin before cutting into ribbons.

For ribbons of zucchini and yellow summer squash, choose squash that are straight. Peel off long strips, rotating the squash when you get to the seeds.

1. Preheat broiler. Trim ends off zucchini. Cut zucchini lengthwise into $1/4$-inch-thick slices. Lightly coat both sides of slices with cooking spray; place half of the slices in a single layer on a wire rack set on a large baking sheet. Broil 5 to 6 inches from the heat 12 to 14 minutes or until lightly browned, turning once. Repeat with remaining zucchini slices. Reduce oven temperature to 375°F. (If desired, set aside three slices of zucchini.)

2. In a large skillet cook beef, mushrooms, and garlic until meat is browned. Drain off fat. Remove from heat. Stir in the next five ingredients (through fennel seeds). In a bowl combine egg and ricotta cheese.

3. To assemble lasagna, spread 1 cup of the sauce mixture over the bottom of a 13×9-inch baking pan. Top with enough of the zucchini slices to cover sauce mixture. Drop half of the ricotta mixture by spoonfuls on top of the zucchini; use the back of the spoon to lightly spread ricotta mixture over zucchini. Sprinkle with $3/4$ cup of the mozzarella cheese. Top with half of the remaining sauce mixture. Repeat layers once more, ending with sauce mixture.

4. Bake, uncovered, 20 minutes. If desired, top with reserved zucchini slices. Sprinkle with the remaining $1/2$ cup cheese. Bake 10 to 15 minutes more or until cheese is melted. Let stand 10 minutes before serving.

PER SERVING: 209 cal., 8 g total fat (3 g sat. fat), 58 mg chol., 565 mg sodium, 15 g carb. (3 g fiber, 10 g sugars), 20 g pro.

Zucchini-Noodle Lasagna

SERVINGS 12 (1 piece each)
CARB. PER SERVING 15 g
PREP 15 minutes   BROIL 12 minutes
BAKE 30 minutes   STAND 10 minutes

- 2 lb. zucchini (about 2 large or 3 medium)
-    Nonstick cooking spray
- 1 lb. extra-lean ground beef
- 2 cups chopped fresh portobello mushrooms
- 2 cloves garlic, minced
- 1 24- to 26-oz. jar chunky-style pasta sauce
- 1 8-oz. can tomato sauce
- 1 tsp. dried basil, crushed
- 1 tsp. dried oregano, crushed
- 1 tsp. fennel seeds, crushed
- 1 egg, lightly beaten
- 1 15-oz. container fat-free ricotta cheese
- 2 cups shredded part-skim mozzarella cheese (8 oz.)

Cashew-Cilantro Pesto with Veggie Noodles

SERVINGS 5 (1 cup each)
CARB. PER SERVING 26 g
START TO FINISH 30 minutes

- 1 English cucumber, peeled (about 7 oz.)
- 1 daikon radish, peeled (about 12 oz.)
- 3 carrots (about $3^1/_2$ oz.)
- 2 cups thinly sliced savoy cabbage or napa cabbage
- $^1/_2$ tsp. kosher salt
- 1 cup raw cashews
- $^3/_4$ cup snipped fresh cilantro
- 3 green onions, chopped
- $^1/_2$ cup lime juice
- 2 Tbsp. raw agave nectar
- 1 fresh jalapeño chile pepper, seeded and finely chopped (about $1^1/_2$ Tbsp.) (tip, *below*)
- 1 Tbsp. tamari sauce
- 2 tsp. grated fresh ginger
- 2 tsp. sesame oil
- 3 cloves garlic

1. Using a vegetable peeler, cut the cucumber, daikon radish, and carrots lengthwise into long julienne "noodles" or "ribbons." In an extra-large bowl toss together the vegetable noodles, cabbage, and salt. Set aside while preparing the pesto. Reserve any liquid that is released from the vegetables as they stand.

2. For pesto, in a food processor or blender combine cashews, $^1/_2$ cup of the cilantro, and the remaining ingredients. Cover and blend or process until smooth. If necessary, add some of the liquid from the salted vegetables or a little water to thin mixture to sauce consistency.

3. Toss the vegetable noodles with the pesto; sprinkle with the remaining $^1/_4$ cup cilantro.

PER SERVING: 248 cal., 15 g total fat (3 g sat. fat), 0 mg chol., 443 mg sodium, 26 g carb. (4 g fiber, 12 g sugars), 6 g pro.

TEST KITCHEN TIP

Chile peppers contain oils that can irritate your skin and eyes. Wear plastic or rubber gloves when working with them.

Spaghetti Squash

This squash is the original pasta impersonator. After roasting, the "spaghetti" strands are relatively dry and hold sauces well.

Pesto Burgers with Spaghetti Squash

SERVINGS 4 (1 patty + 1 cup squash mixture each)

CARB. PER SERVING 26 g carb.

PREP 40 minutes   GRILL 12 minutes

- 1 3-lb. spaghetti squash
- 1/2 cup water
- 1 lb. extra-lean ground beef
- 1/4 cup snipped fresh basil
- 2 Tbsp. purchased basil pesto
- 2 cloves garlic, minced
- 1/2 tsp. salt
- 1/4 tsp. black pepper
- 1 large red sweet pepper, seeded and cut into quarters
- 1 medium onion, cut into 1/2-inch-thick slices
- Nonstick cooking spray
- 2 Tbsp. white balsamic vinegar
- 1/4 cup finely shredded Parmesan cheese

1. Cut squash in half lengthwise; remove and discard seeds. Place one squash half, cut side down, in a 2-qt. baking dish; add 1/4 cup of the water. Cover with vented plastic wrap. Microwave about 10 minutes or until tender. Remove squash half; keep warm. Repeat with the remaining squash half and the remaining 1/4 cup water.

2. Meanwhile, in a bowl combine beef, basil, the pesto, garlic, 1/4 tsp. of the salt, and 1/8 tsp. of the black pepper. Using your hands, shape mixture into four 3/4-inch-thick patties. Lightly coat sweet pepper quarters and onion slices with cooking spray.

3. Grill patties, peppers, and onion, covered, over medium heat. Grill patties 12 to 14 minutes or until done (160°F), turning once. Grill peppers and onion 7 to 8 minutes or until just tender, turning once.

4. When squash is cool enough to handle, use a fork to shred squash pulp into strands. Measure 4 cups into a large bowl. (Reserve and refrigerate any remaining squash for another use.) Remove any charred skin from the pepper quarters and discard. Chop the pepper and onion slices; add to squash along with vinegar, remaining 1/4 tsp. salt, and 1/8 tsp. black pepper. Toss to combine.

5. Top squash mixture with patties. Sprinkle with Parmesan cheese and, if desired, additional basil leaves.

PER SERVING: 322 cal., 12 g total fat (4 sat. fat), 76 mg chol., 563 mg sodium, 26 g carb. (5 g fiber, 13 g sugars), 29 g pro.

NOODLE NOTE

Spaghetti squash has pale yellow flesh with a mild, neutral flavor that lends itself to both sweet and savory uses.

Halve and roast spaghetti squash until tender. Let it cool slightly, then use a fork to gently rake the flesh from the edge to the center, separating it into pastalike strands.

Spaghetti Squash with Chicken and Mushroom Sauce

SERVINGS 4 (1 cup squash + $^3/_4$ cup sauce each)
CARB. PER SERVING 30 g
START TO FINISH 45 minutes

- 1 3-lb. spaghetti squash
- $^1/_2$ cup water
- 1 Tbsp. olive oil
- 2 cups sliced fresh mushrooms
- $^1/_4$ cup chopped onion
- 2 cloves garlic, minced
- 2 links cooked desired-flavor chicken sausage, halved lengthwise and sliced
- 1 14.5-oz. can no-salt-added diced tomatoes, undrained
- 1 8-oz. can no-salt-added tomato sauce
- $1^1/_2$ tsp. dried Italian seasoning, crushed
- $^1/_4$ tsp. salt
- $^1/_4$ tsp. black pepper
- Shaved or grated Parmesan cheese (optional)

1. Cut squash in half lengthwise; remove and discard seeds. Place one squash half, cut side down, in a 2-qt. rectangular baking dish; add $^1/_4$ cup of the water. Cover with vented plastic wrap. Microwave about 10 minutes or until tender. Remove squash half; keep warm. Repeat with the remaining squash half and the remaining $^1/_4$ cup water.

2. Meanwhile, for sauce, in a medium saucepan heat oil over medium heat. Add mushrooms, onion, and garlic; cook about 7 minutes or until tender. Stir in the next six ingredients (through pepper). Bring to boiling; reduce heat. Simmer, uncovered, 15 to 20 minutes or until sauce reaches desired consistency, stirring frequently.

3. Use a fork to shred and separate the squash pulp into strands. Drain as directed in tip, *below.* Serve squash with sauce. If desired, sprinkle with Parmesan cheese.

PER SERVING: 201 cal., 7 g total fat (1 g sat. fat), 25 mg chol., 509 mg sodium, 30 g carb. (8 g fiber, 14 g sugars), 11 g pro.

TEST KITCHEN TIP

Cooking the spaghetti squash in a microwave results in moister strands of squash. To remove any excess liquid, place shredded squash strands in a colander; press the strands with a rubber scraper or the back of a spoon until no more liquid drips out. Fluff the drained squash with a fork before serving.

Beyond BREAD

Slim down traditional bread offerings with thinner versions of rolls, alternatives for wraps, and restructured sandwich presentations.

Mediterranean Chicken-Hummus Stacks

SERVINGS 4 (2 stacks each)
CARB. PER SERVING 22 g
START TO FINISH 30 minutes

- 1 recipe Zucchini-Egg Wraps
- $1/2$ cup plain hummus
- 8 oz. shredded cooked chicken breast
- $1 1/2$ cups grape or cherry tomatoes, halved
- 1 medium yellow sweet pepper, cut into thin bite-size strips
- $1/4$ cup crumbled reduced-fat feta cheese (1 oz.)
- $1/4$ cup sliced pitted Kalamata or black olives (optional)
- 2 tsp. snipped fresh oregano or $1/2$ tsp. dried oregano, crushed (optional)

1. Place two Zucchini-Egg Wraps on each of four plates. Spread 2 Tbsp. hummus over each two wraps. Top with remaining ingredients.
ZUCCHINI-EGG WRAPS In a bowl toss 4 cups shredded zucchini with $1/2$ tsp. coarse salt. Cover and let stand at least 30 minutes or up to 4 hours. Transfer to a colander. Rinse with cold water. Drain well, pressing down gently on zucchini using a rubber spatula. Gently wrap a double thickness of paper towels around zucchini and squeeze gently to remove as much liquid as possible.

In the same bowl combine 1 egg and 2 egg whites, lightly beaten, and 1 Tbsp. olive oil. Stir in zucchini. Sprinkle with $1/3$ cup whole wheat flour and $1/2$ tsp. black pepper. Toss to combine.

Preheat broiler. Line a baking sheet with foil; coat with nonstick cooking spray. Spoon zucchini mixture into 4 mounds onto prepared baking sheet, using 3 Tbsp. mixture per mound. Spread each mound until $1/4$ inch thick and 5 inches in diameter. Broil 4 to 5 inches from the heat 2 to 3 minutes per side or until shells are lightly browned and set, turning once. Repeat with remaining zucchini mixture, making four more wraps.

PER SERVING: 299 cal., 12 g total fat (3 g sat. fat), 100 mg chol., 398 mg sodium, 22 g carb. (5 g fiber, 6 g sugars), 27 g pro.

TEST KITCHEN TIP

Instead of using a hand shredder or box grater, use the shredding blade on a food processor—it will save time and your fingers!

Stack the first batch of cooked wraps between pieces of parchment paper and wrap in foil. Place the wrapped packet on the lowest shelf in oven to keep warm while broiling the rest.

Chicken and Mushroom Bagel Sandwiches

SERVINGS 4 (1 sandwich each)
CARB. PER SERVING 28 g
PREP 20 minutes COOK 10 minutes

$2\frac{1}{2}$ oz. goat cheese (chèvre)
$\frac{1}{4}$ cup dried tomatoes (not oil-pack), cut into thin strips
2 Tbsp. snipped fresh Italian parsley
1 small clove garlic, minced
$\frac{1}{8}$ tsp. dried Italian seasoning, crushed
$\frac{1}{8}$ tsp. black pepper
2 tsp. olive oil
1 lb. skinless, boneless chicken breast halves, cut into bite-size pieces or thin strips
8 oz. sliced fresh cremini mushrooms
4 100% whole wheat bagel thins, split and toasted
2 cups fresh arugula

1. In a food processor combine the first six ingredients (through pepper). Cover and process until smooth.
2. In a large skillet heat oil over medium-high heat. Add chicken; cook and stir about 5 minutes or until chicken is no longer pink. Reduce heat to medium. Add mushrooms; cook and stir about 5 minutes or until mushrooms are tender.
3. Spread goat cheese mixture on cut sides of bagel thins. Divide chicken mixture and arugula among bottom halves of bagel thins. Add top halves.

PER SERVING: 349 cal., 12 g total fat (5 g sat. fat), 87 mg chol., 428 mg sodium, 28 g carb. (6 g fiber, 6 g sugars), 36 g pro.

Asian Beef Cabbage Wraps

SERVINGS 12 (1 wrap each)
CARB. PER SERVING 6 g
PREP 20 minutes
SLOW COOK 8 to 10 hours (low) or
4 to 5 hours (high) + 15 minutes
(high)

- 1 $2^{3}/_{4}$- to 3-lb. boneless beef
  chuck pot roast
- $1^{1}/_{2}$ cups chopped, peeled jicama
  or chopped celery
- $^{1}/_{2}$ cup chopped green onions
- $^{1}/_{4}$ cup rice vinegar
- $^{1}/_{4}$ cup reduced-sodium soy sauce
- 2 Tbsp. hoisin sauce
- 1 Tbsp. grated fresh ginger
- $^{1}/_{2}$ tsp. salt
- $^{1}/_{2}$ tsp. chile oil
- $^{1}/_{4}$ tsp. black pepper
- 2 Tbsp. cornstarch
- 2 Tbsp. cold water
- 12 savoy cabbage leaves
- $^{1}/_{4}$ cup coarsely chopped cashews
  (optional)
- Jicama strips (optional)
- Slivered green onions (optional)
- Crushed red pepper

1. Trim fat from meat. If necessary, cut meat to fit in a $3^{1}/_{2}$- or 4-quart slow cooker. Place meat in the cooker. In a bowl combine the next nine ingredients (through black pepper). Pour over meat.

2. Cover and cook on low 8 to 10 hours or on high 4 to 5 hours. If using low-heat setting, turn cooker to high. In a bowl combine cornstarch and the cold water; stir into mixture in cooker. Cover and cook about 15 minutes more or until thickened.

3. Remove meat from cooker, reserving cooking juices. Shred meat using two forks.

4. Spoon shredded meat onto cabbage leaves. If desired, add cashews, additional jicama strips, and/or slivered green onions. Sprinkle with crushed red pepper. Fold in opposite sides of each cabbage leaf; roll up and secure with a pick. Serve wraps with the reserved cooking liquid for dipping.

PER SERVING: 214 cal., 12 g total fat (5 g sat. fat), 65 mg chol., 413 mg sodium, 6 g carb. (2 g fiber, 2 g sugars), 20 g pro.

Salmon and Quinoa Cake Benedict

SERVINGS 4 (1 quinoa patty + 1 egg + toppers each)

CARB. PER SERVING 15 g

PREP 20 minutes   STAND 20 minutes

COOK 12 minutes

- 3 egg whites, lightly beaten
- 1/2 cup soft bread crumbs
- 1/4 cup grated Parmesan cheese
- 2 Tbsp. chopped green onion
- 1/2 tsp. hot pepper sauce
- 1 3/4 cups cooked quinoa (tip, *below right*)
- Nonstick cooking spray
- 3 Tbsp. light sour cream
- 2 tsp. Dijon-style mustard
- Fat-free milk (optional)
- 1 recipe Poached Eggs
- 2 oz. thinly sliced smoked salmon (lox-style)
- Chopped green onion
- Cracked black pepper

1. In a bowl combine the first five ingredients (through hot pepper sauce). Stir in quinoa. Let stand 20 minutes. Form mixture into four 4-inch-diameter patties. Coat a large nonstick skillet with cooking spray. Heat skillet over medium heat. Cook patties about 3 minutes per side or until golden brown, turning once. Keep warm.

2. For sauce, stir together sour cream and mustard. Thin with milk, if necessary, to reach desired consistency.

3. Prepare Poached Eggs. Top quinoa patties with smoked salmon, eggs, and sauce. Sprinkle with additional chopped green onion and cracked black pepper.

POACHED EGGS In a large skillet combine 4 cups water and 1 Tbsp. vinegar. Bring to boiling; reduce heat to simmering (bubbles should begin to break the surface of the water). Break an egg into a cup and slip egg into the simmering water. Repeat with three more eggs, allowing each egg an equal amount of space in the skillet. Simmer eggs, uncovered, 3 to 5 minutes or until the whites are completely set and yolks begin to thicken but are not hard. Using a slotted spoon, remove eggs from skillet.

PER SERVING: 211 cal., 9 g total fat (3 g sat. fat), 200 mg chol., 562 mg sodium, 15 g carb. (1 g fiber, 1 g sugars), 18 g pro.

TEST KITCHEN TIP

To make 1 3/4 cups cooked quinoa, in a small saucepan combine 1 1/2 cups unsalted chicken stock and 1/3 cup quinoa. Bring to boiling; reduce heat. Simmer, covered, about 15 minutes or until quinoa is tender. If necessary, drain off any excess liquid.

Thai Veggie Pita Pockets

SERVINGS 4 (2 halves each)
CARB. PER SERVING 36 g
PREP 25 minutes   BAKE 15 minutes
COOL 1 hour

- 1 15-oz. can no-salt-added garbanzo beans (chickpeas), rinsed and drained
- 2 Tbsp. olive oil
- $\frac{1}{8}$ tsp. salt
- $\frac{1}{8}$ tsp. black pepper
- 1 small sweet potato (7 oz.)
- 2 Tbsp. peanut sauce
- 1 Tbsp. lime juice
- 2 cloves garlic, peeled and halved
- 4 flax, oat bran, and whole wheat pita bread rounds (such as Joseph's) or low-carb pita bread rounds, halved
- 1 cup fresh baby spinach
- $\frac{1}{2}$ cup purchased julienned carrots
- 2 radishes, shredded

1. Preheat oven to 450°F. Place half of the garbanzo beans in a shallow baking pan. Drizzle with 1 Tbsp. oil and sprinkle with salt and pepper; toss to coat. Roast, uncovered, 15 to 20 minutes or until crisp. Set aside to cool.

2. Meanwhile, pierce the sweet potato with a fork. Microwave 4 to 5 minutes or until tender. Let cool; peel. Transfer pulp to a food processor or blender. Add remaining garbanzo beans, peanut sauce, remaining olive oil, lime juice, and garlic. Cover and process or blend until smooth (if necessary, add 2 to 3 Tbsp. water to make spreadable).

3. Spread hummus in pita pocket halves. Add spinach, carrots, roasted garbanzo beans, and radishes.

PER SERVING: 255 cal., 10 g total fat (1 g sat. fat), 0 mg chol., 459 mg sodium, 36 g carb. (10 g fiber, 6 g sugars), 12 g pro.

Pesto Roast Beef Panini

SERVINGS 4 (1 sandwich each)
CARB. PER SERVING 25 g
START TO FINISH 15 minutes

- 3 Tbsp. purchased basil pesto
- 4 whole wheat sandwich rounds, split
- 4 ultrathin slices provolone cheese
- 2 cups fresh spinach
- 8 oz. low-fat, reduced-sodium sliced cooked roast beef
- 1 medium red or yellow sweet pepper, cut into thin strips
- Nonstick cooking spray

1. Spread pesto evenly on cut sides of sandwich rounds. Fill sandwich rounds with cheese, spinach, roast beef, and sweet pepper strips.

2. Lightly coat a panini sandwich maker or unheated griddle with cooking spray. Preheat panini sandwich maker or griddle over medium heat. Cook sandwiches 3 to 5 minutes in the panini sandwich maker or 6 to 8 minutes on a griddle (if using a griddle, place a heavy skillet on sandwiches) or until cheese is melted and bread is golden brown, turning sandwiches once.

PER SERVING: 300 cal., 12 g total fat (4 g sat. fat), 47 mg chol., 501 mg sodium, 25 g carb. (6 g fiber, 4 g sugars), 25 g pro.

TEST KITCHEN TIP

To make your own pesto, in a food processor or blender place 2 cups packed fresh basil leaves; 1/2 cup finely shredded Parmesan cheese; 1/4 cup olive oil; 3 Tbsp. chopped toasted walnuts; 2 cloves garlic, minced; and 1/4 tsp. salt. Cover and process until smooth. Pesto can be covered and refrigerated up to 3 days or placed in an airtight container and frozen up to 1 month

Crunchy Tilapia Wraps with Lemon-Dill Sauce

SERVINGS 4 (2 wraps each)
CARB. PER SERVING 23 g
START TO FINISH 30 minutes

- 1/2 cup plain fat-free Greek yogurt
- 2 Tbsp. lemon juice
- 1 tsp. dried dill weed
- 1/2 tsp. garlic salt
- 1/4 tsp. white pepper
- 4 4- to 5-oz. fresh or frozen tilapia fillets
- Nonstick cooking spray
- 1/3 cup all-purpose flour
- 1 tsp. ground cumin
- 1/2 tsp. ground coriander
- 1/4 tsp. salt
- 2 egg whites
- 1 cup panko bread crumbs
- 8 small butterhead (Boston or Bibb) lettuce leaves
- Thinly sliced cucumber, tomato, and red onion
- 1/4 cup snipped fresh Italian parsley
- Lemon wedges (optional)

1. For sauce, stir together the first five ingredients (through white pepper). Cover and chill until ready to serve (up to 24 hours).

2. Thaw fish, if frozen. Preheat oven to 425°F. Line a baking sheet with foil. Coat foil with cooking spray. Cut fish in half lengthwise. Rinse fish; pat dry with paper towels.

3. In a shallow dish stir together flour, cumin, coriander, and salt. In a second shallow dish lightly beat egg whites. Place panko in a third shallow dish. Dip fish into flour mixture, then into egg whites. Coat with panko, pressing to adhere. Place on the prepared baking sheet. Lightly coat fish with cooking spray.

4. Bake 10 to 12 minutes or until fish flakes easily, turning once.

5. Divide fish among lettuce leaves. Top with cucumber, tomato, and red onion. Spoon some of the sauce over fish and vegetables; sprinkle with parsley. If desired, roll or wrap lettuce around filling. Serve with lemon wedges (if desired) and the remaining sauce.

PER SERVING: 241 cal., 3 g total fat (1 g sat. fat), 56 mg chol., 414 mg sodium, 23 g carb. (1 g fiber, 3 g sugars), 31 g pro.

Portobello Spinach Eggs Benedict

SERVINGS 4 (1 mushroom cap + 1 egg + 1 Tbsp. sauce each)
CARB. PER SERVING 7 g
PREP 15 minutes   COOK 13 minutes

- 4 small fresh portobello mushrooms (about 3 oz. each), stems and gills removed
- 1/4 tsp. salt
- 1/4 tsp. black pepper
- 4 tsp. olive oil
- 2 Tbsp. plain fat-free yogurt or fat-free sour cream
- 4 tsp. light mayonnaise
- 2 tsp. Dijon-style mustard
- 2 tsp. lemon juice
- 2 tsp. snipped fresh tarragon or thyme
- 10 to 12 drops hot pepper sauce
- 4 cloves garlic, minced
- 4 cups fresh spinach, chopped
- 1/4 cup reduced-sodium chicken broth or vegetable broth
- 1/2 tsp. salt-free Cajun seasoning or seafood seasoning
- 4 eggs

1. Season mushroom caps with the salt and pepper. In a large skillet heat 2 tsp. of the oil over medium heat. Cook mushroom caps in hot oil 8 to 10 minutes or until tender, turning once. Transfer caps to a plate; cover with foil.

2. Meanwhile, for sauce, in a bowl whisk together the next six ingredients (through hot sauce) until smooth.

3. Heat the remaining 2 tsp. oil in the skillet over medium heat. Add garlic; cook and stir 1 minute. Add spinach, broth, and Cajun seasoning; cook and stir about 1 minute until spinach is just wilted. Keep warm. Wipe skillet clean.

4. To poach eggs, fill the skillet halfway with water. Bring water to boiling; reduce heat to simmering (bubbles should begin to break the surface of the water). Break one of the eggs into a small dish. Carefully slide egg into simmering water, holding the lip of the dish as close to the water as possible. Repeat with the remaining eggs, positioning so the eggs don't touch. Simmer, uncovered, 3 to 5 minutes or until egg whites are completely set and yolks begin to thicken but are not hard. Remove eggs from pan with a slotted spoon; blot on a paper towel to remove excess water.

5. To assemble, top mushroom caps with spinach mixture, poached eggs, and sauce. If desired, sprinkle with additional Cajun seasoning.

PER SERVING: 167 cal., 11 g total fat (3 g sat. fat), 188 mg chol., 383 mg sodium, 7 g carb. (2 g fiber, 3 g sugars), 10 g pro.

TEST KITCHEN TIPS

To prepare the mushrooms, wipe the tops clean with a damp paper towel. Trim stems from caps using a sharp paring knife. Gently scrape the dark, soft gills out with a kitchen spoon.

For tips on poaching eggs, see *page 55*.

Turkey and Pickled Strawberry Wraps

SERVINGS 2 (1 wrap each)
CARB. PER SERVING 19 g
PREP 20 minutes STAND 30 minutes

- 1 cup fresh strawberries, hulled and quartered
- 1 small shallot, very thinly sliced
- 1/4 cup white wine vinegar
- 2 Tbsp. water
- 2 8-inch whole wheat low-carb flour tortillas or wraps
- 1 oz. semisoft goat cheese (chèvre) or reduced-fat feta cheese, crumbled
- 1/2 cup fresh spinach or arugula
- 1/4 cup fresh basil leaves
- 4 oz. shredded cooked skinless turkey breast (1 cup)

1. In a bowl combine strawberries, shallot, vinegar, and water. Cover and let stand at room temperature 30 minutes, stirring occasionally. Drain, discarding the liquid.

2. If using goat cheese, spread over tortillas. Top evenly with spinach, basil, turkey, and half of the drained strawberry mixture. If using feta, sprinkle over top. Roll up tortillas and cut in half. Serve the remaining strawberry mixture with the wraps.

PER SERVING: 243 cal., 7 g total fat (3 g sat. fat), 58 mg chol., 351 mg sodium, 19 g carb. (10 g fiber, 4 g sugars), 24 g pro.

Turkey-Swiss Chard Wraps

SERVINGS 6 (1 large or 2 small wraps each)
CARB. PER SERVING 11 g
PREP 20 minutes
SLOW COOK 6 to 7 hours (high) or 3 to 3$\frac{1}{2}$ hours (low)

4 sprigs fresh tarragon or Italian parsley
2 large onions, cut into wedges
1$\frac{1}{4}$ lb. turkey breast tenderloin, cut into 2- to 3-inch pieces
1 14.5-oz. can reduced-sodium chicken broth
3 Tbsp. fig-infused balsamic vinegar or balsamic vinegar
2 Tbsp. olive oil
1 tsp. honey
$\frac{1}{4}$ tsp. black pepper
1 large tart red apple, cored and cut into thin bite-size strips
3 Tbsp. coarsely chopped pistachio nuts
6 large or 12 small Swiss chard leaves, center stems removed, or butterhead (Boston or Bibb) lettuce leaves
$\frac{1}{4}$ cup crumbled blue cheese (1 oz.)

1. Finely snip enough of the tarragon to measure 1 tsp. In a 3$\frac{1}{2}$- or 4-qt. slow cooker combine the remaining tarragon sprigs and onions. Add turkey and broth. Cover and cook on low 6 to 7 hours or on high 3 to 3$\frac{1}{2}$ hours.
2. Using a slotted spoon, remove turkey from broth. Strain broth, discarding solids. Reserve broth for another use. Coarsely shred or chop turkey.
3. In a bowl whisk together the reserved snipped tarragon, vinegar, oil, honey, and pepper. Add turkey, apple, and pistachios; toss gently to coat.
4. For wraps, divide turkey mixture among Swiss chard leaves; sprinkle with cheese. Roll up chard leaves. If necessary, secure with toothpicks.

PER SERVING: 207 cal., 9 g total fat (2 g sat. fat), 46 mg chol., 540 mg sodium, 11 g carb. (2 g fiber, 7 g sugars), 20 g pro.

Uncrusted

Crusts are the most carb- and fat-laden part of pizza, quiche, and pie. Introduce family members to flour-free crusts that improve nutrition and let them all enjoy their favorites.

Cauliflower-Crusted Pizza

SERVINGS 4 (2 wedges each)
CARB. PER SERVING 18 g
PREP 30 minutes
MICROWAVE 3 minutes
BAKE 17 minutes

  4 cups cauliflower florets
  1 egg, lightly beaten
  1/4 cup shredded reduced-fat Italian-blend cheese (1 oz.)
  1/4 cup grated Parmesan cheese
  1/4 cup panko bread crumbs
  1/2 tsp. dried Italian seasoning, crushed
  1/8 tsp. salt
  2 cups sliced fresh mushrooms
  1 cup yellow or green sweet pepper strips
  1 small red onion, cut into thin wedges
  1 tsp. olive oil
  1/2 cup Fast Pizza Sauce or canned pizza sauce
  1 cup shredded Italian cheese blend (4 oz.)
  Snipped fresh basil, oregano, and/or parsley

1. Place the cauliflower in a food processor. Cover and pulse four to six times or until crumbly and mixture resembles the texture of couscous.

2. Place a pizza stone or baking sheet in the oven. Preheat oven to 425°F. Place cauliflower in a large bowl with 2 Tbsp. water. Cover with vented plastic wrap. Microwave 3 to 5 minutes or until tender, stirring once or twice. Cool. Transfer cauliflower to a 100%-cotton flour-sack towel. Wrap towel around cauliflower and squeeze until there is no more liquid (this step is critical).

3. In a bowl stir together cauliflower and the next six ingredients (through salt). On a piece of parchment paper pat cauliflower mixture into a 12-inch circle. Transfer crust on paper to the preheated pizza stone. Bake 12 to 15 minutes or until crisp and starting to brown.

4. Meanwhile, in a large skillet cook and stir mushrooms, sweet pepper, and onion in hot oil 4 to 6 minutes or until crisp-tender. Remove from heat.

5. Spoon pizza sauce over baked crust, spreading evenly. Top with cooked vegetables. Sprinkle evenly with the 1 cup cheese. Bake about 5 minutes more or until heated and cheese is melted. If desired, sprinkle with snipped fresh herb. Cut into eight wedges.

FAST PIZZA SAUCE In a small saucepan cook 1/2 cup chopped onion and 2 cloves garlic, minced, in 1 tsp. hot oil over medium heat about 5 minutes or until onion is tender, stirring occasionally. Stir in one 8-oz. can no-salt-added tomato sauce; 1/2 tsp. each dried oregano and basil, crushed; and 1/4 tsp. each salt and crushed red pepper. Bring to boilng; reduce heat. Simmer, uncovered, about 5 minutes or until sauce reaches desired consistency.

PER SERVING: 245 cal., 12 g total fat (6 g sat. fat), 75 mg chol., 584 mg sodium, 18 g carb. (5 g fiber, 7 g sugars), 17 g pro.

CAULIFLOWER TIP

Do you couscous?
Couscous is a tiny pasta often used as a side dish. Process raw cauliflower with several on/off turns in a food processor until it is crumbly and about the size of cooked couscous, which is a little smaller than uncooked rice.

Swiss Chard and Asparagus Pizza

SERVINGS 4 (2 wedges each)
CARB. PER SERVING 28 g
PREP 40 minutes   BAKE 10 minutes
BROIL 2 minutes   STAND 3 minutes

Nonstick cooking spray
10 oz. fresh Swiss chard or spinach
1 Tbsp. olive oil
$3/4$ cup finely chopped red onion
4 cloves garlic, minced
$1/8$ tsp. salt
6 oz. fresh asparagus spears, trimmed and cut into $1/4$-inch pieces
2 eggs, lightly beaten
1 egg white
$1/4$ tsp. dried oregano, crushed
$1/4$ tsp. black pepper
$1/8$ tsp. ground nutmeg
$1^{1}/2$ cups cooked brown rice, cooled
2 Tbsp. grated Parmesan cheese
1 cup shredded part-skim mozzarella cheese (4 oz.)
$2/3$ cup grape tomatoes, quartered or halved
$1/2$ cup chopped yellow sweet pepper
2 Tbsp. thinly sliced pepperoncini salad peppers
1 Tbsp. snipped fresh Italian parsley
1 Tbsp. red wine vinegar
$1/8$ tsp. black pepper

1. Preheat oven to 400°F. Line a baking sheet with foil. Coat foil with cooking spray. If using chard, separate leaves from stems. Cut stems and leaves into bite-size pieces, keeping them separate.

2. In a large nonstick skillet heat 2 tsp. of the oil over medium-high heat. Add $^2/_3$ cup of the red onion, the garlic, and salt; cook and stir 2 minutes. Add chard stems; cook 5 minutes, stirring frequently. Add chard leaves or spinach (if using); cook about 5 minutes or until chard is wilted and moisture is nearly evaporated, stirring occasionally. Add asparagus; cook and stir about 3 minutes more or until asparagus is crisp-tender. Spread mixture on a plate to cool slightly.

3. For crust, in a medium bowl combine the next five ingredients (through nutmeg). Stir in cooked rice, Parmesan, and chard mixture. Spoon rice mixture onto the prepared baking sheet. Using your hands, press into a 12-inch circle. Bake 10 minutes. Remove from oven.

4. Preheat broiler. Broil crust 4 to 5 inches from the heat 1 to 2 minutes or just until golden. Sprinkle with mozzarella cheese. Broil 1 minute more. Remove from oven. Let stand 2 minutes. Lift one corner of the foil and carefully slide a cutting board under crust; let stand 1 minute more.

5. In a bowl combine the remaining 1 tsp. oil, the remaining red onion, and the remaining ingredients. Cut crust into eight wedges. Top with tomato mixture.

PER SERVING: 284 cal., 12 g total fat (5 g sat. fat), 113 mg chol., 541 mg sodium, 28 g carb. (4 g fiber, 5 g sugars), 16 g pro.

Hearty Vegetable, Bacon, and Quinoa Quiche

SERVINGS 6 (1 wedge each)
CARB. PER SERVING 15 g
PREP 25 minutes   BAKE 55 minutes

Nonstick cooking spray
$^1/_2$ cup quinoa
8 oz. sliced fresh mushrooms
1 cup loosely packed, coarsely chopped fresh spinach
$^1/_2$ cup sliced, halved leeks
4 slices applewood smoked bacon (2 oz.), crisp cooked and coarsely crumbled
4 eggs, lightly beaten
1 cup refrigerated or frozen egg product, thawed
1 12-oz. can evaporated fat-free milk
2 oz. Gruyère or Havarti cheese, shredded ($^1/_2$ cup)
$^1/_2$ tsp. salt
$^1/_8$ tsp. black pepper

1. Preheat oven to 350°F. Coat a deep 10-inch pie plate with cooking spray. Rinse and drain quinoa. Spread quinoa as evenly as possible over the bottom of the prepared pie plate.

2. In a bowl stir together the next four ingredients (through bacon). Spread mushroom mixture over the quinoa. In another bowl whisk together the remaining ingredients. Pour into the pie plate (it will be full).

3. Bake 55 to 60 minutes or until set in the center and browned on top. Cut into six wedges.

PER SERVING: 288 cal., 12 g total fat (4 g sat. fat), 163 mg chol., 571 mg sodium, 15 g carb. (1 g fiber, 4 g sugars), 20 g pro.

Mini Pizzas with Spaghetti Squash Crusts

SERVINGS 6 (1 mini pizza each)
CARB. PER SERVING 17 g
PREP 20 minutes   ROAST 50 minutes
BROIL 7 minutes per batch

1   3$\frac{1}{2}$- to 3$\frac{3}{4}$-lb. spaghetti squash
1   Tbsp. olive oil
Nonstick cooking spray
1   egg, lightly beaten
1   Tbsp. snipped fresh basil or 1 tsp. dried basil, crushed
$\frac{1}{2}$ tsp. salt
$\frac{3}{4}$ cup Quick Marinara Sauce
1$\frac{1}{2}$ cups shredded part-skim mozzarella cheese
6   Tbsp. chopped onion
6   Tbsp. chopped red, yellow, or green sweet pepper
6   Tbsp. sliced fresh mushrooms
3   Tbsp. grated Parmesan cheese

1. Preheat oven to 400°F. Cut squash in half lengthwise; remove and discard seeds. Brush insides of squash halves with oil. Place squash halves, cut sides down, in a 15×10-inch baking pan. Bake 50 to 60 minutes or until tender. Remove from oven; cool slightly.

2. Preheat broiler. Use a fork to shred and separate the squash pulp into strands. Place squash pulp in a colander; press pulp with a spatula to remove any excess moisture.

3. For crusts, line two large baking sheets with foil; coat foil with cooking spray. In a bowl combine egg, basil, and salt. Stir in drained squash. Spoon squash mixture into six mounds (about $\frac{1}{2}$ cup each) onto the prepared baking sheets. Spread each mound into a 6-inch circle; coat with cooking spray.

4. Broil crusts, one baking sheet at a time, 4 to 5 inches from heat about 5 minutes or until lightly browned. Top with Quick Marinara Sauce and remaining toppings. Broil about 2 minutes more or until toppings are heated and cheese(s) are melted.*

QUICK MARINARA SAUCE Place two 28-oz. cans whole tomatoes, undrained, in a food processor or blender. Cover and process or blend until nearly smooth. Stir in 6 Tbsp. snipped fresh basil. In a large skillet heat 2 Tbsp. olive oil over medium heat. Add 2 cloves garlic, minced; cook and stir until garlic is lightly browned. Stir in tomato mixture, 1 tsp. crushed red pepper, and $\frac{1}{2}$ tsp. each salt and black pepper. Bring to boiling; reduce heat. Simmer, uncovered 10 minutes.

*TIP After broiling one pan of mini pizzas, place them on the bottom oven rack to keep warm while broiling the second pan of pizzas.

PER SERVING: 193 cal., 10 g total fat (4 g sat. fat), 51 mg chol., 532 mg sodium, 17 g carb. (4 g fiber, 7 g sugars), 10 g pro.

Sweet Potato-Crusted Quiche

SERVINGS 6 (1 wedge each)
CARB. PER SERVING 13 g
PREP 30 minutes   BAKE 45 minutes
CHILL 6 hours   STAND 10 minutes

    Nonstick cooking spray
- 1 large sweet potato, peeled and thinly sliced (10 oz.)
- 4 slices lower-sodium, less-fat bacon, crisp-cooked, drained, and crumbled
- 1/2 cup chopped green sweet pepper (1 small)
- 3 Tbsp. very finely chopped red onion
- 1/2 cup shredded reduced-fat sharp cheddar cheese (2 oz.)
- 2 oz. Gouda cheese, shredded (1/2 cup)
- 1 3/4 cups refrigerated or frozen egg product, thawed
- 1/2 cup fat-free milk
- 1/4 tsp. hot pepper sauce
    Fresh parsley leaves (optional)

1. Preheat oven to 325°F. Coat a 9-inch pie plate with cooking spray.
2. Place sweet potato slices in a 2-qt. square baking dish. Add 2 Tbsp. water to the baking dish. Cover with vented plastic wrap. Microwave 3 to 5 minutes or just until sweet potatoes are tender. Drain; cool slightly.
3. Arrange sweet potato slices evenly across the bottom and up the sides of the prepared pie plate, overlapping as needed.
4. Sprinkle crumbled bacon over sweet potato; sprinkle with sweet pepper and onion. Top with cheeses. In a bowl whisk together eggs, milk, and hot pepper sauce. Pour egg mixture over vegetables and cheese in the pie plate.
5. Bake about 45 minutes or until a knife inserted near the center comes out clean. Let stand on a wire rack 10 minutes. Cut into six wedges. If desired, garnish with parsley.
TO MAKE AHEAD Prepare and bake as directed. Let cool on a wire rack. Cover and chill at least 6 hours or up to 24 hours. To serve, cut into six wedges. Microwave, one wedge at a time, on 70% (medium-high) power about 2 minutes or until heated.

PER SERVING: 166 cal., 6 g total fat (3 g sat. fat), 20 mg chol., 375 mg sodium, 13 g carb. (2 g fiber, 4 g sugars), 15 g pro.

SLICING TIPS

Knife
Rest the sweet potato on its most stable side, then use a chef's knife to slice the potato as thin as possible.

Mandoline
A mandoline makes it easy to cut very thin, uniform slices. Stop before you get your fingers too close to the slicer!

Chicken Pot Pie with Cauliflower Crust

SERVINGS 4 (1 pot pie each)
CARB. PER SERVING 20 g
PREP 50 minutes   BAKE 30 minutes

Nonstick cooking spray
4 cups coarsely chopped cauliflower
$\frac{1}{2}$ cup finely shredded Parmesan cheese
$\frac{1}{3}$ cup almond meal
$\frac{1}{4}$ tsp. salt
$\frac{1}{4}$ tsp. black pepper
2 tsp. olive oil
$\frac{1}{3}$ cup refrigerated or frozen egg product, thawed, or 1 egg and 1 egg white, lightly beaten
1 cup thinly sliced carrot
$\frac{1}{2}$ cup thinly sliced celery
$\frac{1}{2}$ cup chopped onion
2 cloves garlic, minced
1 cup fat-free milk
$\frac{1}{3}$ cup reduced-sodium chicken broth
2 Tbsp. all-purpose flour
$1\frac{1}{2}$ tsp. snipped fresh thyme or $\frac{1}{2}$ tsp. dried thyme, crushed
Salt
$1\frac{1}{2}$ cups chopped cooked chicken breast

1. Preheat oven to 425°F. Generously coat four 10-oz. custard cups or ramekins with cooking spray; place cups in a 15×10-inch baking pan. Place cauliflower in a food processor. Cover and pulse until cauliflower is finely chopped but not pureed. Set a steamer basket in a large skillet; add water to just below the basket. Bring water to boiling. Add cauliflower to steamer basket. Cover and steam about 5 minutes or until tender. Remove steamer basket with cauliflower from skillet and set over a large plate. Let cauliflower cool completely.

2. In a bowl combine cheese, almond meal, $^1/_4$ tsp. salt, and the pepper. Stir in cooled cauliflower. Transfer $^1/_2$ cup of the cauliflower mixture to a small bowl; add oil and toss to coat. Set aside for topper.

3. Add egg to remaining cauliflower mixture. Stir until well combined. Spoon cauliflower mixture evenly into prepared custard cups; press mixture onto bottoms and up the sides of the cups, leaving $^1/_4$ inch at the tops of the cups.

4. Bake cups in pan about 15 minutes or until edges are browned and centers are set. Transfer pan with cups to a wire rack.

5. Meanwhile, coat a large nonstick skillet with cooking spray. Heat skillet over medium heat. Add carrots, celery, onion, and garlic. Cook about 5 minutes or until tender, stirring occasionally.

6. Whisk together milk, broth, flour, thyme, and dash salt until smooth. Add all at once to carrot mixture. Cook and stir until thickened and bubbly. Stir in chicken.

7. Spoon chicken mixture evenly into crust-lined custard cups. Top each with remaining cauliflower mixture. Bake about 15 minutes or until bubbly and topping is golden brown.

PER SERVING: 300 cal., 12 g total fat (3 g sat. fat), 53 mg chol., 573 mg sodium, 20 g carb. (5 g fiber, 8 g sugars), 29 g pro.

Zucchini, Cheddar, and Sage Crust Pizza with Chicken and Apples

SERVINGS 6 (1 wedge each)
CARB. PER SERVING 15 g
PREP 25 minutes   **BAKE** 30 minutes

- 1 Tbsp. coarse cornmeal
- 2$^1/_2$ cups packed shredded zucchini (2 small)
- 1$^1/_2$ cups shredded reduced-fat cheddar cheese (6 oz.)
- 1 egg, lightly beaten
- $^1/_4$ cup all-purpose flour
- $^1/_4$ cup coarse cornmeal
- 1 Tbsp. snipped fresh sage
- 1 Tbsp. minced garlic
- $^1/_4$ cup purchased dried tomato pesto
- 1 cup shredded cooked chicken
- $^1/_2$ cup finely chopped yellow sweet pepper
- $^1/_2$ cup finely chopped apple
- $^1/_2$ cup chopped pimiento-stuffed green olives (optional)

1. Preheat oven to 425°F. Line a 12-inch pizza pan with parchment paper. Sprinkle with the 1 tablespoon cornmeal.

2. Place shredded zucchini in a colander and press several times with paper towels to remove excess moisture (there should be 2 cups packed after draining).

3. In a bowl combine the drained zucchini, 1 cup of the cheese, and the next five ingredients (through garlic). Spoon mixture onto prepared pan, pressing to an even thickness.

4. Bake 20 minutes or until golden. Cool slightly and loosen crust from paper with a spatula.

5. Reduce oven temperature to 400°F. Spread tomato pesto on crust; top with remaining ingredients. Sprinkle with remaining $^1/_2$ cup cheese. Bake 10 minutes more. Cut into wedges.

PER SERVING: 211 cal., 10 g total fat (5 g sat. fat), 72 mg chol., 441 mg sodium, 15 g carb. (2 g fiber, 3 g sugars), 17 g pro.

Cauliflower-Crusted Dinner Quiche

SERVINGS 6 (1 wedge each)
CARB. PER SERVING 11 g
PREP 30 minutes   COOK 8 minutes
BAKE 50 minutes   STAND 10 minutes

    4   cups cauliflower florets
    2   Tbsp. water
  $1/4$ cup refrigerated or frozen egg
        product, thawed, or 1 egg,
        lightly beaten
    1   cup shredded reduced-fat
        cheese, such as mozzarella or
        cheddar (4 oz.)
    2   Tbsp. whole wheat panko
        bread crumbs
    2   Tbsp. snipped fresh chives
    1   medium green sweet pepper,
        cut into thin bite-size strips
  $1/2$ cup chopped onion
    1   Tbsp. olive oil
    3   fully cooked chicken with
        spinach and feta cheese
        sausage links, chopped*
 $1^{1}/4$ cups refrigerated or frozen egg
        product, thawed, or 4 eggs,
        lightly beaten
  $1/4$ cup fat-free half-and-half
    1   Tbsp. all-purpose flour
  $1/2$ cup chopped, seeded tomato
  $1/4$ cup torn fresh basil

1. Preheat oven to 375°F. Coat a
9-inch pie plate with *nonstick cooking
spray.* In a food processor place half of
the cauliflower. Process until finely
chopped. Remove chopped cauliflower
to a large bowl. Repeat with remaining
cauliflower.
2. Combine water with cauliflower.
Cover with vented plastic wrap.
Microwave 3 to 5 minutes or until
tender, stirring once. Cool slightly.

Transfer cauliflower to a 100%-cotton
flour-sack towel. Wrap towel around
cauliflower and squeeze until there is
no more liquid (this step is critical).
3. In a bowl stir together the $1/4$ cup
egg product, $1/2$ cup of the cheese, the
panko, and chives. Stir in the
cauliflower until well combined. Spoon
cauliflower mixture into prepared pie
plate, pressing mixture onto bottom
and up the sides of the plate.
4. Bake 25 minutes or until golden.
Place crust on a wire rack. Decrease
oven temperature to 325°F.
5. Meanwhile, in a large skillet cook
green pepper and onion in hot oil over
medium heat 5 minutes, stirring
occasionally. Add sausage. Cook
3 minutes more, stirring occasionally.
Spoon sausage mixture into
cauliflower crust, spreading evenly. In a
bowl whisk together the $1^{1}/4$ cups egg
product, half-and-half, and flour. Pour
over sausage mixture in crust.
6. Bake, uncovered, 30 to 40 minutes
or until a knife inserted near center
comes out clean (cover edges of
quiche with foil, if needed, to keep
crust from overbrowning). Sprinkle
with remaining $1/2$ cup cheese. Bake
3 minutes more. Let stand on a wire
rack 10 minutes. Sprinkle with tomato
and basil. Cut into six wedges.
*TIP Save the remaining chicken
sausage from the package to cut up and
add to omelets and scrambled eggs.

PER SERVING: 214 cal., 9 g total fat
(3 g sat. fat), 40 mg chol., 552 mg sodium,
11 g carb. (2 g fiber, 4 g sugars), 21 g pro.

CRUST HOW-TO

The crust mixture for this
quiche is relatively loose.
Working quickly before the egg
product is absorbed, use your
fingers to press the mixture
evenly over the bottom and
sides of dish. It will hold its
shape after baking.

Cook
FRESH

Learn to think out of the box(es)—those on the supermarket shelves. Fresh and whole is more healthful than processed. So make an effort to spend more time in the perimeter of the store, where fresh produce, meats, and dairy are found. Incorporate as many fresh ingredients as you can into a variety of recipes. You'll cut carbs and sodium while boosting the overall nutrition of your meals.

Fresh
BEDS

Replace common carb-loaded rice, pasta, and grains with vegetables, greens, and beans.

Balsamic Marinated Flank Steak on Shaved Parmesan Asparagus

SERVINGS 4 (3 oz. beef + 1 cup asparagus each)

CARB. PER SERVING 4 g

PREP 30 minutes

MARINATE 20 minutes

GRILL 17 minutes

1 lb. beef flank steak
$^1/_3$ cup balsamic vinegar
2 tsp. packed brown sugar*
3 cloves garlic, minced
$^1/_2$ tsp. salt
$^1/_2$ tsp. dried Italian seasoning, crushed
1 lb. fresh thick asparagus spears, trimmed
1 lemon
2 tsp. olive oil
$^1/_4$ cup finely shredded Parmesan cheese
$^1/_4$ tsp. cracked black pepper

1. Trim fat from steak. Score steak on both sides by making shallow cuts at 1-inch intervals in a diamond pattern. Place steak in a plastic bag set in a shallow dish. For marinade, combine vinegar, brown sugar, two cloves of the garlic, $^1/_4$ tsp. of the salt, and the Italian seasoning. Pour over steak; seal bag. Marinate in the refrigerator 30 minutes to 2 hours, turning bag occasionally.

2. Meanwhile, remove 1 tsp. zest and squeeze 1 Tbsp. juice from lemon and place in a large bowl. Add the olive oil, remaining garlic clove, and the remaining $^1/_4$ tsp. salt. Whisk to combine. Hold asparagus spears flat on a cutting board and use a vegetable peeler to cut them into thin ribbons. Add to the bowl with the dressing. Toss to combine.

3. Drain steak, discarding marinade. Grill steak, uncovered, over medium heat until desired doneness, turning once. Allow 17 to 21 minutes for medium (160°F). Thinly slice steak. Spoon asparagus mixture onto a platter. Sprinkle with Parmesan cheese and cracked black pepper. Top with sliced steak.

*SUGAR SUBSTITUTE Choose Splenda Brown Sugar Blend. Follow package directions to use produce amount equivalent to 2 tsp. brown sugar.

PER SERVING: 236 cal., 12 g total fat (5 g sat. fat), 77 mg chol., 318 mg sodium, 4 g carb. (1 g fiber, 2 g sugars), 27 g pro.

PER SERVING WITH SUBSTITUTE: Same as above.

TEST KITCHEN TIP

If asparagus spears are too thin to peel into ribbons, quarter or halve them lengthwise.

Pumpkin Seed Salmon with Maple-Spice Carrots

SERVINGS 4 (1 fish fillet and + $^1/_2$ cup carrots each)

CARB. PER SERVING 31 g

PREP 15 minutes   BAKE 20 minutes

- 4 4- to 5-oz. fresh or frozen salmon fillets
- 1 lb. carrots, cut diagonally into $^1/_4$-inch slices
- $^1/_4$ cup pure maple syrup
- $^1/_2$ tsp. salt
- $^1/_2$ tsp. pumpkin pie spice
- 8 multigrain saltine crackers, finely crushed
- 3 Tbsp. finely chopped salted, roasted pumpkin seeds (pepitas)
- Nonstick cooking spray
- 2 tsp. salted, roasted pumpkin seeds (pepitas)

1. Thaw fish, if frozen. Rinse fish; pat dry with paper towels. Preheat oven to 425°F. Line a 15×10-inch baking pan with foil.

2. In a large bowl combine carrots, 3 Tbsp. of the maple syrup, $^1/_4$ tsp. of the salt, and the pumpkin pie spice. Arrange carrots on one side of the prepared baking pan. Bake 10 minutes.

3. Meanwhile, in a shallow dish combine crushed crackers, 3 Tbsp. pumpkin seeds, and the remaining $^1/_4$ teaspoon salt. Brush tops of fish with the remaining 1 Tbsp. maple syrup. Sprinkle with cracker mixture, pressing to adhere. Place fish in baking pan next to carrots. Lightly coat tops of fish with cooking spray. Bake 10 to 15 minutes more or until fish flakes easily and carrots are tender.

4. To serve, sprinkle carrots with the 2 tsp. pumpkin seeds; top with salmon.

PER SERVING: 359 cal., 15 g total fat (2 g sat. fat), 62 mg chol., 519 mg sodium, 31 g carb. (4 g fiber, 19 g sugars), 28 g pro.

Tortilla Chip Flounder with Black Bean Salad

SERVINGS 4 (1 fish fillet + $^2/_3$ cup bean salad each)

CARB. PER SERVING 35 g

PREP 30 minutes   BAKE 8 minutes

- 4 3- to 4-oz. fresh or frozen flounder fillets or other white fish fillets
- 4 oz. multigrain tortilla chips
- $^1/_8$ to $^1/_4$ tsp. cayenne pepper
- $^1/_3$ cup refrigerated or frozen egg product, thawed
- 1 15-oz. can no-salt-added black beans, rinsed and drained
- $^1/_2$ cup halved cherry tomatoes
- $^1/_2$ cup chopped green sweet pepper
- $^1/_4$ cup finely chopped red onion
- 2 Tbsp. snipped fresh oregano
- 2 Tbsp. snipped fresh parsley
- 1 Tbsp. lemon juice
- 2 tsp. olive oil
- $^1/_4$ tsp. salt
- $^1/_4$ tsp. ground cumin
- $^1/_4$ cup crumbled queso fresco

1. Thaw fish, if frozen. Rinse fish; pat dry with paper towels. Preheat oven to 425°F. Line a baking sheet with foil. Coat foil with *nonstick cooking spray*.

2. In a food processor combine chips and cayenne pepper. Cover; process until very finely crushed. Transfer to a shallow dish. Pour egg into another shallow dish. Dip fish in egg, then in crushed chips, turning to coat and pressing to adhere. Place fish on the prepared baking sheet. Lightly coat tops of fish with cooking spray. Bake 8 to 10 minutes or until fish flakes easily.

3. Meanwhile, for bean salad, combine the remaining ingredients. Serve fish on salad. Sprinkle with queso fresco and, if desired, additional parsley.

PER SERVING: 361 cal., 11 g total fat (2 g sat. fat), 46 mg chol., 401 mg sodium, 35 g carb. (8 g fiber, 3 g sugars), 28 g pro.

Pork Paprikash with Cauliflower "Rice"

SERVINGS 4 ($1\frac{1}{4}$ cups meat mixture + 1 cup cauliflower "rice" each)
CARB. PER SERVING 24 g
START TO FINISH 30 minutes

- 1 1-lb. natural pork tenderloin
- 6 cups chopped cauliflower ($1\frac{1}{2}$ lb.)
- 2 Tbsp. olive oil
- $\frac{1}{8}$ tsp. salt
- 1 medium onion, cut into thin wedges
- $1\frac{1}{2}$ Tbsp. paprika
- $\frac{1}{2}$ tsp. black pepper
- $\frac{1}{4}$ tsp. salt
- 1 14.5-oz. can no-salt-added diced tomatoes with basil, garlic, and oregano, undrained
- 1 cup reduced-sodium chicken broth
- $\frac{1}{4}$ cup mild banana peppers, finely chopped
- $\frac{1}{3}$ cup light sour cream
- 2 Tbsp. all-purpose flour

1. Trim fat from meat. Cut meat into bite-size pieces. Place cauliflower in a food processor. Cover; process with several on/off pulses until cauliflower is chopped into rice-size pieces.
2. In an extra-large nonstick skillet heat 1 Tbsp. of the oil over medium-high heat. Add cauliflower and $\frac{1}{8}$ tsp. salt. Cook 8 to 10 minutes or until golden brown flecks appear throughout, stirring occasionally.
3. Meanwhile, in a large skillet heat the remaining 1 Tbsp. oil over medium-high heat. Add meat and onion; cook about 3 minutes or until meat starts to brown, stirring occasionally. Sprinkle with paprika, black pepper, and $\frac{1}{4}$ tsp. salt. Cook and stir 1 minute more.
4. Add tomatoes, broth, and banana peppers. Bring to boiling; reduce heat to medium-low. Cover and cook 5 minutes. Increase heat to medium-high. Cook, uncovered, 4 to 6 minutes or until slightly thickened, stirring frequently. Combine sour cream and flour; stir into meat mixture. Cook and stir until thickened and bubbly.
5. Serve meat mixture over cauliflower "rice." If desired, top with additional sour cream and a sprinkle of paprika.

PER SERVING: 319 cal., 12 g total fat (3 g sat. fat), 79 mg chol., 593 mg sodium, 24 g carb. (11 g fiber, 11 g sugars), 31 g pro.

Seared Scallops over Lemony Roasted Fennel

SERVINGS 4 (3 or 4 scallops + $^1/_2$ cup fennel each)
CARB. PER SERVING 16 g
PREP 15 minutes   ROAST 35 minutes

Nonstick cooking spray
1 lemon
2 large or 3 small fennel bulbs
2 Tbsp. canola oil
2 cloves garlic, minced
$^1/_4$ tsp. black pepper
$^1/_2$ tsp. fennel seeds, crushed
$1^1/_4$ to $1^1/_2$ lb. fresh sea scallops (12 to 16 scallops)
$^1/_8$ tsp. salt
2 Tbsp. shredded Parmesan cheese

1. Preheat oven to 375°F. Coat a 3-qt. rectangular baking dish with cooking spray.
2. Remove $^1/_2$ tsp. zest and squeeze 3 Tbsp. juice from lemon. Quarter fennel bulbs; remove cores. Cut bulbs into $^1/_2$-inch-thick slices (you should have about 3 cups). Place fennel in the prepared baking dish. Stir in 2 Tbsp. of the lemon juice, 1 Tbsp. of the oil, the garlic, and pepper.
3. Roast, uncovered, 25 minutes, stirring occasionally. Stir in the remaining 1 Tbsp. lemon juice and the fennel seeds. Roast, uncovered, 10 minutes more or until fennel is tender and browned on the edges. Remove from oven. Stir in lemon zest.
4. Meanwhile, rinse scallops; pat dry with paper towels. Sprinkle scallops with salt. Coat an extra-large nonstick skillet with cooking spray. Heat the remaining 1 Tbsp. oil in skillet over medium-high heat. Add scallops. Cook 7 to 8 minutes or until scallops are opaque and lightly browned, turning once. Top roasted fennel with scallops and Parmesan cheese.

PER SERVING: 256 cal., 9 g total fat (1 g sat. fat), 49 mg chol., 443 mg sodium, 16 g carb. (5 g fiber, 0 g sugars), 27 g pro.

TEST KITCHEN TIP

Select a skillet that's large enough to allow some space around each scallop. This helps the scallops brown evenly.

Sweet-and-Sour Pork

SERVINGS 4 (1 cup napa cabbage + about 1 cup pork mixture each)
CARB. PER SERVING 23 g or 21 g
PREP 35 minutes
MICROWAVE 4 minutes
STAND 10 minutes

- 1 large red sweet pepper, quartered and seeded
- 1 tsp. water
- 1 8-oz. can pineapple chunks (juice pack)
- 2 Tbsp. reduced-sodium soy sauce
- 1 Tbsp. packed brown sugar*
- 1 Tbsp. cornstarch
- 2 tsp. grated fresh ginger
- 2 cloves garlic
- 2 tsp. rice vinegar
- 4 tsp. canola oil
- 1 medium green sweet pepper, seeded and cut into 1-inch pieces
- 1 8-oz. can bamboo shoots, drained
- 12 oz. boneless pork loin, trimmed of fat and bias-sliced across the grain into strips
- 4 cups shredded napa cabbage

1. Place red sweet pepper quarters, cut sides down, in a dish. Add the water. Cover with plastic wrap. Microwave 4 to 5 minutes or until tender. Let stand about 10 minutes or until skin can easily be peeled from flesh; remove and discard skin. Place red sweet pepper in a food processor; cover and process until smooth. Drain pineapple chunks, reserving $1/3$ cup of the juice; set pineapple chunks aside. Add the $1/3$ cup pineapple juice and the next six ingredients (through rice vinegar) to food processor. Cover and process until combined.

2. In a large skillet heat 1 tsp. of the oil over medium-high heat. Add green sweet pepper; cook and stir about 2 minutes or until crisp-tender. Add bamboo shoots; cook and stir 30 seconds. Remove vegetables from skillet. Add the remaining 3 tsp. oil to skillet. Add pork strips; cook and stir 2 to 3 minutes or just until done. Add the red sweet pepper mixture; cook and stir about 30 seconds or until thickened and bubbly. Cook and stir 2 minutes more. Stir in vegetables and pineapple chunks; heat through. Serve over cabbage.

*SUGAR SUBSTITUTE Choose Splenda Brown Sugar Blend. Follow package directions to use product amount equivalent to 1 Tbsp. brown sugar.

PER SERVING: 252 cal., 8 g total fat (1 g sat. fat), 58 mg chol., 333 mg sodium, 23 g carb. (3 g fiber, 16 g sugars), 22 g pro.

PER SERVING WITH SUBSTITUTE: Same as above, except 246 cal., 21 g carb. (14 g sugars).

TEST KITCHEN TIP

Use a large chef's knife to cut the head of napa cabbage in half. Then cut into thin shreds to equal 4 cups.

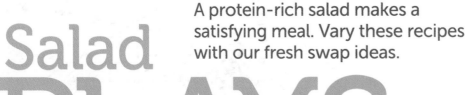

Cook Fresh

Salad
PLAYS

A protein-rich salad makes a satisfying meal. Vary these recipes with our fresh swap ideas.

Strawberry-Turkey Salad with Creamy Curry Dressing

SERVINGS 4 ($2^{1}/4$ cups each)
CARB. PER SERVING 18 g
PREP 15 minutes

- 2 cups chopped cooked turkey breast
- 1 recipe Creamy Curry Dressing
- 6 cups baby spinach
- 1 cup sliced strawberries
- 2 oranges, peeled and sectioned
- $^{1}/4$ cup chopped peanuts
- 2 green onions, sliced
- Lemon wedges (optional)

1. In a bowl toss together the chopped turkey and Creamy Curry Dressing.

2. Arrange greens on a large platter. Top with turkey mixture, strawberries, and oranges. Sprinkle with peanuts and green onions. If desired, serve with lemon wedges.

CREAMY CURRY DRESSING In a bowl whisk together 2 Tbsp. each plain fat-free Greek yogurt and light mayonnaise, 1 tsp. curry powder, $^{1}/8$ tsp. salt, and a dash black pepper. Stir in enough of 2 to 3 Tbsp. fat-free milk to reach desired consistency.

PER SERVING: 241 cal., 8 g total fat (1 g sat. fat), 51 mg chol., 326 mg sodium, 18 g carb. (6 g fiber, 9 g sugars), 27 g pro.

MIX IT UP
Use mixed power greens for the spinach as another nutrient-packed option.

NUTS FOR YOU

Trade 1/4 cup toasted sliced almonds for the peanuts.

BERRY NICE

Add 1 cup fresh blackberries and/or raspberries for the orange sections.

POULTRY PAIRING

When making another meal, prepare an extra chicken breast to use for the turkey in this salad.

GREAT GREENS
Try tender baby kale as an alternative to arugula.

HEARTY GRAINS
Leftover cooked barley or wild rice mix can sub for the farro.

MAKE IT MEATLESS

Swap one 15-oz. can no-salt-added cannellini beans or garbanzo beans, rinsed and drained, for the pork.

PICK A DIFFERENT FRUIT

For a slightly different flavor or color, use apple for the pear and dried apricots or cranberries for the raisins.

TEST KITCHEN TIP

If you can't find packaged cooked farro, place $3/4$ cup uncooked farro and $2 1/4$ cups water in a medium saucepan. Bring to boiling; reduce heat. Simmer, covered, about 30 minutes or until tender. Drain any excess water.

Roasted Pork, Marinated Pear and Farro Salad

SERVINGS 4 ($1 1/2$ cups salad + 3 oz. pork each)
CARB. PER SERVING 42 g
PREP 10 minutes   **ROAST** 25 minutes
STAND 5 minutes

1	1-lb. natural pork tenderloin
$1/4$	tsp. salt
$1/4$	tsp. pepper
1	medium pear, cored and thinly sliced
1	recipe Golden Balsamic Dressing
1	5-oz. pkg. arugula
1	8.5-oz. pkg. precooked farro (tip, *below left*)
4	green onions, thinly sliced
$1/4$	cup golden raisins
1	oz. white cheddar or Gouda cheese, cut into $1/4$-inch cubes
1	Tbsp. thinly sliced fresh basil

1. Preheat oven to 425°F. Place pork tenderloin on a rack in a shallow roasting pan. Sprinkle with the salt and pepper. Roast 25 to 30 minutes or until done (145°F). Let stand 5 minutes. Meanwhile, in a large bowl combine pear and 3 Tbsp. of the Golden Balsamic Dressing. Cover and let stand while pork roasts.

2. To serve, arrange arugula on a platter. Stir farro, onions, raisins, and cheese into pear mixture; spoon over arugula. Slice pork and arrange on top of salad. Drizzle with remaining dressing and top with basil.

GOLDEN BALSAMIC DRESSING In a small bowl whisk together 3 Tbsp. white balsamic vinegar; 2 Tbsp. canola oil; 2 cloves garlic, minced; 1 tsp. honey; $1/4$ tsp. salt; and $1/8$ tsp. crushed red pepper.

PER SERVING: 388 cal., 12 g total fat (3 g sat. fat), 81 mg chol., 406 mg sodium, 42 g carb. (4 g fiber, 18 g sugars), 29 g pro.

Steak Salad with Creamy Horseradish Dressing

SERVINGS 4 (2$\frac{1}{4}$ cups salad + 3 oz. steak + 3 Tbsp. dressing each)
CARB. PER SERVING 22 g
PREP 15 minutes **ROAST** 25 minutes
COOK 15 minutes **STAND** 5 minutes

- 8 oz. new potatoes, quartered
- 8 oz. fresh green beans, trimmed
- 1 small red onion, cut into $\frac{1}{2}$-inch-thick wedges
- 1 Tbsp. olive oil
- 2 8-oz. boneless beef top sirloin steaks, cut 1 inch thick
- $\frac{1}{4}$ tsp. cracked black pepper
- 6 cups torn Bibb lettuce
- 1 recipe Creamy Horseradish Dressing

1. Preheat oven to 425°F. Arrange potatoes, beans, and onion in a shallow baking pan. Drizzle with oil and sprinkle with $\frac{1}{4}$ tsp. *salt.* Roast 25 to 30 minutes or until tender, stirring once.

2. Meanwhile, trim fat from steaks. Sprinkle steaks with $\frac{1}{4}$ tsp. *salt* and the pepper. Coat a large skillet with *nonstick cooking spray.* Heat over medium-high heat. Add steaks. Reduce heat to medium; cook 15 to 20 minutes or until desired doneness (145°F for medium rare or 160°F for medium). Let stand 5 minutes. Slice steaks across the grain into $\frac{1}{4}$-inch-thick slices.

3. Arrange greens on a platter. Top with potato mixture. Arrange steak slices over potato mixture. Drizzle with Creamy Horseradish Dressing.

CREAMY HORSERADISH DRESSING In a bowl combine one 5.3-oz. carton plain fat-free Greek yogurt, 1 Tbsp. each prepared horseradish and snipped fresh chives, 1 tsp. each honey and red wine vinegar, and a dash salt. Stir in 3 to 4 Tbsp. milk for desired consistency.

PER SERVING: 294 cal., 9 g total fat (2 g sat. fat), 68 mg chol., 450 mg sodium, 22 g carb. (4 g fiber, 8 g sugars), 33 g pro.

SWEET STRIPS

Replace the green beans with 1 cup sweet pepper strips in desired color.

RED FISH FOR RED MEAT
Boost omega-3s in your diet by using salmon fillets for the steak.

CRUNCH IT UP
Try a combo of romaine lettuce and Bibb lettuce for a little extra crunch.

CRUNCH IT UP
Coarsely chop romaine to swap for the mixed baby greens.

Greens and Grain Italian Salad

SERVINGS 4 (2^1/$_2$ cups each)
CARB. PER SERVING 35 g
PREP 20 minutes

1^1/$_3$ cups cooked and cooled pearled barley
6 cups mixed baby greens
1 15-oz. can no-salt-added red kidney beans or cannellini beans, rinsed and drained
1 cup coarsely shredded fresh basil
1 cup halved cherry tomatoes
1 recipe Balsamic Dressing
1 oz. shaved Parmesan cheese

1. Spread barley on a large platter. Arrange greens, beans, basil, and tomatoes over barley. Drizzle with Balsamic Dressing and sprinkle with shaved Parmesan.

BALSAMIC DRESSING In a bowl whisk together ^{1}/$_4$ cup balsamic vinegar; 2 Tbsp. olive oil; 2 cloves garlic, minced; and ^{1}/$_4$ tsp. each salt and black pepper.

PER SERVING: 267 cal., 10 g total fat (2 g sat. fat), 5 mg chol., 314 mg sodium, 35 g carb. (8 g fiber, 5 g sugars), 10 g pro.

ALTERNATIVE GRAINS
Bump up the protein of this salad with cooked red or regular quinoa for the barley.

EASY CHEESE
Try shredded reduced-fat Italian cheese blend for the Parmesan cheese.

PICK YOUR PROTEIN
Substitute shredded chicken breast or flaked tuna for the canned beans.

131

SAY CHEESE

Alternate another flavorful cheese like crumbled reduced-fat feta cheese for the shaved Parmesan.

POWER UP

Go with a superfood like baby kale for the baby greens.

GO GREEN

Get your greens on with 1 cup broccoli florets for the sweet pepper.

SEA TO SHORE

Trade chicken breast for the tuna steaks (cook chicken for 10 to 12 minutes, turning once, or until 165°F).

Seared Tuna Salad with Creamy Dried Tomato Dressing

SERVINGS 4 ($1^1/2$ cups salad + 3 oz. tuna each)
CARB. PER SERVING 6 g
START TO FINISH 30 minutes

- 2 6-oz. fresh or frozen tuna steaks, cut $^3/4$ inch thick
- 2 tsp. canola oil
- 6 cups mixed baby greens
- 1 yellow or red sweet pepper, cut into bite-size strips
- $^1/2$ of a recipe Creamy Dried Tomato Dressing
- 1 oz. Parmesan cheese, shaved
- 1 Tbsp. fresh oregano leaves (optional)

1. Thaw fish; if frozen. Rinse fish; pat dry with paper towels. In a large skillet heat oil over medium-high heat. Add fish; cook 4 to 6 minutes or until just slightly pink in center, turning once.
2. Arrange greens on a platter. Break fish into chunks and arrange over greens. Top with sweet pepper. Drizzle with dressing. Top with shaved Parmesan cheese and, if desired, fresh oregano leaves.

CREAMY DRIED TOMATO DRESSING Place $^1/4$ cup dried tomatoes (not oil-packed), chopped, in a small heatproof bowl; add boiling water to cover. Let stand 10 minutes; drain, reserving the soaking liquid. In a blender combine drained tomatoes; $^1/2$ cup low-fat buttermilk; 2 Tbsp. canola oil; 1 Tbsp. each chopped shallot, cider vinegar, and fresh oregano; and $^1/4$ cup of the soaking liquid. Cover and blend until smooth, adding additional soaking liquid to reach desired consistency. Store leftovers in an airtight container in the refrigerator up to 3 days.

PER SERVING: 205 cal., 8 g total fat (2 g sat. fat), 39 mg chol., 190 mg sodium, 6 g carb. (2 g fiber, 3 g sugars), 25 g pro.

Finish It Fresh
SLOW COOKER

Liven up the flavor and appearance of slow-cooked meals with colorful, tasty toppers or stir-ins.

Roasted Beet and Carrot Salad

SERVINGS 4 (3 cups each)
CARB. PER SERVING 37 g
PREP 25 minutes
SLOW COOK 4 to $4^1/2$ hours (high)

- $2^1/4$ to $2^1/2$ lb. medium beets, trimmed, peeled, and each cut into $^3/4$-inch-thick wedges (6 cups)
- 1 Tbsp. + 2 tsp. olive oil
- $^1/4$ tsp. black pepper
- $^1/8$ tsp. salt
- 3 medium carrots, cut into 1-inch pieces
- 1 lime
- 1 Tbsp. honey
- 2 cloves garlic, minced
- $^1/2$ tsp. ground cumin
- $^1/2$ tsp. grated fresh ginger
- 6 cups chopped romaine and/or baby spinach

1. Place beets in a $3^1/2$- to 4-qt. slow cooker. Add 1 tsp. of the olive oil and half of the pepper and salt; stir to coat. Cover; cook on high 2 hours. Place carrots in the center of a 12-inch piece of heavy foil. Drizzle with 1 tsp. of the olive oil and sprinkle with the remaining pepper and salt. Bring up edges of foil over carrots and fold. Fold in sides to seal. Place on top of beets in cooker. Cover; cook on high 2 to $2^1/2$ hours more or until beets are fork-tender.

2. Meanwhile, remove $^1/2$ tsp. zest and squeeze 1 Tbsp. juice from lime. Reserve lime zest. For dressing, in a bowl whisk together the remaining 1 Tbsp. olive oil, the lime juice, honey, garlic, cumin, and ginger.

3. Place romaine and/or spinach on a platter. Carefully remove carrot packet from cooker. Spoon beets over spinach. Carefully open carrot packet; top beets with carrots. Drizzle beets and carrots with dressing. Sprinkle with lime zest and Toppers.

PER SERVING: 241 cal., 9 g total fat (3 g sat. fat), 10 mg chol., 417 mg sodium, 37 g carb. (9 g fiber, 25 g sugars), 7 g pro.

TOPPERS
Top with $^1/2$ cup crumbled reduced-fat feta cheese (2 oz.); 2 oranges, peeled, sectioned, and coarsely chopped; $^1/8$ tsp. crushed red pepper; and (if desired) $^1/4$ cup toasted walnuts, coarsely chopped.

STIR-INS

Remove 2 tsp. zest and squeeze 3 Tbsp. juice from a lemon. Stir in zest, juice, and one 5-oz. pkg. fresh baby spinach as directed.

TOPPERS

Top salad with 1 medium avocado, halved, seeded, peeled, and chopped; $^1/_2$ cup crumbled reduced-fat feta cheese (2 oz.); and $^1/_3$ cup pistachio nuts, coarsely chopped.

Lemony White Bean and Carrot Spinach Salad

SERVINGS 12 ($^3/_4$ cup each)
CARB. PER SERVING 21 g
PREP 30 minutes   STAND 1 hour
SLOW COOK 7 to 8 hours (low) or
$3^1/_2$ to 4 hours (high)

- $1^1/_2$ cups dried Great Northern beans
- 5 medium carrots, cut into $^1/_2$-inch pieces
- 1 medium onion, halved and thinly sliced (1 cup)
- 2 cloves garlic, minced
- $^1/_2$ tsp. dried oregano, crushed
- $^1/_4$ tsp. salt
- $^1/_4$ tsp. black pepper
- $4^1/_2$ cups no-salt-added chicken stock
- Lemon wedges (optional)

1. Rinse beans; drain. In a 4- to 5-qt. Dutch oven combine beans and enough water to cover beans by 2 inches. Bring to boiling; reduce heat. Simmer, uncovered, 10 minutes. Remove from heat. Cover and let stand 1 hour. Rinse and drain beans.
2. In a $3^1/_2$- or 4-qt. slow cooker combine the soaked beans and the next six ingredients (through pepper). Pour stock over mixture in cooker.
3. Cover and cook on low 7 to 8 hours or on high $3^1/_2$ to 4 hours. If desired, remove $^1/_2$ cup of the cooking liquid; set aside. Drain bean mixture; discard any remaining cooking liquid. Return bean mixture to the hot cooker. Add Stir-Ins. Let stand, covered, 5 minutes. Transfer bean mixture to a platter. Add Toppers. If desired, drizzle with enough of the reserved cooking liquid to moisten. If desired, serve with lemon wedges.

PER SERVING: 152 cal., 4 g total fat (1 g sat. fat), 1 mg chol., 216 mg sodium, 21 g carb. (7 g fiber, 2 g sugars), 9 g pro.

Blackened Sea Bass with Radish Pickle Banh Mi Topper

SERVINGS 4 (1 fillet + $^1/_2$ cup pickled vegetables + $1^3/_4$ tsp. topper each)

CARB. PER SERVING 6 g

PREP 20 minutes

SLOW COOK $1^1/_2$ to $1^3/_4$ hours (high)

CHILL 1 hour

- 4 4-oz. fresh or frozen sea bass or salmon fillets, about 1 inch thick
- 2 tsp. salt-free Cajun, Creole, or blackened seasoning
- $^1/_2$ cup rice vinegar
- 1 Tbsp. sugar
- $^1/_4$ tsp. salt
- 1 cup thinly sliced bok choy (white and green parts)
- 1 cup thinly sliced radishes
- $^1/_2$ cup thinly sliced red onion

TOPPERS

In a bowl stir together 2 Tbsp. light mayonnaise and 1 tsp. sriracha sauce. Sprinkle with $^1/_4$ cup fresh cilantro leaves and 1 fresh jalapeño peppers, halved, seeded (if desired), and thinly sliced.*

1. Thaw fish, if frozen. Rinse fish; pat dry with paper towels. Sprinkle seasoning over fish; rub in with your fingers.

2. Place one portion of fish in the middle of a 12-inch parchment square. Bring up two opposite sides of parchment and fold several times over fish. Fold remaining ends of parchment and tuck under. Repeat to make three more packets. Place fish packets in a 4- to 5-qt. oval slow cooker. Cover and cook on high $1^1/_2$ to $1^3/_4$ hours or until fish flakes easily.

3. Meanwhile, in small saucepan combine vinegar, sugar, and salt. Bring to boiling; remove from heat. In a large bowl combine bok choy, radishes, and red onion. Pour vinegar mixture over vegetables, tossing gently to coat. Cover and chill at least 1 hour or until ready to serve. Drain and discard liquid before serving.

4. Serve fish with pickled vegetables. Add Toppers.

*TIP Chile peppers contain oils that can irritate your skin and eyes. Wear plastic or rubber gloves when working with them.

PER SERVING: 166 cal., 5 g total fat (1 g sat. fat), 49 mg chol., 247 mg sodium, 6 g carb. (1 g fiber, 4 g sugars), 22 g pro.

Mechoui Pork Wraps with Carrot-Orange Slaw

SERVINGS 6 (1 sandwich each)

CARB. PER SERVING 23 g

PREP 30 minutes SLOW COOK 8 to
10 hours (low) or 4 to 5 hours (high)

- 1 $1^1/_2$- to 2-lb. boneless pork sirloin roast
- 2 tsp. snipped fresh thyme
- 1 tsp. snipped fresh rosemary
- 1 tsp. ground cumin
- $^1/_2$ tsp. ground coriander
- 2 cloves garlic, minced
- $1^1/_2$ cups fresh baby spinach
- 3 low-carb pita bread rounds, halved crosswise
- 1 6-oz. carton plain fat-free Greek yogurt
- 3 Tbsp. dried cranberries

1. Trim fat from roast. In a bowl combine the next five ingredients (through garlic). Sprinkle evenly over roast, pressing gently into meat. Place roast in a $3^1/_2$- or 4-qt. slow cooker. Pour $^1/_2$ cup water around roast.

2. Cover and cook on low 8 to 10 hours or on high 4 to 5 hours.

3. Remove meat from cooker, reserving cooking liquid. Coarsely shred meat into bite-size pieces using two forks; discard any solid fat. Skim fat from cooking liquid. Add enough reserved cooking liquid to meat to moisten.

4. Place spinach in pita halves. Add meat and top with a small amount of the Slaw Topper, the yogurt, and dried cranberries. Serve with any remaining slaw.

PER SERVING: 293 cal., 9 g total fat (2 g sat. fat), 71 mg chol., 186 mg sodium, 23 g carb. (6 g fiber, 10 g sugars), 34 g pro.

SLAW TOPPER

In a bowl combine 2 cups shredded carrots; 2 blood or Cara Cara oranges, peeled and sections, juices reserved; 2 Tbsp. each snipped fresh mint and cider vinegar; and 1 to 2 Tbsp. olive oil.

Rosemary Pork Tenderloin Sandwiches

SERVINGS 6 (1 sandwich each)
CARB. PER SERVING 35 g
PREP 25 minutes
SLOW COOK $1^1/2$ to 2 hours (low)

- 2 cups thinly sliced onions
- $^1/4$ cup water
- 2 12-oz. pork tenderloins
- 2 tsp. olive oil
- 1 Tbsp. snipped fresh rosemary
- 3 cloves garlic, minced
- 2 tsp. reduced-sodium Worcestershire sauce
- 6 $^1/4$-inch slices whole grain bread, toasted (about 10 oz.)
- 3 cups baby arugula
- $^1/2$ cup thinly sliced roasted red sweet peppers

1. Trim fat from meat. Coat an extra-large nonstick skillet with *nonstick cooking spray.* Cook onions, covered, over medium-low heat 13 to 15 minutes or until tender, stirring occasionally. Uncover; cook and stir over medium-high heat 3 to 5 minutes or until onions are tender. Place onions and water in a $3^1/2$- or 4-qt. slow cooker.

2. Brush tenderloins with olive oil. Sprinkle with rosemary and garlic, pressing into meat. In the same skillet cook meat over medium-high heat until browned on all sides, turning occasionally. Place meat on onions in cooker. Cover and cook on low $1^1/2$ to 2 hours or until pork is done (145°F).

3. Transfer meat to a cutting board. Slice meat. Drain onion mixture. Transfer onions to a small bowl. Stir in Worcestershire sauce.

4. To serve, top bread with arugula, roasted sweet peppers, and sliced pork. Spoon onion mixture over pork slices. Top with Horseradish Aïoli.

PER SERVING: 340 cal., 9 g total fat (2 g sat. fat), 77 mg chol., 439 mg sodium, 35 g carb. (2 g fiber, 8 g sugars), 30 g pro.

HORSERADISH AÏOLI

In a bowl stir together $^1/4$ cup light mayonnaise; 1 Tbsp. prepared horseradish; 2 cloves garlic, minced; and $^1/4$ tsp. black pepper. Cover and chill until ready to use.

Shredded Chile Beef over Lime Slaw with Mango Salsa

SERVINGS 6 (1 cup slaw mixture + $^2/_3$ cup meat + 2 Tbsp. salsa each)

CARB. PER SERVING 14 g

PREP 25 minutes **SLOW COOK** 11 to 12 hours (low) or $5^1/_2$ to 6 hours (high)

- $1^3/_4$ to 2 lb. boneless beef chuck pot roast
- 1 onion, cut into wedges
- 1 fresh jalapeño chile pepper, seeded and finely chopped (tip, *page 137*)
- 2 cloves garlic, minced
- $^1/_2$ cup lower-sodium beef broth
- $^1/_2$ tsp. cayenne pepper
- 3 cups finely shredded red cabbage
- 3 cups finely shredded green cabbage
- $^1/_4$ cup light mayonnaise
- 2 Tbsp. lime juice
- $^1/_2$ tsp. salt

1. Trim fat from roast. Place onion, jalapeño, and garlic in a $3^1/_2$- or 4-qt. slow cooker. Top with roast. Pour broth over roast and sprinkle with cayenne pepper.

2. Cover and cook on low 11 to 12 hours or on high $5^1/_2$ to 6 hours.

3. Remove meat from cooker; remove onions with a slotted spoon, reserving cooking liquid. Coarsely shred meat using two forks; discard any solid fat. Skim fat from reserved cooking liquid. Add onions to meat; add enough cooking liquid to the meat to moisten.

4. In a bowl combine the cabbages, mayonnaise, lime juice, and salt. Spoon slaw mixture into shallow bowls. Top with warmed beef mixture and Mango Salsa. Add avocado slices for Topper.

PER SERVING: 285 cal., 12 g total fat (3 g sat. fat), 89 mg chol., 406 mg sodium, 14 g carb. (3 g fiber, 9 g sugars), 31 g pro.

MANGO SALSA

In a bowl combine 1 cup chopped mango, 2 Tbsp. snipped fresh cilantro, 2 tsp. lime juice, and 1 tsp. olive oil.

TOPPER

Top beef mixture with $^1/_2$ of a medium avocado, seeded, peeled, and sliced.

Chicken Pho

SERVINGS 6 (1$\frac{3}{4}$ cups + toppers each)
CARB. PER SERVING 27 g or 26 g
PREP 25 minutes   SLOW COOK 7 to
8 hours (low) or 3$\frac{1}{2}$ to 4 hours (high)

- 6 oz. fresh shiitake mushrooms
- 1 Tbsp. coriander seeds
- 1 3-inch piece fresh ginger, sliced
- 4 whole cloves
- 2 lb. bone-in chicken thighs
- 4 cups water
- 1 32-oz. carton no-salt-added chicken stock
- 1 large onion, sliced
- 1 oz. dried porcini mushrooms, rinsed and broken
- 1 Tbsp. packed brown sugar*
- 5 cloves garlic, sliced
- 1 tsp. salt
- 4 oz. dried rice noodles, prepared according to pkg. directions

1. Rinse shiitakes; remove and reserve stems. Slice caps; cover and chill until ready to use. Place stems, coriander, ginger, and cloves on a square of cheesecloth. Tie with kitchen string.
2. Remove and discard skin from chicken. In a 5- to 6-qt. slow cooker combine chicken, spice bag, and next seven ingredients (through salt). Cover; cook on low 7 to 8 hours or on high 3$\frac{1}{2}$ to 4 hours. Discard spice bag.
3. Remove chicken. Remove bones; discard. Shred chicken; keep warm. Stir noodles and reserved shiitake caps into broth mixture. Cover; cook 10 minutes.
4. Ladle soup into bowls. Top with shredded chicken. Serve with Toppers.
SUGAR SUBSTITUTE Choose Splenda Brown Sugar Blend. Follow package directions to use product amount equivalent to 1 Tbsp. brown sugar.

PER SERVING: 246 cal., 4 g total fat (1 g sat. fat), 85 mg chol., 623 mg sodium, 27 g carb. (3 g fiber, 7 g sugars), 24 g pro.

PER SERVING WITH SUBSTITUTE: Same as above, except 243 cal., 26 g carb. (5 g sugars).

TOPPERS

Fresh cilantro leaves, slivered red onion, shredded carrots, fresh Thai basil leaves, fresh mint leaves, thinly sliced jalapeño chile peppers (tip, *page 137*), sriracha sauce, and/or lime wedges.

141

Finish Fresh

LEAFY GREENS

When spinach leaves top hot foods, they quickly soften and turn emerald green in color, making them a gorgeous garnish for slow-cooked soups and casseroles. The leaves of nutritious arugula, beet greens, chard, and kale do the same trick. Add them at the last minute.

FRESH HERBS

A sprinkling of fat-free snipped fresh green herbs—especially basil, chives, dill, parsley, mint, and thyme—brings garden-fresh flavors to soups, stews, casseroles, and meat dishes.

GREMOLATA

Five minutes is all it takes to make this sunny-bright Italian topper. In a bowl combine the zest of 1 lemon; 1 clove garlic, minced; 2 Tbsp. snipped fresh Italian parsley; and 1 tsp. olive oil. Sprinkle gremolata over slow-cooked meat or potato dishes.

Take slow-cooked fare to wholesome new heights with bright and spunky toppers for side dishes, soups, salads, and meats. These simple, fresh garnishes enhance flavor and texture while boosting nutrition.

SALSA FRESCA

Spicy, slow-cooked Mexican-style casseroles, soups, and stews benefit from a generous crown of pico de gallo (fresh salsa). To make a batch of the nearly calorie-free condiment, chop 4 tomatoes, 1 small onion, ½ cup fresh cilantro leaves, and 2 fresh jalapeño chile peppers (tip, *page 137*); combine. Add lime juice to taste (about 1 Tbsp.).

FRUIT SALSA

You don't even need a recipe to whip up a batch of this terrific topper. Just combine chopped fresh fruit, such as pineapple, strawberries, and kiwifruit, with lime juice and finely chopped fresh jalapeño chile pepper (tip, *page 137*) to taste. Add chopped red onion and sweet peppers if you like. Add lime juice to taste (about 1 Tbsp.). Use it to top slow-cooked poultry and meat dishes.

VEGGIE CONFETTI

Pep up the color, add crunchy texture, and improve the nutritional content of any slow-cooked casserole with this fat-free eye candy. To prepare, simply chop equal amounts of red sweet pepper, peeled carrot, and fresh Italian parsley, then toss lightly.

CHILES

Super-thin slices of fresh chile peppers—such as Anaheim, Fresno, and jalapeño—bring pizzazz to mellow slow-cooked dishes. Float a few on soups, stud stews, and embellish casseroles and meat dishes. To reduce the heat, use a paring knife to remove the seeds and membranes (tip, *page 137*.)

15-Minute FRESH

Fresh can be fast! Use pre-prepped ingredients to quickly compose a complete meal.

Meatless Swiss Chard and Potato-Bean Bowls

SERVINGS 4 (1 bowl each)
CARB. PER SERVING 36 g
START TO FINISH 15 minutes

- 2 cups frozen roasted sweet potato slices with sea salt and olive oil

  Nonstick cooking spray
- 6 cups torn, trimmed fresh Swiss chard
- $\frac{1}{2}$ cup frozen or fresh chopped onion
- $\frac{1}{8}$ tsp. salt
- $\frac{1}{2}$ cup roasted red peppers, thinly sliced
- 3 hard-cooked eggs, peeled and thinly sliced
- $\frac{1}{2}$ cup crunchy Bombay spice or falafel-flavor chickpeas, such as Saffron Road brand
- 1 Tbsp. olive oil
- $\frac{1}{4}$ cup finely shredded Parmesan cheese
- 4 lemon wedges

1. Preheat oven to 425°F. Line a baking sheet with parchment paper. Arrange sweet potato slices in a single layer on prepared baking sheet. Roast 12 minutes.

2. Meanwhile, coat a large nonstick skillet with cooking spray; heat over medium heat. Add chard, onion, and salt. Cook 3 to 5 minutes or until chard is just tender, stirring frequently. Remove from the heat. Stir in pepper slices.

3. Divide greens mixture among four shallow bowls. Add roasted sweet potato slices, egg slices, and chickpeas. Drizzle evenly with olive oil. Top with Parmesan cheese and serve with lemon wedges.

PER SERVING: 300 cal., 12 g total fat (3 g sat. fat), 145 mg chol., 634 mg sodium, 36 g carb. (5 g fiber, 20 g sugars), 13 g pro.

HARD-COOKED EGGS

Place in pan
Place eggs in a single layer in a saucepan. Add enough cold water to cover eggs by 1 inch. Bring to a rapid boil over high heat (water will have large rapidly breaking bubbles). Remove from heat, cover, and let stand 15 minutes; drain.

Cold water
Run cold water over the eggs or place them in ice water until cool enough to handle; drain.

Peel
To peel, gently tap each egg on the countertop. Roll egg between the palms of your hands. Peel off eggshell, starting at the large end.

Chicken Sausage and Asparagus-Quinoa Pilaf

SERVINGS 4 (about 1 cup each)
CARB. PER SERVING 23 g
START TO FINISH 15 minutes

Nonstick cooking spray
1/2 of a 12-oz. pkg. (2) fully cooked red pepper and Asiago or spinach and feta chicken sausages
1 12- to 16-oz. bunch fresh asparagus
1 10-oz. pkg. frozen cooked quinoa and kale with olive oil and sea salt (tip, *right*)
2 Tbsp. white wine vinegar
2 tsp. olive oil
1 tsp. Dijon-style mustard
1/3 cup dried cranberries or dried cherries
2 Tbsp. chopped toasted walnuts or pecans

1. Coat a large skillet with cooking spray; heat over medium heat. Meanwhile, cut sausages crosswise into 1/2-inch slices. Trim asparagus and cut into 2-inch pieces. Add sausage and asparagus to hot skillet; cook 3 minutes, stirring occasionally.

2. Add quinoa mixture to sausage mixture. Cover and cook 3 minutes, stirring occasionally. Meanwhile, in a bowl whisk together vinegar, oil, and mustard. Add to skillet along with cranberries; stir. Sprinkle with walnuts.

PER SERVING: 248 cal., 12 g total fat (2 g sat. fat), 35 mg chol., 461 mg sodium, 23 g carb. (2 g fiber, 8 g sugars), 12 g pro.

TEST KITCHEN TIP

If you can't find frozen quinoa and kale product, substitute 1 1/2 cups cooked quinoa, 1 cup finely chopped fresh kale, and 1/8 tsp. sea salt.

Simple Shrimp Pad Thai

SERVINGS 4 (1 cup each)
CARB. PER SERVING 34 g
START TO FINISH 15 minutes

- 9 oz. frozen cooked peeled and deveined shrimp (remove tails if desired)
- 4 oz. banh pho (wide rice noodles)
- 2 Tbsp. canola oil
- $\frac{1}{2}$ cup refrigerated or frozen egg product, thawed, or 2 eggs, lightly beaten
- 2 cups packaged shredded green cabbage
- $\frac{1}{2}$ cup packaged shredded carrot
- 2 green onions, thinly sliced
- 2 Tbsp. rice vinegar
- 1 Tbsp. honey
- 2 tsp. fish sauce
- $\frac{1}{4}$ to $\frac{1}{2}$ tsp. crushed red pepper
- $\frac{1}{4}$ cup chopped unsalted peanuts
- $\frac{1}{4}$ cup snipped fresh cilantro
  Lime wedges

1. Place shrimp and rice noodles in a large bowl. Add enough boiling water to cover; let stand 5 minutes, stirring occasionally. Drain; add enough additional boiling water to cover. Let stand 5 minutes more, stirring occasionally. Drain well.
2. Meanwhile, in a large nonstick skillet heat 1 Tbsp. of the oil over medium-low heat. Pour egg product into the skillet. Cook until set, using a spatula to lift and fold eggs as they cook to break up into smaller pieces. Remove from skillet; cover and keep warm.
3. Increase heat to medium-high. Add remaining 1 Tbsp. oil to the skillet. Add cabbage, carrot, and green onions. Cook 3 minutes, stirring occasionally.
4. In a bowl stir together vinegar, honey, fish sauce, and crushed red pepper. In another bowl combine peanuts and cilantro.
5. Add drained shrimp mixture to skillet; cook and stir 2 minutes. Gently add egg. Drizzle with vinegar mixture; toss to coat. Sprinkle noodle mixture with peanut mixture. Serve with lime wedges.

PER SERVING: 324 cal., 11 g total fat (1 g sat. fat), 101 mg chol., 551 mg sodium, 34 g carb. (3 g fiber, 7 g sugars), 21 g pro.

Fresh Tomato Sauce with Squash Noodles

SERVINGS 4 (1$\frac{1}{4}$ cups each)
CARB. PER SERVING 9 g
START TO FINISH 15 minutes

3 cups grape tomatoes or coarsely chopped, cored tomatoes
2 Tbsp. water
$\frac{1}{2}$ cup coarsely chopped fresh basil
3 cloves garlic, minced
$\frac{1}{2}$ tsp. salt
$\frac{1}{4}$ tsp. black pepper or crushed red pepper
1$\frac{1}{2}$ cups shredded cooked chicken breast
2 medium yellow summer squash and/or zucchini
2 Tbsp. olive oil
$\frac{1}{2}$ cup finely shredded Parmesan cheese

1. In a large skillet combine tomatoes and water. Cover and cook over medium heat 3 minutes. Uncover; use a potato masher to mash tomatoes slightly. Stir in half of the basil, the garlic, $\frac{1}{4}$ tsp. of the salt, and the pepper. Cook and stir 2 minutes more. Add chicken; cook about 2 minutes more or until heated. Cover; keep warm.

2. Trim ends of summer squash. Using a spiralizer, cut noodles into long thin strands (tip, *right*). Use kitchen scissors to cut through the strands to make them easier to serve.

3. Heat oil in an extra-large nonstick skillet over medium-high heat. Add squash; sprinkle with remaining $\frac{1}{4}$ tsp. salt. Cook and toss with tongs 1 to 2 minutes or until squash is just softened.

4. Serve squash topped with tomato mixture. Sprinkle with remaining basil and the Parmesan cheese.

PER SERVING: 226 cal., 12 g total fat (3 g sat. fat), 52 mg chol., 508 mg sodium, 9 g carb. (2 g fiber, 5 g sugars), 22 g pro.

TEST KITCHEN TIP

If you don't have a spiralizer, cut the summer squash lengthwise, then thinly slice crosswise into half-moons. Cook as directed in Step 3 for 4 or 5 minutes or until just tender.

Bistro Pizza

SERVINGS 2 ($^1/_2$ pizza each)
CARB. PER SERVING 19 g
START TO FINISH 15 minutes

- 1 rosemary and olive oil artisan pizza thin-crust flatbread
- 3 Tbsp. light ricotta cheese
- $^1/_4$ cup thinly sliced dried tomatoes (not oil-packed)
- 3 Tbsp. crumbled basil-and-tomato-flavor feta cheese
- 3 Tbsp. shredded Parmesan cheese
- Nonstick cooking spray
- 2 eggs
- 1 cup arugula
- 2 tsp. bottled balsamic glaze
- $^1/_4$ tsp. cracked black pepper
- $^1/_8$ tsp. kosher salt

1. Preheat oven to 450°F. Place the pizza crust on a baking sheet. Bake 4 minutes.

2. Spread the ricotta on the crust and top with the dried tomatoes, feta, and Parmesan cheese. Bake 3 to 5 minutes more or until cheese is melted and crust is golden brown.

3. Meanwhile, coat a large nonstick skillet with cooking spray. Heat skillet over medium heat. Break eggs into skillet. Add 1 Tbsp. water to the skillet; cover. Reduce heat to low. Cook eggs, covered, 3 to 4 minutes or until the whites are set and yolks are thickened but not hard.

4. In a bowl combine the arugula, balsamic glaze, $^1/_8$ tsp. of the pepper, and the salt. Top pizza with arugula salad. Gently place the eggs on top of the salad. Sprinkle with remaining $^1/_8$ tsp. pepper. Cut in half; serve immediately.

PER SERVING: 242 cal., 11 g total fat (5 g sat. fat), 205 mg chol., 552 mg sodium, 19 g carb. (2 g fiber, 6 g sugars), 17 g pro.

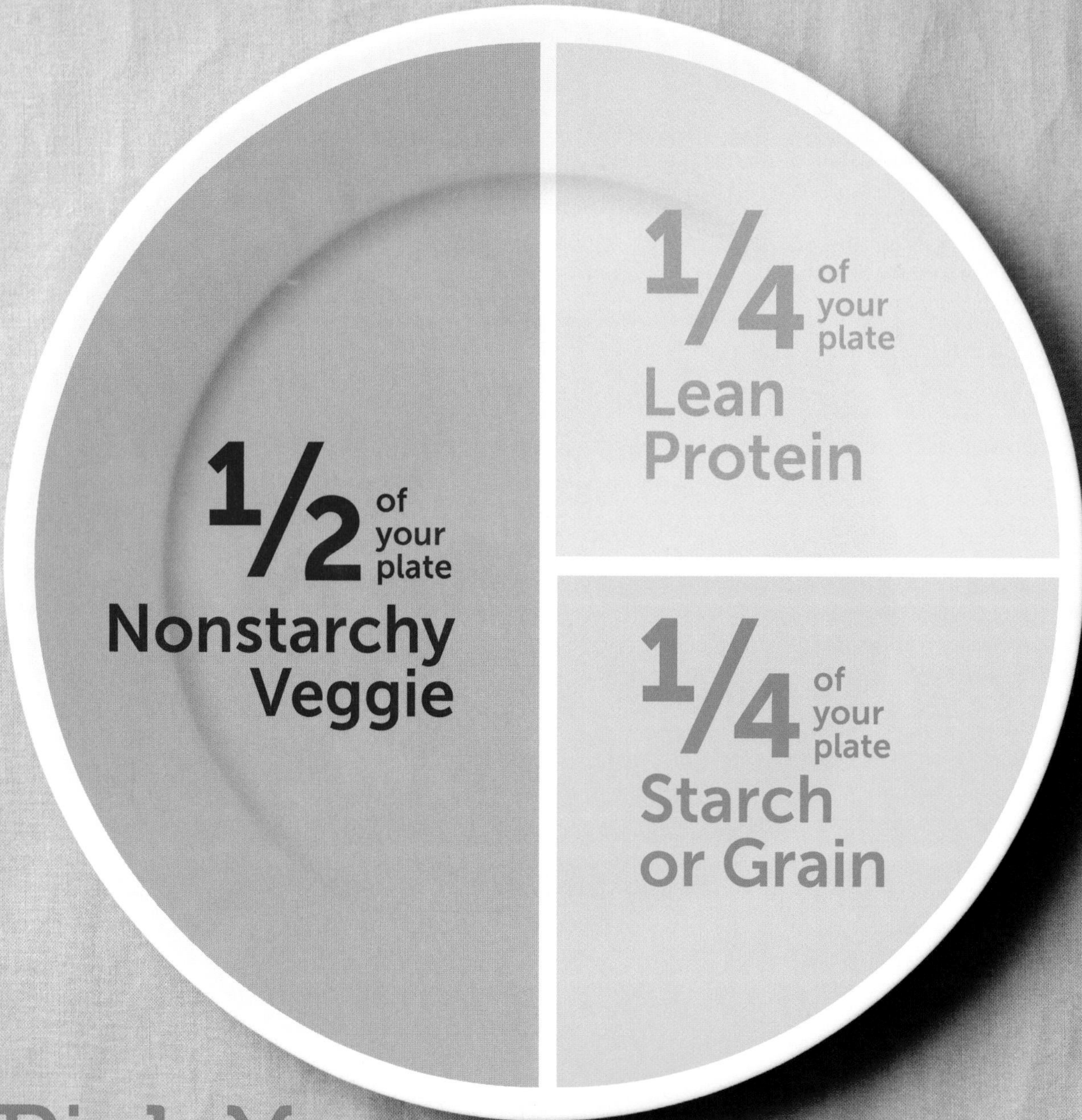

1/2 of your plate
Nonstarchy Veggie

1/4 of your plate
Lean Protein

1/4 of your plate
Starch or Grain

Pick Your PORTION

Give your plate a face-lift by filling it as shown here. Mix and match from the lists *opposite* to create meals. Get started with the combos that follow.

Choose 1 Nonstarchy Veggie

 Green beans

 Baby Mixed Greens Salad *Page 165*

 Asparagus and Wild Mushrooms *Page 163*

 Sugar snap peas

 Tomato-Cucumber Salad *Page 157*

 Brussels sprouts

 Tri-Color Summer Veggies *Page 155*

 Sweet pepper strips

Choose 1 Starch or Grain

 Parmesan Mashed Pototoes *Page 159*

 Butternut Squash and Quinoa Pilaf *Page 161*

 ½ cup corn

 Spiced Sweet Potato Wedges *Page 155*

 ½ cup brown rice

 ½ cup green peas

 Roasted Red Pepper-Spinach Pasta *Page 165*

 New Potato Salad with Cucumber and Jalapeño *Page 153*

Choose 1 Lean Protein

 Balsamic Chicken *Page 153*

 Tuna canned in water (3 oz.)

 Steak with Watercress Pesto *Page 159*

 95% lean ground beef patty (4 oz.)

 Sweet Barbecue-Glazed Turkey *Page 157*

 Low-fat cheese (1½ oz.)

 Maple Pecan Pork Chops *Page 161*

 Spice-Rubbed Salmon *Page 163*

Balsamic
Chicken

New Potato Salad
with Cucumber
and Jalapeño

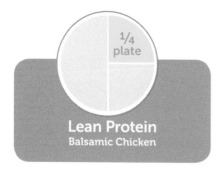

Lean Protein
Balsamic Chicken

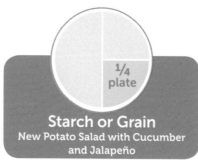

Starch or Grain
New Potato Salad with Cucumber and Jalapeño

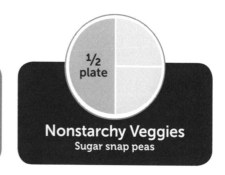

Nonstarchy Veggies
Sugar snap peas

Balsamic Chicken

SERVINGS 4 (1 breast half each)
CARB. PER SERVING 8 g
PREP 25 minutes   COOK 19 minutes

- 1 Tbsp. snipped fresh rosemary or 1 tsp. dried rosemary, crushed
- 2 cloves garlic, minced
- ¼ tsp. salt
- ⅛ tsp. black pepper
- 4 small bone-in chicken breast halves, skinned (2 lb. total)
- ½ cup reduced-sodium chicken broth
- ¼ cup balsamic vinegar
- 4 orange wedges
- Orange zest

1. Preheat oven to 425°F. In a bowl combine rosemary, garlic, salt, and pepper. Sprinkle herb mixture evenly over skinned sides of the chicken breast halves; rub in with your fingers.
2. Coat an unheated extra-large nonstick skillet with *nonstick cooking spray*. Heat over medium heat. Add chicken pieces, herb sides down. Cook 4 to 6 minutes or until browned. Turn chicken pieces over. Remove skillet from the heat. Carefully add broth and vinegar to the skillet. Return skillet to heat. Cover and cook 15 to 20 minutes or until done (170°F), spooning broth mixture over chicken occasionally.
3. Spoon pan juices over chicken. Serve with orange wedges; top with zest.

PER SERVING: 181 cal., 2 g total fat (1 g sat. fat), 72 mg chol., 287 mg sodium, 8 g carb. (1 g fiber, 6 g sugars), 30 g pro.

New Potato Salad with Cucumber and Jalapeño

SERVINGS 8 (¾ cup each)
CARB. PER SERVING 17 g
PREP 30 minutes   COOK 12 minutes
CHILL 2 hours

- 1½ lb. tiny new potatoes
- 1 6-oz. carton plain low-fat Greek yogurt
- 2 Tbsp. white balsamic vinegar
- 1 Tbsp. yellow mustard
- 1 Tbsp. honey
- 1 Tbsp. snipped fresh dill weed
- ¼ tsp. salt
- ⅛ tsp. black pepper
- 2 cups chopped cucumber
- ¾ cup chopped red onion
- ¼ cup chopped fresh jalapeño chile pepper (tip, *page 137*)
- 2 hard-cooked eggs, chopped

1. Halve any large potatoes. In a covered large saucepan cook potatoes in enough boiling water to cover 12 to 15 minutes or just until tender. Drain; cool. Quarter or halve potatoes.
2. In a bowl combine the next seven ingredients (through black pepper). Stir in cucumber, red onion, and jalapeño pepper. Add the cooked potatoes and eggs; toss gently to coat. Cover and chill 2 to 4 hours. Toss before serving.
TO STORE Refrigerate salad in an airtight container up to 2 days. Before serving, stir in a splash of fat-free milk.

PER SERVING: 107 cal., 2 g total fat (1 g sat. fat), 48 mg chol., 129 mg sodium, 17 g carb. (2 g fiber, 7 g sugars), 5 g pro.

START WITH A 9-INCH PLATE

Portion control is easier when your plate is no more than 9 inches wide. If your dinnerware plates are larger than that, fill just inside the rim. A shallow rimmed bowl (like a pasta bowl) is also a good option as long as it measures 9 inches wide. Along with a right-size plate, use a 1-cup glass for milk, a ½-cup dish for fruit or dessert, and a 1-cup bowl for cereal or soup.

Tri-Color
Summer
Veggies

Spiced
Sweet Potato
Wedges

154

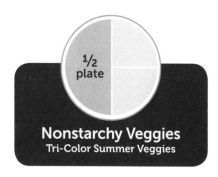

Nonstarchy Veggies
Tri-Color Summer Veggies

Starch or Grain
Spiced Sweet Potato Wedges

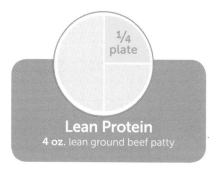

Lean Protein
4 oz. lean ground beef patty

Tri-Color Summer Veggies

SERVINGS 4 (1 cup each)
CARB. PER SERVING 11 g
PREP 25 minutes   COOK 8 minutes

- 1 Tbsp. butter
- 1¼ cups coarsely chopped yellow summer squash
- 1¼ cups coarsely chopped zucchini
- 1 cup frozen shelled edamame
- ¾ cup coarsely chopped red sweet pepper
- ¾ cup thinly sliced red onion
- 2 cloves garlic, minced
- 1 Tbsp. champagne vinegar or white wine vinegar
- 1½ tsp. snipped fresh oregano
- 1 tsp. snipped fresh thyme
- ¼ tsp. salt
- ¼ tsp. black pepper

1. In a large skillet melt butter over medium heat. Add the next six ingredients (through garlic). Cook and stir about 8 minutes or until vegetables are crisp-tender. Stir in remaining ingredients. Serve immediately.

PER SERVING: 109 cal., 5 g total fat (2 g sat. fat), 8 mg chol., 177 mg sodium, 11 g carb. (4 g fiber, 5 g sugars), 6 g pro.

Spiced Sweet Potato Wedges

SERVINGS 4 (4 wedges each)
CARB. PER SERVING 22 g or 21 g
PREP 10 minutes   ROAST 25 minutes

- 2 sweet potatoes (about 10 oz. each)
- 1 Tbsp. olive oil
- 1 tsp. packed brown sugar*
- ¼ tsp. kosher salt
- ¼ tsp. smoked paprika
- ¼ tsp. black pepper
- ¼ tsp. pumpkin pie spice
- ¼ tsp. hot chili powder

1. Preheat oven to 425°F. Place a baking sheet in oven to preheat.
2. Scrub sweet potatoes; cut each potato lengthwise into 8 wedges (16 wedges total). In a large bowl combine potato wedges and olive oil; toss to coat. In a small bowl combine remaining ingredients. Sprinkle spice mixture over wedges; toss to coat.
3. Arrange wedges in a single layer on the hot baking sheet. Roast 25 to 30 minutes or until tender and browned, turning wedges once.

*SUGAR SUBSTITUTE Choose Splenda Brown Sugar Blend. Follow package directions to use product amount equivalent to 1 tsp. brown sugar.

PER SERVING: 124 cal., 3 g total fat (0 g sat. fat), 0 mg chol., 184 mg sodium, 22 g carb. (3 g fiber, 5 g sugars), 2 g pro.

PER SERVING WITH SUBSTITUTE: Same as above, except 123 cal., 21 g carb.

DIVIDE YOUR PLATE

The plate method is a simple strategy to get your eating on track. If you mentally divide your plate into sections, it is easier to plan a balanced meal with the right mix of nutrients (including carbohydrate, protein, and fat) for better control of glucose and weight. This is how you should divide your plate.

½ nonstarchy vegetables

Make nonstarchy vegetables the star of your meal. For variety, pick two nonstarchy vegetables per meal.

¼ starch or grain

This can be a serving of bread, pasta, rice, beans, or starchy vegetable. (Men may need two servings of starch.) Choose whole grains and beans to give meals a fiber boost.

¼ protein

Lean meat, fish, tofu, eggs, cheese, or nuts play a smaller than traditional role.

Tomato-Cucumber
Salad with Garlic
Buttermilk Dressing

Sweet Barbecue-
Glazed Turkey

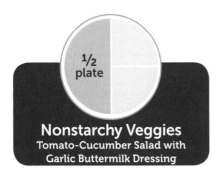

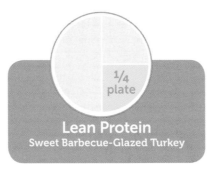

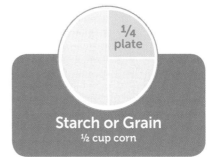

Nonstarchy Veggies
Tomato-Cucumber Salad with
Garlic Buttermilk Dressing

Lean Protein
Sweet Barbecue-Glazed Turkey

Starch or Grain
½ cup corn

Tomato-Cucumber Salad with Garlic Buttermilk Dressing

SERVINGS 4 ($^3/_4$ cup each)
CARB. PER SERVING 8 g
START TO FINISH 25 minutes

  2 cloves garlic
  ¼ tsp. coarse kosher or sea salt
  2 Tbsp. light mayonnaise
  1 Tbsp. cider vinegar
  ⅓ cup buttermilk
  2 Tbsp. snipped fresh basil
  3 medium tomatoes (about 1 lb.),
     cored and thinly sliced
  1 cup thinly sliced cucumber
     Freshly ground black pepper

1. For dressing, mince the garlic on a cutting board. Sprinkle garlic with the salt; use the side of a chef's knife to mash and rub the garlic and salt together into a paste. Transfer garlic mixture to a bowl. Whisk in mayonnaise and vinegar until smooth. Slowly whisk in buttermilk until smooth. Stir in basil.
2. Layer tomato and cucumber slices on serving plates, sprinkling pepper lightly between the layers. Drizzle salads with dressing.

PER SERVING: 56 cal., 2 g total fat (0 g sat. fat), 2 mg chol., 207 mg sodium, 8 g carb. (2 g fiber, 5 g sugars), 2 g pro.

Sweet Barbecue-Glazed Turkey

SERVINGS 4 (3 oz. cooked turkey +
about 1 Tbsp. sauce each)
CARB. PER SERVING 5 g
START TO FINISH 30 minutes

  ⅔ cup reduced-sugar ketchup
  ¼ cup orange juice
  2 Tbsp. snipped fresh cilantro
  1 clove garlic, minced
  ¼ tsp. ground cumin
  ¼ tsp. black pepper
  1 large turkey breast tenderloin
     (about 1 lb.), split in half
     horizontally, or 4 skinless,
     boneless chicken breast halves
     (1 to 1¼ lb. total)

1. For sauce, in a small saucepan the first six ingredients (through pepper). Bring to boiling over medium heat, stirring constantly; reduce heat. Simmer, uncovered, 5 minutes. Reserve ⅓ cup of the sauce in a bowl and keep remaining sauce warm.
2. Grill turkey, uncovered, over medium heat 12 to 16 minutes (allow 12 to 15 minutes for boneless, skinless chicken) or until done (165°F), turning once and brushing with the reserved ⅓ cup sauce the last 2 minutes of grilling.
3. Slice turkey. Serve with remaining sauce. If desired, sprinkle with additional snipped fresh cilantro.

PER SERVING: 143 cal., 1 g total fat (0 g sat. fat), 70 mg chol., 511 mg sodium, 5 g carb. (0 g fiber, 4 g sugars), 28 g pro.

GO EASY ON EXTRAS

When using items like salad dressings, sauces, and spreads, choose low-fat versions and keep the servings as skimpy as you can. When dining out, ask for dressings on the side and ask for substitutions.

Parmesan Mashed
Potatoes

Steak with
Watercress Pesto

Lean Protein
Steak with Watercress Pesto

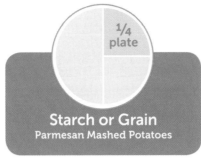

Starch or Grain
Parmesan Mashed Potatoes

Nonstarchy Veggies
Sweet pepper strips

Steak with Watercress Pesto

SERVINGS 4 (1 steak + 1 Tbsp. pesto each)

CARB. PER SERVING 3 g

PREP 20 minutes   GRILL 7 minutes

  1 cup lightly packed fresh watercress, tough stems removed
  ½ cup lightly packed fresh mint or fresh Italian parsley
  3 Tbsp. slivered almonds, toasted
  2 cloves garlic, minced
  ¼ tsp. kosher salt
  2 Tbsp. water
  1 Tbsp. olive oil
  4 4-oz. beef chuck top blade (flat iron) steaks, cut ¾ inch thick
  ⅛ tsp. kosher salt
  ⅛ tsp. black pepper

1. For pesto, in a food processor or blender combine the first five ingredients (through ¼ tsp. salt). Cover and pulse to chop the watercress and mint. With the processor running, gradually add water and oil through the feed tube until well combined, scraping sides of bowl as needed.
2. Sprinkle steaks with the ⅛ tsp. salt and the pepper. Grill steaks, covered, over medium heat to desired doneness, turning once. Allow 7 to 9 minutes for medium rare (145°F) or 10 to 12 minutes for medium (160°F). Serve steaks with the pesto.

PER SERVING: 200 cal., 12 g total fat (3 g sat. fat), 56 mg chol., 248 mg sodium, 3 g carb. (1 g fiber, 0 g sugars), 20 g pro.

Parmesan Mashed Potatoes

SERVINGS 4 (⅔ cup each)

CARB. PER SERVING 23 g

PREP 15 minutes   COOK 20 minutes

  12 oz. medium round red potatoes
  8 oz. parsnips
  4 tsp. light butter or tub-style vegetable oil spread
  Dash black pepper
  2 to 3 Tbsp. fat-free milk
  ½ cup finely shredded Parmesan cheese (2 oz.)

1. Scrub potatoes and cut in half. Peel parsnips and cut into 2-inch pieces. In a large saucepan cook potatoes and parsnips, covered, in enough boiling water to cover about 20 minutes or until tender; drain.
2. Mash potatoes and parsnips. Add butter and pepper. Gradually work in enough milk to make mixture light and fluffy. Stir in cheese.

PER SERVING: 157 cal., 5 g total fat (3 g sat. fat), 12 mg chol., 226 mg sodium, 23 g carb. (4 g fiber, 4 g sugars), 6 g pro.

WATCH THE HEIGHT

Don't fall into the trap of piling food too high on your plate to make up for the plate's smaller size. Food should be no more than ½ inch high.

½ inch

Butternut
Squash and
Quinoa Pilaf

Maple-Pecan
Pork Chops

Lean Protein
Maple-Pecan Pork Chops

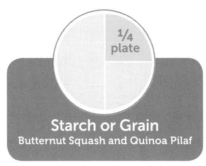

Starch or Grain
Butternut Squash and Quinoa Pilaf

Nonstarchy Veggies
Green beans

Maple-Pecan Pork Chops

SERVINGS 4 (1 pork chop each)
CARB. PER SERVING 3 g
START TO FINISH 15 minutes

- 4 pork loin rib chops, about ¾ inch thick (1½ lb. total)
- ¼ tsp. salt
- ¼ tsp. black pepper
- 1 Tbsp. canola oil
- 2 Tbsp. finely chopped shallot
- 2 Tbsp. chopped pecans, toasted
- 2 Tbsp. sugar-free maple-flavor syrup
- 2 tsp. butter, melted
- 1 Tbsp. snipped fresh thyme

1. Sprinkle pork chops with the salt and pepper. In an extra-large skillet heat oil over medium-high heat. Add shallot; cook and stir 1 minute. Add chops; cook 8 to 10 minutes or until done (145°F), turning once. Cover chops with foil and let rest 3 minutes.
2. Meanwhile, in a bowl combine the remaining ingredients. Top pork chops with pecan mixture.

PER SERVING: 216 cal., 12 g total fat (3 g sat. fat), 62 mg chol., 224 mg sodium, 3 g carb. (1 g fiber, 1 g sugars), 23 g pro.

Butternut Squash and Quinoa Pilaf

SERVINGS 4 (½ cup each)
CARB. PER SERVING 19 g
PREP 25 minutes   ROAST 30 minutes

- 2 cups cubed, peeled butternut squash
- 3 cloves garlic, minced
- Pinch crushed red pepper
- 3 tsp. olive oil
- 2 Tbsp. sliced almonds
- 1 cup cooked quinoa
- 1½ tsp. snipped fresh sage
- ¼ tsp. salt

1. Preheat oven to 425°F. In a bowl combine squash, garlic, and crushed red pepper. Drizzle with 1½ tsp. of the oil; toss to coat. Spread squash in a 15×10-inch baking pan. Roast 30 minutes, stirring once and adding the sliced almonds the last 4 minutes of roasting.
2. In a large bowl combine quinoa, the remaining 1½ tsp. oil, the sage, and salt. Stir in roasted squash mixture. If desired, top with fresh sage leaves.

PER SERVING: 137 cal., 6 g total fat (1 g sat. fat), 0 mg chol., 152 mg sodium, 19 g carb. (3 g fiber, 2 g sugars), 4 g pro.

ON THE SIDE

For at least one meal each day, and as your calorie allowance permits, enjoy a cup of low-fat milk or light yogurt and a small piece of fruit or ½ cup cut-up fruit. When you pick low-fat options, a meal with these side items and each of the three plate components typically totals less than 50 grams of carbohydrate and less than 500 calories.

Spice-Rubbed
Salmon

Asparagus
and Wild
Mushrooms

162

Nonstarchy Veggies
Asparagus and Wild Mushrooms

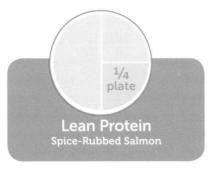

Lean Protein
Spice-Rubbed Salmon

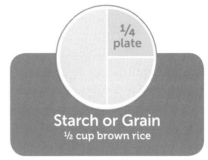

Starch or Grain
½ cup brown rice

Asparagus and Wild Mushrooms

SERVINGS 4 (5 asparagus spears + ⅓ cup mushrooms each)
CARB. PER SERVING 5 g
PREP 20 minutes **ROAST** 15 minutes

- 3 cups halved cremini, shiitake, and/or button mushrooms
- 2 Tbsp. white wine
- 2 tsp. snipped fresh tarragon
- 1 lb. fresh asparagus
- 1 Tbsp. olive oil
- ¼ tsp. salt
- ¼ tsp. black pepper

1. Preheat oven to 400°F. In a bowl toss together mushrooms, wine, and tarragon.

2. Snap off and discard woody bases from asparagus. Place asparagus in a 15×10-inch baking pan. Drizzle with oil and sprinkle with the salt and pepper. Toss to coat.

3. Roast, uncovered, 5 minutes. Add mushroom mixture to the pan; toss gently to combine. Return to oven; roast about 10 minutes more or until asparagus is crisp-tender. If desired, garnish with additional fresh tarragon.

PER SERVING: 64 cal., 4 g total fat (1 g sat. fat), 0 mg chol., 151 mg sodium, 5 g carb. (2 g fiber, 2 g sugars), 4 g pro.

Spice-Rubbed Salmon

SERVINGS 4 (1 portion salmon each)
CARB. PER SERVING 0 g
PREP 10 minutes **BAKE** 15 minutes

- 1 lb. fresh or frozen salmon fillet (with skin)
  Nonstick cooking spray
- ½ tsp. ground coriander
- ¼ tsp. salt
- ¼ tsp. fennel seeds, crushed
- ¼ tsp. black pepper

1. Thaw fish, if frozen. Preheat oven to 425°F. Line a 2-qt. rectangular baking dish with foil; lightly coat foil with nonstick spray. Rinse salmon; pat dry with paper towels. Place salmon in prepared dish, skin side down. In a bowl combine the remaining ingredients. Sprinkle over salmon. Bake 15 to 20 minutes or until fish flakes easily. Cut salmon into portions.

PER SERVING: 162 cal., 7 g total fat (1 g sat. fat), 62 mg chol., 196 mg sodium, 0 g carb. (0 g fiber, 0 g sugars), 23 g pro.

MAKING FAIR TRADES

When you are calculating your servings of fruit, milk, and starch, trade one for another to keep your carbs in check. For example, if you want two pieces of bread for a sandwich, skip the milk or fruit for that meal. The fruit, milk, or starch serving can also be traded for a cup of broth-base soup or even ½ cup low-fat ice cream.

Baby Mixed
Green Salad

Roasted Red Pepper-
Spinach Pasta

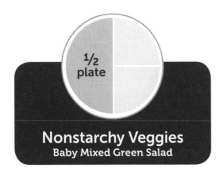

Nonstarchy Veggies
Baby Mixed Green Salad

Starch or Grain
Roasted Red Pepper-Spinach Pasta

Lean Protein
3 oz. tuna canned in water

Baby Mixed Green Salad

SERVINGS 4 (1^{1}/2 cups each)
CARB. PER SERVING 5 g
START TO FINISH 15 minutes

- 5 cups baby mixed greens
- 1 cup sliced fresh mushrooms
- ½ cup thinly sliced red onion
- 1 Tbsp. white wine vinegar
- 1 Tbsp. lemon juice
- 1 Tbsp. olive oil
- 1 tsp. snipped fresh thyme
- 1 clove garlic, minced
- ¼ tsp. salt
- ¼ tsp. black pepper

1. In a bowl toss together the baby greens, mushrooms, and red onion. For dressing, in a small bowl whisk together the remaining ingredients. Pour dressing over greens; toss to coat.

PER SERVING: 54 cal., 4 g total fat (1 g sat. fat), 0 mg chol., 156 mg sodium, 5 g carb. (1 g fiber, 2 g sugars), 2 g pro.

Roasted Red Pepper-Spinach Pasta

SERVINGS 4 (^{3}/4 cup each)
CARB. PER SERVING 22 g
START TO FINISH 20 minutes

- 4 oz. dried whole grain or multigrain penne pasta
- ½ cup roasted red sweet peppers, chopped
- ¼ tsp. salt
- 1 cup coarsely chopped fresh spinach

1. Cook pasta in lightly salted water according to package directions. Before draining pasta, reserve ½ cup of the pasta cooking water. Drain pasta and return to the pan.
2. Add the reserved pasta cooking water, roasted sweet peppers, and salt to the pasta. Cook and stir over medium heat 1 to 2 minutes or until liquid is nearly absorbed. Remove from the heat. Stir in spinach.

PER SERVING: 107 cal., 1 g total fat (0 g sat. fat), 0 mg chol., 152 mg sodium, 22 g carb. (4 g fiber, 1 g sugars), 4 g pro.

PLATING COMBOS

You can use the plate method with mixed dishes such as casseroles, pizza, tacos, and sandwiches, too. Just think of the ingredients separately. A salad with grilled chicken and croutons could cover every section of the plate: greens, carrots, and tomatoes for the nonstarchy vegetables; chicken for the protein; and croutons for the starch or grain. Assemble casseroles in layers so you can see how much meat versus vegetables you are getting. When in doubt, put the serving for a casserole with pasta, rice, or beans in the starch section of your plate.

Re-create
FAMILY
FAVORITES

Please the whole family with lightened versions of typically fat-and-carb-loaded comfort foods. Discover simple ways to substitute ingredients to improve nutrition while keeping the wholesome quality and great taste. Try these tricks and techniques to convert your own family favorites for better health.

REDUCED-FAT CHEESE

Use reduced-fat cheese so you can top this skillet meal with a satisfying amount.

Chili-Mac Skillet

SERVINGS 4 (1 cup each)
CARB. PER SERVING 40 g
PREP 15 minutes   COOK 20 minutes
STAND 2 minutes

- 8 oz. lean ground beef
- 1/2 cup finely chopped onion
- 1 15-oz. can no-salt-added tomato puree
- 1 8-oz. can no-salt-added tomato sauce
- 1 cup dried elbow macaroni
- 1/2 cup finely chopped green sweet pepper
- 1/4 cup water
- 1 Tbsp. chili powder
- 1/2 tsp. garlic salt
- 1/2 cup shredded reduced-fat cheddar cheese (2 oz.)

1. In a large skillet cook ground beef and onion over medium-high heat until meat is browned. Drain off fat.
2. Stir in the next seven ingredients (through garlic salt). Bring to boiling; reduce heat. Simmer, covered, about 20 minutes or until macaroni is tender, stirring frequently.
3. Remove skillet from heat; sprinkle meat mixture with cheese. Cover and let stand about 2 minutes or until cheese is melted.

PER SERVING: 321 cal., 10 g total fat (4 g sat. fat), 47 mg chol., 380 mg sodium, 40 g carb. (6 g fiber, 10 g sugars), 21 g pro.

TOMATO PUREE & SAUCE

No-salt-added tomato products give you control over the sodium content in this recipe.

168

Beef and Vegetable Biscuit Bake

SERVINGS 5 ($1^1/_4$ cups meat mixture + 1 biscuit each)
CARB. PER SERVING 34 g
PREP 25 minutes **ROAST** 20 minutes
COOK 10 minutes **BAKE** 18 minutes

Nonstick cooking spray
12 oz. fresh Brussels sprouts, halved
$2^1/_2$ cups sliced carrots
2 tsp. olive oil
1 tsp. dried thyme, crushed
$1/_4$ tsp. black pepper
8 oz. 95% lean ground beef
$1/_2$ cup chopped onion
5 tsp. butter
3 Tbsp. all-purpose flour
$1/_8$ tsp. salt
1 cup fat-free milk
$3/_4$ cup water
4 oz. fresh mushrooms, chopped
$1/_2$ of a 12-oz. pkg. refrigerated biscuits (5)

1. Preheat oven to 400°F. Coat a 2-qt. square or oval baking dish with cooking spray. Line a 15×10-inch baking pan with foil. Place Brussels sprouts and carrots in the prepared baking pan. In a bowl combine oil, thyme, and pepper. Drizzle over vegetables; toss to combine. Spread vegetables in a single layer in baking pan. Roast, uncovered, 20 to 25 minutes or until vegetables are browned and tender, stirring once.
2. Meanwhile, in a large skillet cook meat and onion over medium heat until meat is browned and onion is tender, stirring occasionally. Remove from skillet; drain.
3. In the same large skillet melt butter over medium heat. In a bowl stir together flour and salt; carefully whisk about half of the flour mixture into milk until smooth. Whisk the remaining flour mixture into melted butter. Add milk mixture and the water all at once to skillet. Cook and stir until thickened and bubbly; cook and stir 2 minutes more. Stir in mushrooms, roasted vegetables, and cooked meat mixture; bring to boiling. Spoon into the prepared baking dish.
4. Bake 10 minutes. Quickly top with the biscuits. Bake 8 to 11 minutes more or until biscuits are golden brown and casserole is bubbly.

PER SERVING: 311 cal., 13 g total fat (5 g sat. fat), 39 mg chol., 562 mg sodium, 34 g carb. (6 g fiber, 10 g sugars), 18 g pro.

BRUSSELS SPROUTS & CARROTS

Bulk up the casserole with lots of rich-flavored roasted vegetables.

90% LEAN GROUND BEEF

Choose lean ground beef for a lean but moist meat loaf.

FAT-FREE MILK

In dishes in which milk is used for moisture and binding, fat-free milk is a good option.

EGG PRODUCT

Using egg product instead of whole eggs cuts fat by 5 grams and cholesterol by 185 milligrams per egg.

Our Best Meat Loaf

SERVINGS 8 (1 slice each)
CARB. PER SERVING 14 g or 12 g
PREP 20 minutes
BAKE 1 hour 10 minutes
STAND 10 minutes

- ½ cup refrigerated or frozen egg product, thawed, or 2 eggs
- ¾ cup fat-free milk
- ⅔ cup fine dry bread crumbs or 2 cups soft bread crumbs
- ¼ cup finely chopped onion
- 2 Tbsp. snipped fresh parsley
- ¾ tsp. salt
- ½ tsp. dried sage, basil, or oregano, crushed
- ⅛ tsp. black pepper
- 1½ lb. 90% lean ground beef, lamb, or pork
- ¼ cup ketchup
- 2 Tbsp. packed brown sugar*
- 1 tsp. dry mustard

1. Preheat oven to 350°F. In a large bowl combine eggs and milk; stir in the next six ingredients (through pepper). Add ground meat; mix well. Lightly pat mixture into an 8×4-inch loaf pan.
2. Bake 1 to 1¼ hours or until 160°F in center. Spoon off fat. In a bowl combine ketchup, brown sugar, and dry mustard; spread over meat loaf. Bake 10 minutes more.
3. Let stand 10 minutes before serving. If desired, sprinkle with additional parsley.

*SUGAR SUBSTITUTE Choose Splenda Brown Sugar Blend. Follow package directions to use product amount equivalent to 2 Tbsp. brown sugar.

PER SERVING: 226 cal., 9 g total fat (4 g sat. fat), 56 mg chol., 456 mg sodium, 14 g carb. (1 g fiber, 7 g sugars), 21 g pro.

PER SERVING: Same as above, except 221 cal., 12 g carb. (5 g sugars).

IS IT DONE?

The internal color of a meat loaf is not a reliable doneness indicator. A beef, lamb, or pork loaf cooked to 160°F is safe, regardless of color. To measure the doneness of a meat loaf, insert an instant-read thermometer into the center of the loaf to a depth of 2 to 3 inches.

TEST KITCHEN TIP

Use two metal spatulas to carefully lift the meat loaf from the pan and place on a cutting board. For the best slicing, use a serrated knife and cut gently with a back-and-forth motion.

RICOTTA & MOZZARELLA

Light ricotta cheese and part-skim mozzarella contribute plenty of cheesy goodness without the fat.

SPAGHETTI SAUCE

Make the effort to find a low-sodium spaghetti sauce to keep sodium in check. Look at labels to choose the one with the lowest numbers.

GROUND TURKEY BREAST

Ground turkey breast and ground chicken breast are great alternatives to extra-lean ground beef.

Skillet Lasagna

SERVINGS 5 (1 cup each)
CARB. PER SERVING 37 g
START TO FINISH 45 minutes

- Nonstick cooking spray
- 8 oz. 95% lean ground beef
- 3/4 cup chopped green sweet pepper
- 1/2 cup chopped onion
- 2 cloves garlic, minced
- 1 23.5-oz. jar low-sodium spaghetti sauce, such as Prego Heart Smart Traditional brand
- 1 cup water
- 2 cups sliced fresh mushrooms
- 4 oz. dried lasagna noodles, broken into 1 1/2-inch pieces, or mini farfalle
- 1/2 cup light ricotta cheese
- 2 Tbsp. grated Parmesan or Romano cheese
- 1 Tbsp. snipped fresh parsley or 1/2 tsp. dried Italian seasoning, crushed
- 1/2 cup shredded part-skim mozzarella cheese (2 oz.)
- Snipped fresh herbs (optional)

1. Coat an extra-large skillet with cooking spray; heat skillet over medium heat. Cook beef, sweet pepper, onion, and garlic in hot skillet until meat is browned. Drain off any fat. Stir in spaghetti sauce and water. Bring to boiling. Add mushrooms and noodles; stir to separate noodles. Return to boiling; reduce heat. Cover and gently boil about 20 minutes or until pasta is tender, stirring frequently.
2. Meanwhile, in a bowl stir together ricotta, Parmesan, and parsley. Drop cheese mixture by spoonfuls into 10 small mounds on the pasta mixture in the skillet. Sprinkle each mound with mozzarella. Reduce heat to low. Cover and cook 4 to 5 minutes or until

cheese mixture is heated and mozzarella is melted. Remove from heat; let stand, covered, 10 minutes. If desired, sprinkle with additional fresh herbs.

PER SERVING: 303 cal., 8 g total fat (3 g sat. fat), 43 mg chol., 562 mg sodium, 37 g carb. (4 g fiber, 15 g sugars), 22 g pro.

Cheeseburger Shepherd's Pie

SERVINGS 8 ($1^1/_3$ cups each)
CARB. PER SERVING 30 g
PREP 25 minutes   COOK 15 minutes
BAKE 20 minutes

$1^3/_4$ lb. russet potatoes, peeled and cut into $1^1/_2$-inch pieces
  2 cups cauliflower florets
$^1/_2$ cup light sour cream
$^1/_4$ cup fat-free milk
$^1/_4$ tsp. salt
  1 cup shredded reduced-fat cheddar cheese (4 oz.)
$1^1/_2$ lb. 95% lean ground beef
$^3/_4$ cup chopped red sweet pepper
$^1/_2$ cup chopped onion
  2 cloves garlic, minced
$1^1/_2$ cups frozen whole kernel corn
  1 15-oz. can no-salt-added tomato sauce
$^1/_3$ cup chopped dill pickles
  3 Tbsp. yellow mustard
  1 tsp. dried oregano, crushed
  Sliced green onions (optional)

1. Preheat oven to 350°F. In a large saucepan cook potatoes and cauliflower in enough boiling water to cover about 15 minutes or until tender; drain. Mash potatoes and cauliflower. Gradually add sour cream, milk, and salt, mashing until light and fluffy. Stir in $^1/_2$ cup of the cheese.

2. Meanwhile, in a large skillet cook beef, sweet pepper, onion, and garlic over medium heat until browned. Drain off any fat. Stir in the next five ingredients (through oregano). Bring to boiling; reduce heat. Simmer, uncovered, 5 minutes to blend flavors.

3. Spoon beef mixture into a 3-qt. baking dish. Spoon mashed potato mixture in mounds over beef mixture. Sprinkle with remaining $^1/_2$ cup cheese. Bake about 20 minutes or until heated. If desired, top with green onions.

PER SERVING: 294 cal., 9 g total fat (5 g sat. fat), 67 mg chol., 402 mg sodium, 30 g carb. (5 g fiber, 6 g sugars), 26 g pro.

CAULIFLOWER

Adding cauliflower to the mashed potato topping cuts carbs and contributes valuable antioxidants in the form of vitamin C.

Five-Spice Sloppy Joes

SERVINGS 4 (2 stuffed cabbage leaves each)
CARB. PER SERVING 20 g
START TO FINISH 45 minutes

- 1 lb. 95% lean ground beef
- $1\frac{1}{2}$ cups finely chopped fresh cremini mushrooms
- $\frac{1}{2}$ cup chopped red sweet pepper
- $\frac{1}{2}$ cup chopped onion
- 4 cloves garlic, minced
- 1 8-oz. can no-salt-added tomato sauce
- 2 tsp. reduced-sodium soy sauce
- 1 to 2 tsp. sriracha sauce
- $\frac{1}{2}$ tsp. five-spice powder
- $\frac{1}{4}$ tsp. salt
- 8 small napa or green cabbage leaves
- 1 cup toppers, such as slivered red sweet pepper strips, thinly sliced green onions, and/or snipped fresh cilantro
- 1 recipe Crispy Wonton Strips

1. In a large skillet cook the first five ingredients (through garlic) over medium heat until meat is browned. Drain off any fat. Stir in the next five ingredients (through salt). Reduce heat and cook, uncovered, 5 minutes to blend flavors, stirring occasionally.

2. Spoon beef mixture into cabbage leaves. Garnish each with toppers and Crispy Wonton Strips.

CRISPY WONTON STRIPS Preheat oven to 375°F. Use a sharp knife to cut 4 wonton wrappers in half. Cut each half crosswise into thin strips Arrange strips on a baking sheet. Lightly coat with nonstick cooking spray; toss to coat. Spread evenly on sheet. Bake about 4 minutes or until edges are golden brown.

PER SERVING: 243 cal., 6 g total fat (2 g sat. fat), 70 mg chol., 405 mg sodium, 20 g carb. (5 g fiber, 9 g sugars), 28 g pro.

TOMATO SAUCE & SOY SAUCE
These reduced-sodium products give these sandwiches an Asian flair without all the sodium

CABBAGE
Using cabbage leaves instead of buns is a carb, fat, and sodium controller.

Creamy Corn Soup with Crispy Bacon

SERVINGS 4 (1^1/$_3$ cups each)
CARB. PER SERVING 31 g
PREP 25 minutes   COOK 31 minutes
COOL 10 minutes

- 2 Tbsp. unsalted butter
- 1 cup chopped onion
- 1 cup thinly sliced celery
- ^{1}/$_2$ cup thinly sliced carrot
- 2 cloves garlic, minced
- ^{1}/$_4$ tsp. salt
- 1 Tbsp. all-purpose flour
- 2 cups fat-free milk
- 1 14.5-oz. can reduced-sodium chicken broth
- 2 cups frozen whole kernel corn, thawed
- 2 sprigs fresh thyme or ^{1}/$_2$ tsp. dried thyme, crushed
- 2 bay leaves
- 4 slices lower-sodium, less-fat bacon, crisp-cooked and crumbled

1. In a 4-qt. Dutch oven melt butter over medium heat. Add the next five ingredients (through salt); cook and stir about 10 minutes or until vegetables are soft, stirring frequently. If desired, set aside about ^{1}/$_2$ cup cooked vegetables to use as a topper. Stir in flour. Cook and stir 1 minute more.

2. Add milk and broth all at once, whisking to combine. Stir in corn, thyme, and bay leaves. Bring to boiling; reduce heat. Simmer, covered, 10 minutes, stirring frequently.

3. Remove soup from heat; cool 10 minutes. Remove and discard thyme sprigs (if using) and bay leaves. Using an immersion blender, blend soup until smooth. (Or transfer part of the soup to a blender; cover and blend until smooth. Repeat with the remaining soup, blending in batches. Return all of the soup to the Dutch oven.) Heat. Top soup with reserved vegetables (if using) and crumbled bacon.

PER SERVING: 231 cal., 8 g total fat (4 g sat. fat), 21 mg chol., 540 mg sodium, 31 g carb. (3 g fiber, 11 g sugars), 11 g pro.

REDUCED-SODIUM BROTH
Sodium is kept under control with reduced-sodium broth and by not using canned creamed corn.

FAT-FREE MILK
This soup gets its creaminess by blending it at the end, so no cream is needed.

FROZEN CORN

Using frozen corn instead of canned corn reduces sodium and adds a fresher flavor.

Spicy Skillet Pork Chops

SERVINGS 4 (1 pork chop + about $^1/_2$ cup corn mixture each)
CARB. PER SERVING 33 g
PREP 35 minutes   **COOK** 10 minutes

- 1$^1/_2$ cups frozen whole kernel corn
- 1 10-oz. can diced tomatoes and green chiles, undrained
- 2 cloves garlic, minced
- $^1/_2$ tsp. ground cumin
- $^1/_4$ tsp. hot pepper sauce
- 4 boneless pork loin chops, cut $^3/_4$ inch thick
- $^1/_2$ tsp. chili powder
- 2 tsp. vegetable oil
- 1 medium onion, cut into thin wedges
- 1$^1/_3$ cups hot cooked brown rice
  Fresh cilantro (optional)

1. In a bowl combine the first five ingredients (through hot pepper sauce).

2. Trim fat from chops. Sprinkle both sides of chops with chili powder. In an extra-large skillet heat oil over medium-high heat. Add chops; cook about 4 minutes or until browned, turning once. Remove chops, reserving drippings in skillet.

3. Add onion to skillet; cook and stir over medium heat 3 minutes. Stir in corn mixture; top with chops. Bring to boiling; reduce heat. Simmer, covered, 10 to 12 minutes or until chops are 145°F. Serve over rice and top with cilantro.

PER SERVING: 378 cal., 9 g total fat (2 g sat. fat), 95 mg chol., 450 mg sodium, 33 g carb. (3 g fiber, 4 g sugars), 45 g pro.

Loaded Barbecue Sweet Potatoes

SERVINGS 4 (1 loaded sweet potato half each)
CARB. PER SERVING 35 g
PREP 20 minutes   **COOK** 10 minutes
BAKE 50 minutes

- 2   8- to 10-oz. sweet potatoes
- 12 oz. pork tenderloin or lean boneless pork
- 2   tsp. canola oil
- 1   small onion, halved and sliced
- 1   small fresh poblano chile pepper, seeded and cut into bite-size strips (tip, *page 137*)
- 1/3 cup barbecue sauce
- 1/4 cup light sour cream
- 1/4 cup shredded reduced-fat cheddar cheese (1 oz.)
- 1/4 cup sliced green onions
- 4   slices lower-sodium, less-fat bacon, crisp-cooked and crumbled

1. Preheat oven to 425°F. Scrub potatoes; pat dry. Prick potatoes with a fork. Wrap potatoes individually in foil and place in a 15x10-inch baking pan. Bake 50 to 60 minutes or until tender.

2. Meanwhile, cut pork into bite-size strips. In a large nonstick skillet heat oil over medium-high heat. Add pork; cook and stir about 4 minutes or until no pink remains. Remove meat from skillet. Add onion and poblano chile to skillet; cook and stir 4 to 6 minutes or until tender. Remove from heat. Return pork to skillet. Drizzle with barbecue sauce; toss to combine.

3. Cut baked sweet potatoes in half lengthwise. Top cut sides with pork mixture. Top with sour cream, cheese, green onions, and bacon.

PER SERVING: 317 cal., 8 g total fat (3 g sat. fat), 68 mg chol., 461 mg sodium, 35 g carb. (4 g fiber, 13 g sugars), 24 g pro.

SWEET POTATO

Sweet potatoes provide a healthy dose of vitamin A in the form of beta-carotene. Eat the skin for extra fiber.

Pork Tenderloin Sandwiches with Chimichurri Sauce

SERVINGS 4 (1 sandwich each)
CARB. PER SERVING 30 g
PREP 25 minutes   **COOK** 5 minutes

- 1 cup packed fresh Italian parsley
- 2 Tbsp. snipped fresh oregano
- 2 Tbsp. finely chopped shallot
- 2 Tbsp. red wine vinegar
- 2 Tbsp. lime juice
- 1 Tbsp. olive oil
- 3 cloves garlic, minced
- $\frac{1}{2}$ tsp. crushed red pepper
- 1 lb. pork tenderloin, trimmed
- $\frac{1}{4}$ tsp. salt
- $\frac{1}{4}$ tsp. black pepper
- 2 tsp. olive oil
- 8 slices whole grain bread, toasted
- 4 leaves lettuce
- 4 slices tomato

1. For chimichurri sauce, in a food processor or blender combine the first eight ingredients (through crushed red pepper). Cover and blend or process until finely chopped, scraping sides as necessary.

2. Cut tenderloin into four equal pieces. Using the flat side of a meat mallet, flatten tenderloin pieces between two pieces of plastic wrap to about $\frac{1}{4}$ inch thick. Sprinkle pieces evenly with salt and black pepper.

3. In an extra-large nonstick skillet heat the 2 tsp. olive oil over medium-high heat. Reduce heat to medium. Cook tenderloin in hot oil 5 to 7 minutes or until just pink inside. Remove from heat.

4. Top 4 slices of toast with lettuce, tenderloin, chimichurri sauce, tomato slices, and the remaining toast slices. Serve immediately.

PER SERVING: 343 cal., 10 g total fat (2 g sat. fat), 70 mg chol., 506 mg sodium, 30 g carb. (6 g fiber, 4 g sugars), 32 g pro.

PORK

Pork tenderloin is a naturally lean cut. It does not need to be breaded and fried to make a delicious sandwich.

Scalloped Root Vegetables and Ham

SERVINGS 5 (1$\frac{1}{4}$ cups each)
CARB. PER SERVING 31 g
PREP 25 minutes   COOK 20 minutes
BAKE 55 minutes   STAND 10 minutes

- $\frac{1}{2}$ cup chopped onion
- 1 Tbsp. butter
- 3 Tbsp. all-purpose flour
- 1 12-oz. can evaporated low-fat milk (2%)
- $\frac{1}{2}$ tsp. dried thyme, crushed
- $\frac{1}{4}$ tsp. salt
- $\frac{1}{4}$ tsp. black pepper
- 10 oz. Yukon gold potatoes (2 medium), cut into $\frac{1}{4}$-inch-thick slices
- 10 oz. sweet potato (2 medium), peeled and cut into $\frac{1}{4}$-inch-thick slices
- 10 oz. turnip (1 large), peeled and cut into $\frac{1}{8}$-inch-thick slices
- $\frac{1}{4}$ cup water
- 8 oz. low-fat, reduced-sodium cooked boneless ham, cut into thin strips
- 2 Tbsp. finely shredded Parmesan cheese
- Snipped fresh parsley

1. Preheat oven to 350°F. For sauce, in a medium saucepan cook onion in melted butter over medium heat 5 to 7 minutes or until tender. Stir in flour. Gradually whisk in milk. Cook and stir until thickened and bubbly. Stir in thyme, salt, and pepper.

2. Meanwhile, in a 2-qt. oval or rectangular baking dish combine Yukon gold potatoes, sweet potatoes, turnips, and the $\frac{1}{4}$ cup water. Cover with vented plastic wrap. Microwave about 8 minutes or just until tender. Carefully drain in a colander.

3. In the same ungreased baking dish layer half of the ham, half of the potatoes and turnips, and half of the sauce. Top with the remaining potatoes and turnips and the remaining ham. Spoon remaining sauce over all.

4. Bake, covered, 45 minutes. Uncover and sprinkle with Parmesan cheese. Bake, uncovered, about 10 minutes more or until 160°F. Let stand 10 minutes before serving. Sprinkle with parsley.

PER SERVING: 228 cal., 5 g total fat (2 g sat. fat), 34 mg chol., 562 mg sodium, 31 g carb. (4 g fiber, 11 g sugars), 14 g pro.

SWEET POTATOES & TURNIPS

Cut calories and carbs by swapping sweet potatoes and turnips for some of the regular potatoes. Turnips add vitamin C, and sweet potatoes bring the vitamin A.

HAM

Sodium is usually a big issue with this favorite dish. Look for low-fat, reduced-sodium ham to help control that.

Almond-Crusted Chicken

SERVINGS 4 (1 chicken breast half +
about 1 cup spinach each)
CARB. PER SERVING 11 g
START TO FINISH 35 minutes

    4   skinless, boneless chicken
        breast halves (1 to 1¼ lb. total)
    1   egg, lightly beaten
    2   Tbsp. buttermilk
    ½   cup finely chopped almonds
    ½   cup panko bread crumbs or
        fine dry bread crumbs
    2   tsp. snipped fresh rosemary
    ¼   tsp. salt
    1   Tbsp. peanut oil or canola oil
    2   Tbsp. sliced shallot
    8   cups fresh spinach
    ¼   tsp. salt
        Freshly ground black pepper
        Fresh mint leaves (optional)

PANKO CRUMBS & ALMONDS

Because panko is lighter and fluffier, you use less cup for cup than
fine dry bread crumbs and get crispier results. By using a chopped
almond-panko combination, you cut carbs and increase protein
in this coating.

1. Using the flat side of a meat mallet,
flatten chicken between two pieces of
plastic wrap to ¼ to ½ inch thick.
2. In a shallow dish combine egg and
buttermilk. In another shallow dish stir
together almonds, bread crumbs,
rosemary, and ¼ teaspoon salt. Dip
chicken into egg mixture, then into
almond mixture, turning to coat.
3. In an extra-large nonstick skillet
cook chicken, half at a time if
necessary, in hot oil over medium heat
4 to 6 minutes or until no longer pink,
turning once. Remove chicken,
reserving drippings in skillet. Keep
chicken warm.

4. Cook shallot over medium heat
in reserved drippings 3 to 5 minutes
or just until tender, stirring frequently.
Add spinach and ¼ teaspoon salt;
cook and toss about 1 minute or
just until spinach is wilted. Serve
chicken with wilted spinach. Sprinkle
with pepper and, if desired, garnish
with mint.

PER SERVING: 276 cal., 11 g total fat
(1 g sat. fat), 66 mg chol., 456 mg sodium,
11 g carb. (3 g fiber, 2 g sugars), 33 g pro.

Chicken Pot Pies

SERVINGS 4 (1 casserole each)
CARB. PER SERVING 34 g
PREP 45 minutes   ROAST 25 minutes
BAKE 15 minutes   STAND 10 minutes

- 1 whole bulb garlic
- 1 Tbsp. olive oil
- 2 cups sliced fresh mushrooms
- 2 medium carrots, cut into $\frac{1}{2}$-inch slices
- 1 medium parsnip, cut into $\frac{1}{2}$-inch slices
- $\frac{1}{2}$ cup chopped onion
- $\frac{1}{2}$ cup reduced-sodium chicken broth
- 1 tsp. dried thyme, crushed
- $\frac{1}{2}$ tsp. salt
- $\frac{1}{4}$ tsp. black pepper
- 2 cups fat-free milk
- 3 Tbsp. flour
- 2 cups cubed cooked chicken breast (about 10 oz.)
- 4 sheets frozen phyllo dough (14×9-inch rectangles), thawed
  Nonstick cooking spray
  Black pepper (optional)

1. Preheat oven to 425°F. Peel away the dry outer layers of skin from the garlic bulb, leaving skins and cloves intact. Cut off the pointed top portion (about $\frac{1}{4}$ inch), leaving bulb intact but exposing the individual cloves. Place the garlic bulb, cut side up, in a custard cup. Drizzle with about $\frac{1}{2}$ tsp. of the olive oil. Cover with foil. Roast 25 to 35 minutes or until the cloves feel soft when pressed. Set aside just until cool enough to handle. Squeeze out the garlic paste from individual cloves.

2. Meanwhile, heat the remaining oil in a large skillet. Add next four ingredients (through onion). Cook 10 minutes, stirring occasionally. Add next four ingredients (through $\frac{1}{4}$ tsp. pepper). Bring to boiling; reduce heat. Simmer, covered, 5 to 10 minutes or just until vegetables are tender. Add garlic paste.

3. In a bowl whisk together milk and flour until smooth; add all at once to mushroom mixture. Cook and stir over medium heat until thickened and bubbly. Stir in chicken. Divide mixture among four 12-oz. individual oven-safe dishes.

4. Unfold phyllo dough; remove one sheet phyllo dough and place on a flat surface. (As you work, cover the remaining phyllo with plastic wrap to prevent them from drying out.) Lightly coat the phyllo sheet with cooking spray. Lay another sheet of phyllo dough on top of the first sheet and lightly coat with cooking spray. Repeat with the remaining two phyllo sheets. Cut phyllo stack in half crosswise. Place one stack on top of the other to make a 9x7-inch stack of 8 sheets.

PHYLLO DOUGH

Replace a traditional fat-filled pastry crust with strips of phyllo dough coated with nonstick cooking spray.

5. Using a pizza cutter, cut phyllo stack into 16 strips. Place four strips in a woven pattern on top of chicken mixture in each baking dish.

6. Bake 15 to 20 minutes or until the filling is bubbly and phyllo is golden brown. Let stand 10 minutes before serving. If desired, sprinkle tops of pot pies with additional pepper.

PER SERVING: 308 cal., 6 g total fat (1 g sat. fat), 61 mg chol., 570 mg sodium, 34 g carb. (3 g fiber, 11 g sugars), 31 g pro.

VEGGIES

This dish is loaded with peas, celery, and carrots to give you almost two veggie servings.

REDUCED-SODIUM CONDENSED CREAM OF CHICKEN SOUP

By using this product instead of the regular condensed cream of chicken soup, you cut the fat by nearly 7 grams per serving. And it has half as much sodium as the regular soup, giving you more control over added sodium.

Chicken and Noodles with Vegetables

SERVINGS 6 (1$\frac{1}{2}$ cups each)
CARB. PER SERVING 42 g
PREP 30 minutes
SLOW COOK 8 to 9 hours (low) or 4 to 4$\frac{1}{2}$ hours (high)

2	cups sliced carrots
1$\frac{1}{2}$	cups chopped onions
1	cup sliced celery
1	bay leaf
4	medium whole chicken legs (drumstick and thigh) (about 2$\frac{1}{2}$ lb. total), skinned
2	10.75-oz. cans reduced-fat and reduced-sodium condensed cream of chicken soup
$\frac{1}{2}$	cup water
1	tsp. dried thyme, crushed
$\frac{1}{4}$	tsp. salt
$\frac{1}{4}$	tsp. black pepper
3	cups dried wide noodles (6 oz.)
1	cup frozen peas

1. In a 3$\frac{1}{2}$- or 4-qt. slow cooker stir together carrots, onions, celery, and bay leaf. Place chicken on top of vegetables. In a bowl stir together the next five ingredients (through pepper). Pour over chicken in cooker.

2. Cover and cook on low 8 to 9 hours or on high 4 to 4$\frac{1}{2}$ hours. Shortly before serving, cook noodles according to package directions; drain. Return noodles to pan; cover and keep warm.

3. Remove chicken from cooker; cool slightly. Remove and discard bay leaf. Stir frozen peas into mixture in cooker. Remove chicken from bones; discard bones. Shred or chop chicken; stir into mixture in cooker. Before serving, stir in cooked noodles.

PER SERVING: 333 cal., 7 g total fat (2 g sat. fat), 94 mg chol., 579 mg sodium, 42 g carb. (5 g fiber, 11 g sugars), 25 g pro.

Bruschetta Chicken Breasts

SERVINGS 4 (1 chicken roll + 2 Tbsp. sauce each)

CARB. PER SERVING 11 g

PREP 40 minutes   **BAKE** 25 minutes

Nonstick cooking spray

2 10-oz. skinless, boneless chicken breast halves

$^3/_4$ tsp. dried basil, crushed

2 Tbsp. snipped oil-packed
carb. per serving 40 g **dried tomatoes**

2 cloves garlic, minced

$^1/_8$ tsp. black pepper

$^1/_3$ cup Italian-seasoned dry bread crumbs

1 egg

$^3/_4$ cup shredded part-skim mozzarella cheese (3 oz.)

$^1/_2$ cup marinara sauce

Snipped fresh basil (optional)

1. Preheat oven to 375°F. Lightly coat a shallow baking pan with cooking spray. Trim any fat from the chicken breasts. Halve each chicken breast half. Using the flat side of a meat mallet, flatten each chicken portion between two pieces of plastic wrap from center to edge to make a rectangle about $^1/_8$ inch thick. Sprinkle $^1/_4$ tsp. of the dried basil over chicken pieces.

2. In a bowl stir together the remaining $^1/_2$ tsp. dried basil, the dried tomatoes, garlic, and pepper. Place bread crumbs in a shallow dish. Place egg in another shallow dish; using a fork, beat egg lightly.

3. Spread a scant tablespoon of the basil mixture on each chicken piece. Place 2 Tbsp. of the shredded mozzarella near an edge of each chicken piece. Fold in sides; starting from the edge with the cheese, roll up jelly-roll style. If necessary, secure with toothpicks.

4. Roll chicken rolls in egg. Dip rolls in bread crumbs, turning to coat evenly.

Place rolls, seam sides down, in prepared pan. Bake, uncovered, 25 to 30 minutes or until 165°F. Remove toothpicks if using. In a small saucepan heat marinara sauce; spoon over chicken rolls. Sprinkle with the remaining $^1/_4$ cup mozzarella. If desired, top with snipped fresh basil.

PER SERVING: 304 cal., 10 g total fat (4 g sat. fat), 149 mg chol., 588 mg sodium, 11 g carb. (1 g fiber, 3 g sugars), 39 g pro.

BREAD CRUMBS

Cut carbs by swapping a bread crumb coating for toasted slices of bread.

183

BASIL & ROSEMARY

Add big flavor with fresh basil and rosemary and you won't need as much salt.

Creamy Basil-Rosemary Chicken and Rice

SERVINGS 4 (1 cup each)
CARB. PER SERVING 21 g
PREP 25 minutes   **COOK** 30 minutes

- 1 tsp. canola oil
- 1½ cups chopped onions
- 1 cup thinly sliced celery
- 1 14.5-oz. can reduced-sodium chicken broth
- 1 cup instant brown rice
- 2 cups chopped cooked chicken breast
- 4 oz. light semisoft cheese with garlic and fine herbs
- ¼ cup water
- 1 clove garlic, minced
- ¼ cup snipped fresh basil
- 1 Tbsp. snipped fresh rosemary
- ⅛ tsp. salt

1. In a medium nonstick skillet heat oil over medium-low heat. Add onions; cook about 15 minutes or until golden brown. Stir in celery; cook about 4 minutes more or until celery is tender. Stir in broth and rice. Bring to boiling; reduce heat. Simmer, covered, about 10 minutes or until liquid is absorbed.

2. Stir in chicken, cheese, the water, and garlic; heat through, stirring occasionally. Stir in basil, rosemary, and salt. If desired, sprinkle with additional snipped fresh basil and/or rosemary.

PER SERVING: 294 cal., 10 g total fat (5 g sat. fat), 80 mg chol., 559 mg sodium, 21 g carb. (3 g fiber, 4 g sugars), 29 g pro.

Spicy Chicken Kabobs with Vegetable Rice

SERVINGS 4 (3 skewers + $^3/_4$ cup rice mixture each)
CARB. PER SERVING 33 g
PREP 25 minutes **GRILL** 8 minutes

- 2 Tbsp. olive oil
- 4 tsp. lemon juice
- $^1/_4$ tsp. crushed red pepper
- $^1/_8$ tsp. salt
- $^1/_8$ tsp. dried thyme
- $^1/_8$ tsp. black pepper
- 1 medium zucchini
- 1 lb. skinless, boneless chicken breast, cut into 1-inch pieces
- 1 medium red onion, cut into $^1/_2$-inch-thick wedges
- 24 red and/or yellow cherry tomatoes
  Nonstick cooking spray
- $^3/_4$ cup chopped red sweet pepper
- 2 cloves garlic, minced
- 4 cups chopped kale
- $^1/_4$ cup reduced-sodium chicken broth
- $^3/_4$ tsp. Cajun seasoning
- $1^1/_3$ cups cooked brown rice

1. If using wooden skewers, soak twelve 8-inch skewers in water 30 minutes. In a bowl whisk together the first six ingredients (through black pepper). Cut zucchini in half crosswise. Chop half of the zucchini; cut the remaining zucchini lengthwise into thin slices. Add zucchini slices, chicken, onion, and tomatoes to oil mixture; toss to coat. Alternately thread chicken pieces, zucchini slices, onion wedges, and tomatoes on skewers, leaving $^1/_4$ inch between pieces.

2. Grill skewers, covered, over medium heat 8 to 10 minutes or until chicken is no longer pink, turning occasionally.

3. Meanwhile, for rice, coat a large skillet with cooking spray. Heat skillet over medium heat. Add chopped zucchini, sweet pepper, and garlic. Cook and stir 3 minutes. Add kale, broth, and Cajun seasoning. Simmer, covered, about 5 minutes or until kale is tender. Stir in cooked rice; heat. Serve skewers with rice mixture.

PER SERVING: 300 cal., 10 g total fat (2 g sat. fat), 47 mg chol., 264 mg sodium, 33 g carb. (5 g fiber, 8 g sugars), 22 g pro.

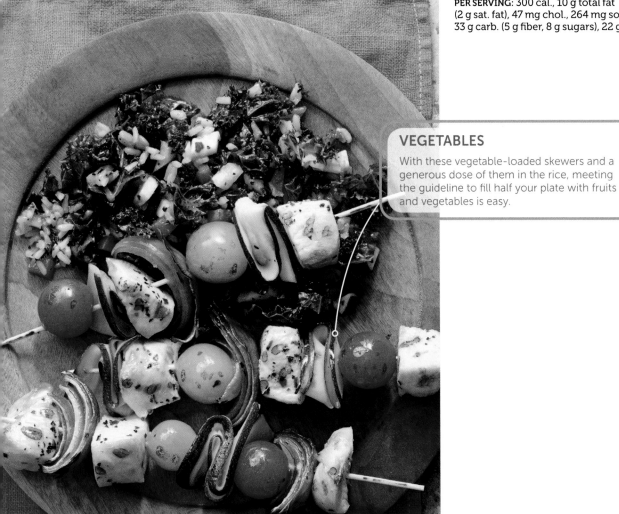

VEGETABLES

With these vegetable-loaded skewers and a generous dose of them in the rice, meeting the guideline to fill half your plate with fruits and vegetables is easy.

Honey Chicken Stir-Fry

SERVINGS 8 (^{3}/4 cup chicken mixture + ^{1}/3 cup rice each)
CARB. PER SERVING 34 g
START TO FINISH 30 minutes

HONEY STIR-FRY SAUCE

Most prepared stir-fry sauces are very high in sodium. Make your own using reduced-sodium ingredients.

- 1^1/2 lb. skinless, boneless chicken breast halves, cut into thin bite-size strips
- ^{1}/4 tsp. salt
- ^{1}/4 tsp. black pepper
- 2 tsp. olive oil
- 1 16-oz. pkg. frozen stir-fry vegetables with broccoli, thawed and drained
- 1 recipe Honey Stir-Fry Sauce
- 2^2/3 cups hot cooked brown rice
- ^{1}/4 cup sliced green onions
- ^{3}/4 cup chow mein noodles (optional)

1. Sprinkle chicken with salt and pepper. In a large skillet heat oil over medium heat. Add half of the chicken; cook and stir 3 to 4 minutes or until no longer pink. Remove from skillet. Repeat with the remaining chicken.

2. Return all of the chicken to skillet. Stir in thawed vegetables and Honey Stir-Fry Sauce. Cook and stir until thickened and bubbly. Cook and stir 2 minutes more.

3. Serve chicken mixture over rice. Sprinkle with green onions. If desired, serve with chow mein noodles.

HONEY STIR-FRY SAUCE In a bowl combine 6 Tbsp. honey; ^{1}/4 cup reduced-sodium chicken broth; 3 Tbsp. reduced-sodium soy sauce; 2 Tbsp. cider vinegar; 4 cloves garlic, minced; 1 tsp. toasted sesame oil; ^{1}/4 tsp. ground ginger; and ^{1}/8 tsp. cayenne pepper. Stir in 1 Tbsp. cornstarch until dissolved.

PER SERVING: 262 cal., 5 g total fat (1 g sat. fat), 54 mg chol., 428 mg sodium, 34 g carb. (2 g fiber, 15 g sugars), 21 g pro.

Chicken Ragout

SERVINGS 8 (1 cup chicken mixture + about $\frac{1}{3}$ cup noodles each)
CARB. PER SERVING 33 g
PREP 20 minutes
SLOW COOK 8 to 10 hours (low)
COOK 8 minutes

- 8 bone-in chicken thighs (about $3\frac{1}{2}$ lb. total), skinned
- 2 14.5-oz. cans no-salt-added diced tomatoes, drained
- 3 cups 2-inch carrot pieces or packaged baby carrots
- 1 large onion, cut into wedges
- $\frac{1}{3}$ cup reduced-sodium chicken broth
- 2 Tbsp. white wine vinegar
- 1 tsp. dried rosemary, crushed
- 1 tsp. dried thyme, crushed
- $\frac{1}{4}$ tsp. black pepper
- 8 oz. fresh mushrooms, sliced
- 1 tsp. olive oil
- 3 cups hot cooked whole wheat noodles
  Snipped fresh parsley (optional)

1. Place chicken thighs in a $3\frac{1}{2}$- or 4-qt. slow cooker. In a bowl stir together the next eight ingredients (through pepper). Pour over chicken in cooker. Cover and cook on low 8 to 10 hours.

2. Just before serving, in a large nonstick skillet cook and stir mushrooms in hot oil over medium-high heat 8 to 10 minutes or until golden brown. Stir mushrooms into mixture in cooker. Serve chicken mixture over hot cooked noodles. If desired, sprinkle with parsley.

PER SERVING: 234 cal., 4 g total fat (1 g sat. fat), 57 mg chol., 163 mg sodium, 33 g carb. (7 g fiber, 7 g sugars), 20 g pro.

WHOLE WHEAT NOODLES
Use whole grain pasta instead of regular to boost fiber and protein.

Oven-Fried Chicken with Tomato Gravy

SERVINGS 4 (2 pieces chicken + $^1/_4$ cup tomato gravy)
CARB. PER SERVING 33 g
PREP 15 minutes   BAKE 15 minutes

Nonstick cooking spray
1 6-oz. carton plain fat-free Greek yogurt
2 Tbsp. honey
2$^3/_4$ cups cornflakes, coarsely crushed, or 1$^1/_2$ cups panko bread crumbs
$^1/_2$ cup snipped fresh basil (optional)
4 skinless, boneless chicken breast halves (about 1$^1/_4$ lb. total), each halved crosswise
$^1/_8$ tsp. salt
Black pepper
1 14.5-oz. can fire-roasted tomatoes with garlic, undrained
2 tsp. reduced-sodium Worcestershire sauce
Finely shredded Parmesan cheese (optional)
Hot cooked noodles (optional)

1. Preheat oven to 425°F. Lightly coat a baking sheet with cooking spray.
2. In a shallow dish combine yogurt and honey. In another shallow dish combine cornflakes and, if desired, $^1/_4$ cup of the snipped basil. Using the flat side of a meat mallet, flatten chicken lightly between two pieces of plastic wrap to a uniform thickness. Sprinkle chicken with $^1/_8$ tsp. salt and pepper to taste. Dip chicken into yogurt mixture, turning to coat; dip into cornflake mixture, turning to coat. Arrange on the prepared baking sheet. Lightly coat with cooking spray. Bake 15 to 18 minutes or until chicken is crisp and golden brown on the outside and no longer pink on the inside (165°F), turning once.
3. Meanwhile, in a small saucepan combine tomatoes, Worcestershire sauce, and, if desired, the remaining $^1/_4$ cup snipped basil. Cook and stir over medium-low heat until heated.
4. Serve tomato gravy with chicken. If desired, garnish with Parmesan cheese and serve with hot cooked noodles.

PER SERVING: 326 cal., 4 g total fat (1 g sat. fat), 103 mg chol., 514 mg sodium, 33 g carb. (3 g fiber, 15 g sugars), 39 g pro.

TEST KITCHEN TIP

Skinless, boneless chicken breast halves vary in size, and some can be as large as 10 oz. Weigh those you purchase because you only need about 20 oz. total. Cut the halves crosswise into about 2$^1/_2$-oz. pieces before flattening with a meat mallet.

TOMATO-BASED SAUCE
Replace classic fat-filled gravy with a flavorful tomato-based sauce.

COOKING SPRAY
Coating crumb-covered chicken pieces with cooking spray and baking is a more healthful cooking technique than frying.

Chicken-Waffle à la King

SERVINGS 4 (1 waffle + 1 cup chicken mixture + 5 Tbsp. gravy each)
CARB. PER SERVING 36 g
PREP 20 minutes   **COOK** 15 minutes
BAKE per waffle baker's directions

- 1   4-oz. can (drained weight) no-salt-added sliced mushrooms or mushroom stems and pieces
  Nonstick cooking spray
- 1½ tsp. canola oil
- 1   lb. skinless, boneless chicken thighs, cut into 1-inch pieces
- 1   cup frozen baby broccoli florets
- 1   cup frozen sliced carrots
- ¼ cup frozen chopped onions
- ½ tsp. minced garlic
- 1   cup water
- 1   0.87-oz. pkg. low-sodium chicken gravy mix
- 1   Tbsp. cornstarch
- ½ tsp. dried thyme, crushed
- ¼ tsp. celery seeds
- ¾ cup low-fat pancake and baking mix
- ⅔ cup fat-free milk
- ¼ cup cornmeal
- 1   egg white, lightly beaten
- 1   Tbsp. canola oil
- 2   tsp. dried sage, crushed

1. Drain mushrooms, reserving the liquid. Coat a large nonstick skillet with cooking spray. Add the 1½ tsp. canola oil to skillet; heat over medium-high heat. Cook chicken in hot oil about 10 minutes or until browned and cooked through, stirring occasionally. Remove chicken from skillet. Add drained mushrooms and the next four ingredients (through garlic) to skillet. Cook and stir about 5 minutes or until vegetables begin to soften and mixture is heated. Return chicken to skillet; heat.

2. In a small saucepan stir together reserved mushroom liquid and the next five ingredients (through celery seeds). Cook and stir until boiling; reduce heat. Simmer 1 minute. Remove from heat; keep warm.

3. In a bowl stir together the next six ingredients (through sage). Add one-fourth of the batter to a preheated, lightly greased waffle baker. Bake according to manufacturer's directions. (Do not open baker until done.) Use a fork to lift waffle off grid. Repeat with the remaining batter. Top waffles with chicken mixture and gravy.

PER SERVING: 368 cal., 12 g total fat (2 g sat. fat), 108 mg chol., 613 mg sodium, 36 g carb. (4 g fiber, 7 g sugars), 28 g pro.

WAFFLES

Instead of biscuits, spoon this veggie-filled gravy mixture over waffles lightened with lower-fat ingredients and egg whites.

MILK & FLOUR

Make a creamy gravy by combining fat-free milk with flour to thicken the soup.

Chicken and Cornmeal Dumplings

SERVINGS 4 (1^1/$_2$ cups chicken mixture + 2 dumplings each)

CARB. PER SERVING 47 g

PREP 25 minutes

SLOW COOK 7 to 8 hours (low) or 3^1/$_2$ to 4 hours (high) + 20 minutes (high)

- 2 cups thinly sliced carrots
- 1 cup thinly sliced celery
- ^{2}/$_3$ cup fresh or frozen whole kernel corn
- 1 medium onion, thinly sliced
- 3 cloves garlic, minced
- 2 tsp. snipped fresh rosemary or 1 tsp. dried rosemary, crushed
- ^{1}/$_2$ tsp. black pepper
- 4 bone-in chicken thighs, skinned
- 2 cups reduced-sodium chicken broth
- 1 cup fat-free milk
- 2 Tbsp. all-purpose flour
- 1 recipe Cornmeal Dumplings

1. In a 3^1/$_2$- or 4-qt. slow cooker combine the first seven ingredients (through black pepper). Top with chicken. Pour broth over all in cooker.

2. Cover and cook on low 7 to 8 hours or high 3^1/$_2$ to 4 hours.

3. If using low setting, turn to high. Remove chicken from cooker. Transfer chicken to a cutting board; cool slightly. When cool enough to handle, remove chicken from bones; discard bones. Cut up chicken; return to slow cooker. In a bowl whisk together milk and flour until smooth. Stir into mixture in cooker.

4. Prepare Cornmeal Dumplings. Using two spoons, drop dough into eight mounds on top of hot chicken mixture. Cover and cook 20 to 25 minutes more (do not lift cover) or until a toothpick inserted into a dumpling comes out clean. If desired, sprinkle each serving with *coarsely ground black pepper*.

CORNMEAL DUMPLINGS In a medium bowl combine 1 cup all-purpose flour, 1 cup shredded cheddar cheese, ^{2}/$_3$ cup yellow cornmeal, 2 teaspoons baking powder, and ^{1}/$_2$ teaspoon salt. In a small bowl combine 1 egg and ^{1}/$_4$ cup each milk and melted butter. Add egg mixture to flour mixture. Stir with a fork until moistened.

PER SERVING: 369 cal., 10 g total fat (1 g sat. fat), 55 mg chol., 582 mg sodium, 47 g carb. (5 g fiber, 9 g sugars), 24 g pro.

Herbed Chicken, Orzo, and Zucchini

SERVINGS 4 (1 chicken breast half + about $1^{1}/_{4}$ cups orzo mixture each)
CARB. PER SERVING 35 g
START TO FINISH 20 minutes

- 1 cup dried orzo pasta
- 4 skinless, boneless chicken breast halves (1 to $1^{1}/_{4}$ lb. total)
- 1 tsp. dried basil, crushed
- 3 Tbsp. olive oil
- 2 medium zucchini and/or yellow summer squash, halved lengthwise and sliced
- 2 Tbsp. red wine vinegar
- 1 Tbsp. snipped fresh dill weed
- $^{1}/_{4}$ tsp. salt
- $^{1}/_{4}$ tsp. black pepper

1. Cook orzo according to package directions; drain. Return orzo to hot pan; cover and keep warm.

2. Meanwhile, sprinkle chicken with basil. In a large skillet heat 1 Tbsp. of the oil over medium-high heat. Add chicken; cook about 12 minutes or until no longer pink (165°F), turning once. (Reduce heat to medium if chicken browns too quickly.) Remove chicken from skillet.

3. Add zucchini and/or yellow squash to skillet; cook and stir about 3 minutes or until crisp-tender. Stir in cooked orzo, the remaining 2 Tbsp. oil, and the remaining ingredients. Serve chicken with orzo mixture. If desired, sprinkle with additional snipped fresh dill weed.

PER SERVING: 390 cal., 12 g total fat (2 g sat. fat), 66 mg chol., 366 mg sodium, 35 g carb. (3 g fiber, 3 g sugars), 33 g pro.

VINEGAR & DILL WEED

Tangy red wine vinegar and fresh dill weed give bright, intense flavor to this pasta dish in a low-fat vinaigrettelike sauce.

Southwestern White Chili

SERVINGS 8 (1 cup each)
CARB. PER SERVING 27 g
PREP 20 minutes
SLOW COOK 8 hours to 10 hours (low) or 4 to 5 hours (high)

- 3 15-oz. cans no-salt-added Great Northern beans, rinsed and drained
- 4 cups reduced-sodium chicken broth
- 3 cups chopped cooked chicken breast
- 2 4-oz. cans diced green chiles, undrained
- 1 cup chopped onion
- 4 cloves garlic, minced
- 2 tsp. ground cumin
- 1 tsp. dried oregano, crushed
- $1/4$ tsp. cayenne pepper
- $1^{1}/2$ cups shredded Monterey Jack cheese (6 oz.)

Sour cream (optional)
Fresh cilantro leaves (optional)

1. In a $3^{1}/2$- to 6-qt. slow cooker combine the first nine ingredients (through cayenne pepper).
2. Cover and cook on low 8 to 10 hours or high 4 to 5 hours. Stir in cheese until melted. If desired, top each serving with sour cream and cilantro.

PER SERVING: 316 cal., 10 g total fat (5 g sat. fat), 63 mg chol., 575 mg sodium, 27 g carb. (10 g fiber, 3 g sugars), 30 g pro.

BEANS & BROTH
Keep sodium in check with no-salt-added beans and reduced-sodium broth.

Spaghetti Squash Pie

SERVINGS 6 (1 wedge each)
CARB. PER SERVING 16 g
PREP 20 minutes BAKE 35 minutes
BAKE 45 minutes STAND 20 minutes

1 2-lb. spaghetti squash
Nonstick cooking spray
2 Tbsp. refrigerated or frozen egg product, thawed, or 1 egg white, lightly beaten
1/4 cup finely shredded Parmesan cheese
2 tsp. dried Italian seasoning, crushed
1/8 tsp. salt
8 oz. ground turkey
1/2 cup chopped onion
1/2 cup chopped green or red sweet pepper
1/2 cup finely chopped carrot
2 cloves garlic, minced
1/4 tsp. fennel seeds, crushed
1 8-oz. can no-salt-added tomato sauce
1/4 tsp. crushed red pepper
2/3 cup shredded part-skim mozzarella cheese (2.5 oz.)
3/4 cup low-fat cottage cheese (2%)
Chopped fresh basil or oregano (optional)

1. Preheat oven to 400°F. Line a 15×10-inch baking pan with parchment paper or foil. Cut squash in half lengthwise; remove and discard seeds. Place squash, cut sides down, in prepared pan. Bake about 35 minutes or until squash is tender. Remove from oven; cool slightly. Reduce oven temperature to 350°F.

2. Coat a 9-inch pie plate with cooking spray. Using a fork, remove squash pulp from shells into a bowl; add egg product, Parmesan cheese, 1 tsp. of the Italian seasoning, and salt. Press into bottom and up sides of prepared pie plate. Bake 20 minutes.

3. Meanwhile, in a large skillet cook the next six ingredients (through fennel seeds) over medium heat until turkey is browned. Drain off any fat. Stir in tomato sauce, crushed red pepper, and the remaining 1 tsp. Italian seasoning. Heat. Sprinkle half of the mozzarella over squash crust; top with cottage cheese, then turkey mixture.

4. Bake, uncovered, 20 minutes, placing a foil-lined baking sheet on the rack below the dish. Sprinkle with remaining mozzarella cheese. Bake 5 minutes more or until cheese is melted. Let stand 20 minutes before serving. Cut into wedges. If desired, top with basil or oregano.

PER SERVING: 188 cal., 7 g total fat (3 g sat. fat), 42 mg chol., 343 mg sodium, 16 g carb. (4 g fiber, 7 g sugars), 16 g pro.

TEST KITCHEN TIP

Spaghetti squash is about 92 percent water by weight, so it is low in calories. Prebaking the squash crust does help to dry and set it; however, a slight bit of water will be released during baking.

SPAGHETTI SQUASH

Spaghetti squash replaces pasta to reduce carbs and add fiber and other nutrients.

COTTAGE CHEESE

Use low-fat cottage cheese instead of whole-milk ricotta to cut the fat without sacrificing flavor.

Turkey Tetrazzini Bake

SERVINGS 6 (1 cup each)
CARB. PER SERVING 30 g
PREP 30 minutes **BAKE** 15 minutes
STAND 5 minutes

Nonstick cooking spray
6 oz. dried multigrain farfalle pasta (2$\frac{1}{2}$ cups)
$\frac{1}{3}$ cup soft whole wheat bread crumbs
2 Tbsp. freshly grated Parmesan cheese
2 Tbsp. snipped fresh Italian parsley
2 tsp. olive oil
1$\frac{1}{2}$ cups frozen pepper stir-fry vegetables (green, red, and yellow sweet peppers and onion)
1 tsp. minced garlic
2 Tbsp. all-purpose flour
1 tsp. dried thyme, crushed
$\frac{1}{2}$ tsp. salt
$\frac{1}{4}$ tsp. cracked black pepper
1 cup evaporated low-fat milk (2%)
$\frac{1}{2}$ cup unsalted chicken stock
2 oz. reduced-fat cream cheese (Neufchâtel), cut up and softened
1 Tbsp. Dijon-style mustard
2 cups chopped cooked turkey breast
$\frac{1}{2}$ cup frozen peas, thawed

EVAPORATED MILK
Using evaporated low-fat milk produces a richness similar to cream sauce with less fat.

1. Preheat oven to 375°F. Coat a 1$\frac{1}{2}$-qt. gratin dish or baking dish with cooking spray. Cook pasta according to package directions. Drain, reserving 1 cup of the cooking water.

2. Meanwhile, in a bowl combine bread crumbs, Parmesan cheese, and parsley. In a large nonstick skillet heat oil over medium-high heat. Add frozen stir-fry vegetables and garlic. Cook and stir 4 minutes. Sprinkle flour, thyme, salt, and black pepper over vegetables.

Cook and stir 2 minutes more. Add evaporated milk and stock. Cook and stir about 5 minutes more or until boiling and slightly thickened.

3. Remove skillet from heat. Add cream cheese and mustard to hot mixture in skillet, stirring until cream cheese melts. Stir in turkey, peas, and cooked pasta. Stir in enough of the reserved cooking water, $\frac{1}{4}$ cup at a time, to make desired consistency.

Transfer to prepared baking dish. Sprinkle with bread crumb mixture; coat with cooking spray. Bake 15 to 20 minutes or until edges are bubbly and top is browned. Remove from oven. Let stand 5 minutes before serving.

PER SERVING: 281 cal., 6 g total fat (2 g sat. fat), 54 mg chol., 429 mg sodium, 30 g carb. (3 g fiber, 7 g sugars), 25 g pro.

Turkey Reubens

SERVINGS 6 (1 open-face sandwich each)
CARB. PER SERVING 28 g
PREP 15 minutes
SLOW COOK 7 to 8 hours (low) or $3^1/_2$ to 4 hours (high) + 30 minutes (high)   **BROIL** 2 minutes

2	stalks celery, cut crosswise into thirds
1	medium onion, cut into wedges
1	cup water
$^1/_2$	tsp. caraway seeds, crushed
$^1/_4$	tsp. celery seeds
$^1/_4$	tsp. salt
$^1/_4$	tsp. black pepper
2	to $2^1/_2$ lb. bone-in turkey breast halves
6	cups shredded fresh cabbage
2	cups purchased coarsely shredded carrots
6	slices rye bread
6	$^3/_4$-oz. slice reduced-fat Swiss cheese
$^1/_2$	cup reduced-calorie Thousand Island salad dressing

1. Place celery and onion in a $3^1/_2$- or 4-qt. slow cooker. Add the water to cooker. In a bowl combine caraway seeds, celery seeds, salt, and pepper. Sprinkle over turkey. Place turkey on celery and onions in cooker.
2. Cover and cook on low 7 to 8 hours or high $3^1/_2$ to 4 hours. If using low setting, turn to high. Add cabbage and carrots to cooker; cover and cook 30 minutes more.
3. Preheat broiler. Using tongs, remove cabbage and carrots from cooker; set aside. Transfer turkey to a cutting board; remove and discard skin. Thinly slice or shred turkey. Discard celery and onion from cooker. Place bread slices on a large baking

sheet. Broil 3 to 4 inches from the heat 1 to 2 minutes or until tops are lightly toasted. Turn bread slices over and top each with a slice of cheese. Broil 1 to 2 minutes more or until cheese is melted.
4. Place $^3/_4$ cup turkey and $^3/_4$ cup cabbage mixture on each cheese-topped bread slice. Top sandwiches with salad dressing. If desired, sprinkle with additional celery seeds.

PER SERVING: 341 cal., 8 g total fat (3 g sat. fat), 86 mg chol., 591 mg sodium, 28 g carb. (4 g fiber, 8 g sugars), 41 g pro.

TURKEY

Enjoy a better-tasting sandwich with less sodium and no nitrates by cooking the turkey yourself instead of buying processed turkey slices.

Seafood Enchiladas

SERVINGS 8 (1 enchilada each)
CARB. PER SERVING 22 g
PREP 40 minutes BAKE 35 minutes
STAND 5 minutes

- 1¼ lb. fresh or frozen medium shrimp
- 8 oz. fresh or frozen halibut
- 5 cups water
- ¾ cup chopped red sweet pepper
- 2 fresh poblano chile peppers, stemmed, seeded, and chopped (tip, *page 137*)
- ½ cup chopped onion
- 2 tsp. canola oil
- 2 cloves garlic, minced
- 8 8-inch low-carb whole wheat flour tortillas
- 4 oz. reduced-fat cream cheese (Neufchâtel), softened
- 1 8-oz. carton light sour cream
- 2 Tbsp. all-purpose flour
- ¼ tsp. salt
- ¼ tsp. black pepper
- ¾ cup fat-free milk
- ½ cup thinly sliced green onions

1. Thaw shrimp and halibut, if frozen. Peel and devein shrimp. Rinse shrimp and halibut; pat dry with paper towels. Preheat oven to 350°F. Grease a 3-qt. rectangular baking dish. In a large saucepan bring the water to boiling. Add shrimp; cook 1 to 3 minutes or until shrimp are opaque, stirring occasionally. Rinse shrimp with cold water; drain and chop.

2. Measure thickness of fish. Place a steamer insert in a large skillet or 4-quart Dutch oven with a tight-fitting lid. Add water to the skillet to just below the steamer insert. Bring water in skillet to boiling. Place fish in the steamer insert. Cover and steam over medium heat 4 to 6 minutes per ½-inch thickness or until fish flakes easily, adding more water as needed to maintain steam. Flake fish into bite-size pieces.

3. In a large nonstick skillet cook sweet pepper, chile peppers, and onion in hot oil over medium heat 5 to 10 minutes or until tender, stirring occasionally. Stir in garlic; cook 1 minute. Remove from heat. Stir in shrimp and halibut.

4. Meanwhile, stack tortillas; wrap tightly in foil. Bake about 10 minutes or until heated. For sauce, in a bowl beat cream cheese with a mixer on medium until smooth. Beat in the next four ingredients (through black pepper). Gradually beat in milk until smooth.

5. Stir ½ cup of the sauce into the shrimp mixture. Divide shrimp mixture among tortillas, spooning it near one side of each tortilla. Roll up tortillas. Place filled tortillas, seam sides down, in prepared baking dish. Pour the remaining sauce over enchiladas.

6. Bake, covered, about 35 minutes or until heated. Let stand 5 minutes before serving. Sprinkle with green onions.

PER SERVING: 283 cal., 11 g total fat (4 g sat. fat), 139 mg chol., 540 mg sodium, 22 g carb. (9 g fiber, 3 g sugars), 24 g pro.

TEST KITCHEN TIP

Halibut is a mild, sturdy white fish. If you have cod, tilapia, or sea bass in your freezer, pull it out to use in place of the halibut.

CREAM CHEESE, SOUR CREAM & MILK
Reduced-fat dairy products replace heavy cream to make a cheesy cream sauce.

LOW-CARB TORTILLAS
Cut carbs (about 10 g per tortilla) by using low-carb tortillas.

Shrimply Divine Pasta

SERVINGS 4 (1 cup each)
CARB. PER SERVING 37 g
START TO FINISH 20 minutes

- 12 oz. fresh or frozen medium shrimp in shells
- 6 oz. dried rotini or other small pasta (2 cups)
- 1 Tbsp. olive oil
- 3 cloves garlic, minced
- 1/2 cup Italian salad dressing
- 1 tsp. dried Italian seasoning, crushed
- 1 5- to 6-oz. pkg. fresh baby spinach or 8 cups torn fresh spinach

Finely shredded Parmesan cheese

1. Thaw shrimp, if frozen. Cook pasta according to package directions; drain. Return pasta to pan; cover and keep warm.

2. Meanwhile, peel and devein shrimp, leaving tails intact if desired. Rinse shrimp; pat dry with paper towels.

3. In a large skillet heat oil over medium-high heat. Add garlic; cook and stir 15 seconds. Add shrimp; cook and stir 2 to 3 minutes or until shrimp are opaque. Remove shrimp from skillet. Add salad dressing and Italian seasoning to skillet. Bring to simmering. Add spinach; cook and stir 1 to 2 minutes or just until wilted. Return shrimp to skillet.

4. Add cooked pasta to shrimp mixture; toss gently to combine. Serve with Parmesan cheese.

PER SERVING: 340 cal., 11 g total fat (2 g sat. fat), 120 mg chol., 438 mg sodium, 37 g carb. (2 g fiber, 4 g sugars), 22 g pro.

SALAD DRESSING

Use a light-tasting bottled Italian dressing to make a pasta "sauce" instead of a heavy cream sauce.

Barley Vegetable Soup

SERVINGS 6 (about 1 cup)
CARB. PER SERVING 44 g
PREP 25 minutes
SLOW COOK 8 to 10 hours (low) or
4 to 5 hours (high)

- 2 cups sliced fresh mushrooms
- 1 15-oz. can small red beans, rinsed and drained
- 1 14.5-oz. can stewed tomatoes, undrained
- 1 10-oz. pkg. frozen whole kernel corn
- 1 cup chopped onion
- $^1/_2$ cup regular pearled barley
- $^1/_2$ cup sliced carrot
- $^1/_2$ cup sliced celery
- 2 tsp. dried Italian seasoning, crushed
- 3 cloves garlic, minced
- $^1/_4$ tsp. black pepper
- 5 cups reduced-sodium vegetable broth or chicken broth

1. In a 3$^1/_2$- to 5-qt. slow cooker combine the first 11 ingredients (through pepper). Pour broth over mixture in cooker.

2. Cover and cook on low 8 to 10 hours or high 4 to 5 hours.

PER SERVING: 208 cal., 1 g total fat (0 g sat. fat), 0 mg chol., 447 mg sodium, 44 g carb. (10 g fiber, 9 g sugars), 9 g pro.

BROTH

Keep sodium low with reduced-sodium broth. This broth-based soup is super low in fat and loaded with veggies.

Two-Bean Enchilada Casserole

SERVINGS 6 (about 1 cup + 1 Tbsp. yogurt + $^1/_2$ Tbsp. taco sauce each)
CARB. PER SERVING 42 g
PREP 35 minutes BAKE 45 minutes

- 2 tsp. canola oil
- 1 Tbsp. all-purpose flour
- 2 8-oz. cans no-salt-added tomato sauce
- $^3/_4$ cup reduced-sodium chicken broth
- 2 Tbsp. chili powder
- 2 tsp. dried oregano, crushed
- 1 tsp. ground cumin
- $^1/_2$ tsp. salt
- $^1/_4$ tsp. ground cinnamon
- $^1/_8$ to $^1/_4$ tsp. cayenne pepper
- 1 15-oz. can no-salt-added black beans, rinsed and drained
- 1 15-oz. can no-salt-added pinto beans, rinsed and drained
- 1 cup chopped onion
- $^3/_4$ cup chopped green sweet pepper
- 1 4-oz. can diced green chile peppers, undrained

  Nonstick cooking spray
- 9 6-inch corn tortillas, cut into wedges
- $1^1/_4$ cups shredded sharp cheddar cheese (5 oz.)
- 6 Tbsp. plain fat-free Greek yogurt
- 3 Tbsp. mild or medium taco sauce

TOMATO SAUCE, BROTH & BEANS

Purchased enchilada sauce is a high-sodium product. Make your own using reduced-sodium products. And use no-salt-added beans to control sodium content.

1. Preheat oven to 350°F. For sauce, in a small saucepan heat oil over medium heat. Add flour, stirring until smooth. Stir in the next eight ingredients (through cayenne pepper). Cook and stir until thickened and bubbly. Cook and stir 1 minute more.

2. In a bowl combine the next five ingredients (through green chile peppers).

3. Coat a 2-qt. baking dish with cooking spray. Spread $^1/_2$ cup of the sauce over bottom of the prepared baking dish. Layer one-third of the tortilla wedges on sauce. Top with one-third of the bean mixture. Spoon one-third (about $^2/_3$ cup) of the remaining sauce over all. Sprinkle with $^1/_4$ cup of the cheese. Repeat layers twice, starting with tortilla wedges. Do not add the final layer of cheese.

4. Cover with foil. Bake 35 minutes. Sprinkle with the remaining $^1/_2$ cup cheese. Bake, uncovered, about 10 minutes more or until cheese melts. Serve with yogurt and taco sauce.

PER SERVING: 329 cal., 11 g total fat (5 g sat. fat), 25 mg chol., 606 mg sodium, 42 g carb. (11 g fiber, 7 g sugars), 17 g pro.

Veggie Mac and Cheese

SERVINGS 8 (1 cup each)
CARB. PER SERVING 34 g
START TO FINISH 45 minutes

- $\frac{1}{2}$ cup panko bread crumbs
- $\frac{1}{4}$ tsp. paprika
- 8 oz. dried whole grain elbow macaroni (about 2 cups)
- 1 cup sliced carrots
- 1 cup green beans cut into 1-inch pieces
- $\frac{2}{3}$ cup finely chopped onion
- 2 cups small broccoli florets
- $1\frac{3}{4}$ cups fat-free milk
- 3 Tbsp. all-purpose flour
- $\frac{1}{2}$ tsp. salt
- $\frac{1}{8}$ tsp. black pepper
- 3 oz. reduced-fat cream cheese (Neufchâtel)
- $1\frac{1}{2}$ tsp. Dijon-style mustard
- 2 cups shredded reduced-fat Mexican-style four-cheese blend (8 oz.)
- Nonstick cooking spray

1. Preheat broiler. In a bowl stir together panko and paprika.

2. In a large saucepan cook macaroni, carrots, green beans, and onion according to package directions for macaroni, except omit salt; add broccoli the last 3 minutes of cooking time. Drain. Return cooked macaroni and vegetables to hot saucepan; keep warm.

3. Meanwhile, in a medium saucepan whisk together milk, flour, salt, and pepper. Cook and stir over medium heat until slightly thickened and bubbly. Add cream cheese and mustard, stirring until smooth. Remove from heat. Add shredded cheese blend, stirring constantly until melted.

4. Immediately pour cheese mixture over cooked macaroni mixture; toss gently to coat. Spoon into a $2\frac{1}{2}$- or

3-qt. broilerproof oval baking dish. Sprinkle panko mixture over macaroni mixture. Lightly coat panko mixture with cooking spray. Broil 4 to 6 inches from heat 1 to 2 minutes or until golden brown.

PER SERVING: 269 cal., 8 g total fat (5 g sat. fat), 24 mg chol., 495 mg sodium, 34 g carb. (4 g fiber, 6 g sugars), 16 g pro.

CARROTS, BEANS & BROCCOLI
Classic creamy mac and cheese gets a healthful bump when packed with vegetables.

TOMATO SAUCE, BROTH & BEANS

Mashing some of the cooked vegetables allows you to use fat-free milk but still achieve a thick, creamy consistency in this popular soup.

Tater Soup

SERVINGS 4 ($1^1/_2$ cups each)
CARB. PER SERVING 27 g
PREP 20 minutes   COOK 15 minutes

- 4 medium round red, white, or yellow potatoes (about $1^1/_4$ lb.), cut into bite-size pieces
- $^1/_2$ cup sliced carrot
- $^1/_2$ cup sliced celery
- 2 Tbsp. butter
- 2 Tbsp. all-purpose flour
- $^1/_4$ tsp. salt
- $^1/_8$ tsp. white pepper
- $1^1/_2$ cups fat-free milk
- 1 14.5-oz. can reduced-sodium chicken broth
- Shredded reduced-fat cheddar cheese (optional)

1. In a covered large saucepan cook potatoes in enough boiling salted water to cover 5 minutes. Add carrot and celery. Cook about 10 minutes more or until vegetables are tender; drain. Transfer 1 cup of the cooked vegetables to a small bowl; set the remaining cooked vegetables aside. Mash the 1 cup vegetables until nearly smooth.

2. In the same saucepan melt butter over medium heat. Stir in flour, salt, and pepper. Gradually stir in milk. Cook and stir until slightly thickened and bubbly.

3. Stir in the reserved cooked vegetables, the mashed vegetables, and broth. Cook and stir over medium heat until heated through. If necessary, stir in enough additional milk to reach desired consistency. If desired, sprinkle with cheese.

PER SERVING: 186 cal., 6 g total fat (4 g sat. fat), 17 mg chol., 507 mg sodium, 27 g carb. (3 g fiber, 7 g sugars), 7 g pro.

Salmon Noodle Casserole

SERVINGS 4 (1^3/4 cups each)
CARB. PER SERVING 36 g
PREP 20 minutes   COOK 8 minutes
BAKE 30 minutes

- 3 oz. dried medium egg noodles
- 1 small yellow summer squash, halved and thinly sliced (1 cup)
- 1 cup fresh or frozen peas
- 1 12-oz. can evaporated fat-free milk
- 1 Tbsp. all-purpose flour
- 4 oz. reduced-fat cream cheese (Neufchâtel), cut up
- 2 tsp. snipped fresh dill weed or ^{1}/2 tsp. dried dill weed
- 1 tsp. prepared horseradish
- 1 tsp. lemon zest
- ^{1}/4 tsp. salt
- 1 5-oz. pouch skinless, boneless pink salmon, flaked (tip, *below*)
- ^{1}/4 cup slivered red onion
- ^{1}/8 tsp. cracked black pepper

1. Preheat oven to 375°F. In a large saucepan cook noodles, squash, and peas in a large amount of boiling water 3 minutes. Drain; return to saucepan.

2. In a small saucepan whisk milk and flour. Add cream cheese. Cook and whisk over medium heat until cheese melts and sauce is thickened. Remove from heat. Stir in the next five ingredients (through salt). Stir into noodle mixture. Gently fold in salmon.

3. Spoon mixture into a 2-qt. baking dish. Cover; bake 30 minutes or until heated. Top with onion, black pepper, and additional fresh dill weed (if using).

PER SERVING: 308 cal., 9 g total fat (5 g sat. fat), 51 mg chol., 541 mg sodium, 36 g carb. (3 g fiber, 16 g sugars), 20 g pro.

TEST KITCHEN TIP

Cooked tuna, chicken, and turkey are good stand-ins for the salmon.

EVAPORATED MILK & CREAM CHEESE

Make a sauce with evaporated fat-free milk and reduced-fat cream cheese for a thick, rich, and completely satisfying casserole.

SQUASH & PEAS

Mix colorful vegetables into this classic noodle casserole to add to your veggie count for the day.

RESTAURANT REMAKES
at Home

Enjoy favorite restaurant fare without the expense and feeling overly full afterwards. Find popular eating-out recipes made lighter with fresh foods, lower-fat and reduced-sodium ingredients, and sensible portion sizes. Your family will start asking you to "Order up!" at home.

Sesame Honey Chicken and Green Beans

SERVINGS 4 (1 cup chicken mixture + $^1/_3$ cup rice each)

CARB. PER SERVING 35 g

START TO FINISH 40 minutes

- 2 Tbsp. + 2 tsp. honey
- 2 Tbsp. reduced-sodium soy sauce
- 1 Tbsp. grated fresh ginger
- 5 cloves garlic, minced
- Dash crushed red pepper
- Nonstick cooking spray
- 1 lb. skinless, boneless chicken thighs, cut into bite-size pieces
- 2 tsp. canola oil
- 2 tsp. sesame oil
- 2 cups fresh green beans cut into $1^1/_2$-inch pieces
- $^1/_4$ cup chopped shallots
- $1^1/_3$ cups hot cooked brown rice
- 1 tsp. sesame seeds, toasted

1. For sauce, in a bowl combine the first five ingredients (through crushed red pepper).

2. Coat an extra-large nonstick skillet with cooking spray. Heat over medium heat. Add chicken; cook and stir until chicken is no longer pink. Remove chicken from skillet.

3. Heat canola oil and sesame oil in the same skillet over medium-high heat. Add green beans; cook and stir 3 minutes. Add shallots; cook and stir 1 to 2 minutes more or until beans are crisp-tender.

4. Return chicken to skillet. Stir the sauce into chicken mixture in skillet. Cook and stir about 2 minutes or until sauce is thickened. Serve with brown rice. Sprinkle with sesame seeds.

PER SERVING: 333 cal., 10 g total fat (2 g sat. fat), 108 mg chol., 365 mg sodium, 35 g carb. (3 g fiber, 15 g sugars), 26 g pro.

COOKING METHOD HACK

This saucy classic usually features batter-dipped and fried chicken. Stir-frying the chicken substantially reduces the fat and carbs. Adding green beans not only improves nutrition, it makes the dish prettier.

Cilantro-Chicken Chilaquiles with Crumbled Queso Fresco

SERVINGS 4 (1 cup each)
CARB. PER SERVING 27 g
PREP 25 minutes   BAKE 10 minutes
COOL 10 minutes   STAND 5 minutes

- 6 corn tortillas, each cut into 6 wedges
- 1 7-oz. jar salsa verde
- 1 4-oz. can diced green chiles, undrained
- $1/4$ cup water
- 1 Tbsp. olive oil
- 1 cup shredded cooked chicken breast
- 1 cup crumbled queso fresco (4 oz.)
- $1/2$ cup quartered and/or sliced grape tomatoes
- $1/2$ cup snipped fresh cilantro
- $1/3$ cup chopped red onion
- 1 medium lime, cut into wedges
- $1/2$ cup light sour cream (optional)

1. Preheat oven to 350°F. Spread tortilla wedges on a large baking sheet. Bake 10 to 12 minutes or until beginning to lightly brown. Cool on baking sheet on a wire rack 10 minutes. (Tortilla wedges harden as they cool.)

2. Place the cooled tortilla wedges in a medium nonstick skillet. In a bowl stir together the next four ingredients (through olive oil). Pour evenly over tortilla wedges. Top with chicken. Bring to boiling over medium-high heat; reduce heat. Simmer, uncovered, about 3 minutes or until tortilla wedges are slightly softened.

3. Remove from heat. Sprinkle with queso fresco, tomatoes, cilantro, and onion. Cover; let stand 5 minutes. Serve with lime wedges and, if desired, sour cream.

PER SERVING: 246 cal., 9 g total fat (2 g sat. fat), 39 mg chol., 435 mg sodium, 27 g carb. (5 g fiber, 4 g sugars), 18 g pro.

SQUEEZE THE FAT

In a classic chilaquiles recipe, the corn tortillas that form the base for this dish are fried until crisp. Baking them achieves the same effect with less fat and less mess.

209

Chicken and Shrimp Jambalaya

SERVINGS 8 ($1^1/2$ cups each)
CARB. PER SERVING 37 g
PREP 20 minutes
SLOW COOK $4^1/2$ to $5^1/2$ hours (low) or $2^1/4$ to $2^3/4$ hours (high) + 30 minutes (high)

- 1 lb. skinless, boneless chicken breast halves or thighs, cut into $3/4$-inch pieces
- 2 cups thinly sliced celery
- 2 cups chopped onions
- 1 14.5-oz. can diced tomatoes, undrained
- 1 14.5-oz. can reduced-sodium chicken broth
- $1/3$ cup tomato paste
- 1 recipe Homemade Salt-Free Cajun Seasoning or $1^1/2$ tsp. salt-free Cajun seasoning
- 2 cloves garlic, minced
- $1/2$ tsp. salt
- $1^1/2$ cups brown rice
- $3/4$ cup chopped green, red, and/or yellow sweet pepper
- 8 oz. fresh or frozen peeled and deveined cooked shrimp (tails on if desired)
- 2 Tbsp. snipped fresh Italian parsley

1. In a $3^1/2$- or 4-qt. slow cooker combine the first nine ingredients (through salt). Cover and cook on low $4^1/2$ to $5^1/2$ hours or on high $2^1/4$ to $2^3/4$ hours.
2. If using low setting, turn to high. Stir in rice and sweet pepper. Cover and cook about 30 minutes more or until most of the liquid is absorbed and rice is tender.
3. Thaw shrimp, if frozen. Stir shrimp and parsley into chicken mixture. Let stand 5 minutes.

HOMEMADE SALT-FREE CAJUN SEASONING In a bowl stir together $1/4$ tsp. each onion powder, garlic powder, white pepper, paprika, and black pepper and $1/8$ to $1/4$ tsp. cayenne pepper.

PER SERVING: 266 cal., 3 g total fat (1 g sat. fat), 82 mg chol., 562 mg sodium, 37 g carb. (4 g fiber, 6 g sugars), 23 g pro.

Eating Out Carb Check

On those occasions when you dine out, a few key choices when ordering help control carbohydrate intake.

Bread
Halve the carbs in your sandwich by eating it open-face. Ask that the server not bring a basket of complimentary bread.

Go grilled
Grilled meats are virtually carb-free. Avoid breaded items like crispy chicken and pork tenderloin sandwiches.

Sauces and glazes
Eat sauces sparingly. Gravies and sweet or savory sauces contain carbs from the sugar, flour, and milk used to make them.

Starchy sides
A healthful side-dish serving should be about $1/2$ cup. Restaurant portions of rice, beans, and french fries are often out of line, so eat half or less of what's served.

211

Ultimate Spaghetti and Meatballs

SERVINGS 4 ($^1/_2$ cup cooked spaghetti + $1^1/_4$ cups meatball mixture each)
CARB. PER SERVING 37 g
PREP 25 minutes
SLOW COOK 4 to 5 hours (low) or 2 to $2^1/_2$ hours (high)

- 2 cups fresh button or cremini mushrooms, quartered
- 1 cup thinly sliced sweet onion, such as Vidalia, Maui, or Walla Walla
- $^2/_3$ cup thin bite-size strips red or yellow sweet pepper
- 12 1-oz. refrigerated Italian-style cooked turkey meatballs
- 2 8-oz. cans no-salt-added tomato sauce
- $^1/_4$ cup no-salt-added tomato paste
- 2 tsp. dried Italian seasoning, crushed
- 3 cloves garlic, minced
- 3 oz. dried multigrain spaghetti
  Fresh basil leaves (optional)

1. In a $3^1/_2$- or 4-qt. slow cooker combine mushrooms, onion, and sweet pepper. Top with meatballs. In a bowl combine tomato sauce, tomato paste, Italian seasoning, and garlic. Add to cooker.

2. Cover and cook on low 4 to 5 hours or on high 2 to $2^1/_2$ hours.

3. To serve, cook spaghetti according to package directions; drain. Serve meatball mixture over pasta. If desired, top with fresh basil leaves.

PER SERVING: 357 cal., 12 g total fat (3 g sat. fat), 91 mg chol., 435 mg sodium, 37 g carb. (8 g fiber, 13 g sugars), 25 g pro.

PRIMO PRODUCT PICKS

Choose a more sensible portion size instead of the mountain of meatballs and pasta served at your favorite Italian restaurant. In addition, search for purchased meatballs with the best nutritional numbers and use reduced-sodium products. You'll only consume one-fifth of the sodium and cut calories, fat, and carbs by half.

Baked Cavatelli

SERVINGS 8 (¾ cup each)
CARB. PER SERVING 30 g
PREP 30 minutes   COOK 15 minutes
BAKE 40 minutes

- 8 oz. dried cavatelli or dried multigrain penne pasta
- 12 oz. uncooked ground Italian turkey sausage*
- 1 cup chopped eggplant or zucchini
- 1 cup chopped fresh cremini or button mushrooms
- ¾ cup chopped red sweet pepper
- ½ cup chopped onion
- 2 cloves garlic, minced
- 1 14.5-oz. can no-salt-added diced tomatoes, undrained
- 1 8-oz. can no-salt-added tomato sauce
- ¼ cup snipped fresh basil or 1 Tbsp. dried basil, crushed
- 1 Tbsp. snipped fresh oregano or 1 tsp. dried oregano, crushed
- ¼ tsp. salt
- ¼ tsp. black pepper
- 1 cup shredded reduced-fat Italian cheese blend (4 oz.)

1. Preheat oven to 350°F. Cook pasta according to package directions, omitting any salt or oil. Drain.

2. Meanwhile, in an extra-large skillet cook the next six ingredients (through garlic) over medium heat until sausage is browned and vegetables are just tender. Drain off any fat. Add tomatoes, tomato sauce, dried basil and oregano (if using), salt, and black pepper. Bring to boiling; reduce heat. Simmer, covered, 10 minutes, stirring occasionally. Stir in fresh basil and oregano (if using).

3. In an extra-large bowl stir together pasta and sausage mixture. Spoon into a 3-qt. baking dish.

4. Bake, covered, 35 to 40 minutes or until heated. Uncover; sprinkle with cheese. Bake about 5 minutes more or until cheese is melted.

*TIP For a less spicy pasta dish, use half regular ground turkey breast and half Italian turkey sausage.

PER SERVING: 254 cal., 7 g total fat (3 g sat. fat), 34 mg chol., 492 mg sodium, 30 g carb. (3 g fiber, 6 g sugars), 17 g pro.

KNOCK DOWN SODIUM

Sodium and fat are the most significant challenges you face when eating restaurant food. Cut the sodium in home-prepared favorites by choosing reduced or no-salt-added products, such as tomato products, and put down the salt shaker.

213

French Dips with Mushrooms

SERVINGS 6 (1 sandwich each)
CARB. PER SERVING 37 g
PREP 25 minutes
SLOW COOK 8 to 9 hours (low) or 4 to $4^{1}/_{2}$ hours (high)
STAND 10 minutes

- 1 2- to $2^{1}/_{2}$-lb. boneless beef bottom round or round rump roast
- Nonstick cooking spray
- 4 fresh portobello mushrooms (each 3 to 4 inches in diameter), stemmed and sliced $1/_{4}$ inch thick
- 1 cup chopped yellow or white onion
- 1 cup chopped red and/or green sweet pepper
- 1 14.5-oz. can 50%-less-sodium beef broth
- 1 16-oz. loaf French bread or oval-shaped whole wheat bread loaf
- $1/_{2}$ cup thinly sliced red onion
- 3 oz. provolone cheese, shredded ($3/_{4}$ cup) (optional)

1. Trim fat from meat. Lightly coat a large skillet with cooking spray; heat over medium heat. Cook meat in hot skillet until browned on all sides. Transfer meat to a 4- to 5-qt. slow cooker.

2. Add mushrooms, yellow onion, sweet pepper, and $1/_{4}$ tsp. *black pepper* to cooker. Add broth. Cover and cook on low 8 to 9 hours or on high 4 to $4^{1}/_{2}$ hours.

3. Remove meat from cooker; cover and let stand 10 minutes. Using a slotted spoon, remove mushroom mixture from cooking liquid. Thinly slice meat. Pour cooking liquid into a measuring cup; skim off fat.

4. Cut bread in half lengthwise. Hollow out the soft bread from halves, leaving a $1/_{2}$-inch-thick shell.* (If desired, preheat broiler; broil cut sides of bread halves 4 inches from the heat 1 to 2 minutes or until toasted.)

5. Arrange meat, mushroom mixture, and red onion slices on bottom bread half. Drizzle with cooking liquid. If desired, sprinkle with shredded cheese. Add top of bread. Cut sandwich into six portions. Pour remaining liquid into bowls; serve with sandwiches.

*TIP Reserve soft bread to make bread crumbs or cut into cubes to make croutons.

PER SERVING: 388 cal., 8 g total fat (3 g sat. fat), 92 mg chol., 552 mg sodium, 37 g carb. (3 g fiber, 7 g sugars), 42 g pro.

SAVE HALF THE CALORIES

Enjoy a smaller sandwich packed with more veggies than you'll find on a menu. You save almost half the calories and lose 80 percent of the fat. A major issue in a French dip is the sodium. Our version has one-third of what is typical.

Roasted BLT Salad

SERVINGS 4 ($^1/_4$ romaine head + 1 slice bacon + $^1/_4$ cup tomatoes each)
CARB. PER SERVING 31 g
PREP 15 minutes   BAKE 15 minutes
STAND 5 minutes

- 4 slices lower-sodium, less-fat bacon
- 1 cup cherry tomatoes
- 6 tsp. olive oil
- $^1/_2$ baguette, cut into 1$^1/_2$-inch cubes
- 1 head romaine lettuce, quartered lengthwise
- $^1/_4$ tsp. salt
- $^1/_4$ tsp. black pepper

1. Preheat oven to 400°F. In a large skillet cook bacon over medium heat until crisp; drain on paper towels. Break bacon into large pieces.

2. Meanwhile, line a 15x10-inch baking pan with foil. Add tomatoes; toss with 2 tsp. of the olive oil. Bake 10 minutes. Transfer tomatoes and their juices to a bowl. Place bread cubes and romaine on the pan. Drizzle romaine with 2 tsp. of the olive oil. Return pan to oven; bake about

5 minutes or until bread is golden and romaine is browned on edges.

3. Add bread to the tomatoes. Toss gently to combine. Let stand 5 minutes to allow bread to absorb some of the tomato juices. Transfer tomatoes, bread, romaine, and bacon to a platter. Drizzle with the remaining olive oil. Sprinkle with salt and pepper.

PER SERVING: 239 cal., 8 g total fat (1 g sat. fat), 3 mg chol., 525 mg sodium, 31 g carb. (2 g fiber, 2 g sugars), 7 g pro.

NIX 2,000 MG OF SODIUM

Juice from the roasted tomatoes and a little olive oil serve as the dressing for this salad that uses only four slices of a healthier bacon. You still have a delicious salad but with one-third the calories, one-tenth the fat, and a savings of nearly 2,000 mg sodium.

Alfredo-Sauced Chicken with Fettuccine

SERVINGS 6 ($^3/_4$ cup chicken mixture + $^1/_3$ cup pasta each)
CARB. PER SERVING 34 g
START TO FINISH 40 minutes

- 6 oz. dried whole grain fettuccine
- Nonstick cooking spray
- 3 tsp. butter
- 1 lb. skinless, boneless chicken breast halves, cut into bite-size pieces
- 1 cup sliced fresh mushrooms
- $^1/_4$ cup finely chopped onion
- 1 clove garlic, minced
- $^1/_2$ cup dry white wine or reduced-sodium chicken broth
- 1$^1/_2$ cups fat-free half-and-half
- 3 Tbsp. all-purpose flour
- $^1/_2$ cup light sour cream
- $^1/_2$ tsp. salt
- $^1/_8$ tsp. black pepper
- 1 cup halved cherry tomatoes
- $^1/_2$ cup finely shredded Parmesan cheese (2 oz.)
- 2 Tbsp. thinly sliced green onion
- 2 Tbsp. finely shredded Parmesan cheese

1. Cook fettuccine according to package directions,* except omit the salt. Drain well. Return to pot; cover and keep warm.
2. Meanwhile, coat a large nonstick skillet with cooking spray. Heat over medium heat. Add 2 tsp. of the butter. Add chicken; cook about 8 minutes or until chicken is cooked through, stirring occasionally. Remove chicken; cover and keep warm.
3. Add the remaining 1 tsp. butter to hot skillet. Add mushrooms, onion, and garlic; cook about 3 minutes or until vegetables are tender. Stir wine and cooked chicken into vegetable mixture.

4. Meanwhile, in a bowl whisk together half-and-half and flour until smooth. Whisk in sour cream, salt, and pepper. Stir sour cream mixture into chicken mixture in skillet. Cook and stir over medium heat just until bubbly; cook and stir 2 minutes more. Add tomatoes and the $^1/_2$ cup Parmesan cheese, stirring until cheese is melted.
5. Transfer fettuccine to a platter. Spoon chicken-vegetable mixture over

fettuccine. Sprinkle with green onion and the 2 Tbsp. Parmesan cheese.
*TIP For the best texture, cook the fettuccine just until it is al dente (firm and slightly chewy).

PER SERVING: 340 cal., 10 g total fat (5 g sat. fat), 68 mg chol., 516 mg sodium, 34 g carb. (4 g fiber, 6 g sugars), 26 g pro.

PORTION IS KEY

Control your portion size and use a fat-free half-and-half and light sour cream combo instead of heavy cream to achieve ultimate creaminess in this classic pasta dish.

Bistro Beef Steak with Wild Mushroom Sauce

SERVINGS 6 (3 oz. steak + 7 Tbsp. sauce each)
CARB. PER SERVING 8 g
START TO FINISH 40 minutes

- 5 cloves garlic, minced
- 2 tsp. herbes de Provence
- $\frac{1}{2}$ tsp. black pepper
- $\frac{1}{4}$ tsp. salt
- 3 8-oz. boneless beef top loin steaks, cut $\frac{3}{4}$ inch thick
- 1 Tbsp. olive oil
- $\frac{1}{3}$ cup finely chopped shallots
- 4 cups thinly sliced assorted mushrooms, such as oyster, cremini, and/or shiitake (about 12 oz.), stemmed
- $\frac{1}{4}$ cup dry sherry or 1 Tbsp. balsamic vinegar
- 1 14.5-oz. can 50%-less-sodium beef broth
- 1 Tbsp. cornstarch
- $\frac{1}{8}$ tsp. salt

1. Preheat broiler. In a bowl combine three cloves of the garlic, 1 tsp. of the herbes de Provence, the pepper, and the $\frac{1}{4}$ tsp. salt. Trim fat from steaks. Sprinkle herb mixture on steaks; rub in. Place steaks on the unheated rack of a broiler pan. Broil 3 to 4 inches from heat 9 to 11 minutes for medium rare to medium (145°F to 160°F), turning once.

2. Meanwhile, for mushroom sauce, in a large nonstick skillet heat oil over medium-high heat. Add shallots and the remaining 2 cloves garlic; cook 1 to 2 minutes or until shallots are tender. Add mushrooms; cook 6 to 7 minutes or until mushrooms are tender and any liquid evaporates, stirring occasionally. Remove from heat. Stir in sherry (if using). Return to heat. Bring to boiling. Cook, uncovered, 1 to 2 minutes or until all liquid evaporates.

3. In a bowl stir together broth, balsamic vinegar (if using), cornstarch, the remaining 1 tsp. herbes de Provence, and the $\frac{1}{8}$ tsp. salt. Stir broth mixture into mushroom mixture in skillet. Cook and stir over medium heat until thickened and bubbly. Cook and stir 2 minutes more.

4. Cut each steak in half. Serve steak with mushroom sauce.

PER SERVING: 229 cal., 8 g total fat (2 g sat. fat), 66 mg chol., 324 mg sodium, 8 g carb. (2 g fiber, 2 g sugars), 27 g pro.

HALF THE CALORIES

Steak topped with mushrooms is a classic eating-out indulgence. Instead of a 9-ounce steak, start with a smaller piece of beef. Flavor comes from an herb rub, and broiling controls added fat. The mushrooms are sautéed in olive oil rather than butter, then finished with a cornstarch-thickened, reduced-sodium beef broth sauce instead of cream. These steps cut calories in half and fat by three-fourths. Sodium is reduced from 1,160 mg to 324 mg.

Pulled Pork Sandwiches with Creamy Slaw

SERVINGS 18 (1 sandwich [about $^1/_2$ cup cooked meat] + scant $^1/_4$ cup slaw each)
CARB. PER SERVING 36 g
PREP 30 minutes   CHILL 12 hours
SMOKE 4 hours   STAND 15 minutes

- 1 cup molasses
- $^1/_2$ cup pickling salt
- 8 cups water
- 1 5-lb. boneless pork shoulder roast
- 1 Tbsp. onion powder
- 1 Tbsp. dry mustard
- 1 Tbsp. ground coriander
- 1 Tbsp. ground cumin
- 1 Tbsp. fennel seeds, crushed
- 1 Tbsp. paprika
- 2 tsp. cayenne pepper
- 18 whole wheat hamburger buns or kaiser rolls, split
- 1 recipe Creamy Slaw

1. For brine, in a large deep container combine molasses and salt. Gradually add the water, stirring to dissolve salt. Trim fat from meat. Add meat to brine. Cover and chill at least 12 hours or up to 16 hours.

2. For rub, in a bowl combine the next seven ingredients (through cayenne pepper). Remove meat from brine; pat dry with paper towels. Discard brine. Sprinkle rub evenly over meat; rub in with your fingers.

3. In a smoker arrange preheated coals, wood chunks, and water pan according to the manufacturer's directions. Pour water into pan. Place meat on grill rack over water pan. Cover and smoke 4 to 5 hours or until meat is very tender. Add additional coals and water as needed to maintain temperature and moisture. Do not add wood after the first 2 hours of cooking.

4. Remove meat from smoker. Cover with foil; let stand 15 minutes. Cut meat into thick pieces. Shred pork using two forks. Serve meat in buns with some of the Creamy Slaw. Pass the remaining Creamy Slaw.

CREAMY SLAW In a large bowl combine one 6-oz. carton plain fat-free yogurt, $^1/_4$ cup light mayonnaise, 2 tsp. sugar, 1 tsp. celery seeds, and $^1/_4$ tsp. salt. Add one 14-oz. pkg. shredded cabbage with carrot (coleslaw mix). Toss to coat. Cover; chill 2 to 24 hours. Stir before serving.

PER SERVING: 357 cal., 11 g total fat (3 g sat. fat), 76 mg chol., 684 mg sodium, 36 g carb. (8 g fiber, 6 g sugars), 32 g pro.

HALF THE CARBS AND 8X THE FIBER

Making your own rub, using whole wheat buns, and controlling portion size allow you to eat this favorite sandwich without the guilt. Our pulled pork sandwich saves 200 calories, has one-fourth of the sodium, eight times the fiber, and half the carbs of a comparable sandwich from a big-name barbecue joint. Plus, you get slaw!

Shrimp Tacos with Lime Slaw

SERVINGS 6 (2 tacos each)
CARB. PER SERVING 15 g
START TO FINISH 35 minutes

- 1 lb. fresh or frozen medium shrimp, peeled and deveined
- 1 Tbsp. olive oil
- 3 cloves garlic, minced
- 1 tsp. ground cumin
- 1/2 tsp. chili powder
- 1/2 tsp. salt
- 1 lime
- 3 cups shredded red cabbage
- 1/2 cup sour cream
- 12 6-inch corn tortillas
- 1 tsp. finely chopped canned chipotle pepper in adobo sauce
- Fresh cilantro (optional)
- Lime wedges (optional)

1. If using wooden skewers, soak in water 30 minutes. Thaw shrimp, if frozen. Rinse shrimp; pat dry. In a resealable plastic bag combine the next four ingredients (through chili powder) and 1/4 tsp. of the salt; add shrimp. Seal bag; turn to coat shrimp. Chill 30 minutes.

2. Meanwhile, remove zest and squeeze juice from lime. In a bowl combine lime zest and juice, cabbage, and the remaining 1/4 tsp. salt. Stir together sour cream and chipotle pepper. Wrap tortillas in foil.

3. Thread shrimp on skewers. Grill tortilla packet, covered, over medium heat 5 minutes; turning once. Grill shrimp, covered, over medium heat 5 to 8 minutes or until shrimp turn opaque, turning once.

4. Remove shrimp from skewers. Spread sour cream mixture on tortillas. Top with slaw and shrimp. If desired, top with cilantro; serve with lime wedges.

PER SERVING: 135 cal., 4 g total fat (1 g sat. fat), 62 mg chol., 198 mg sodium, 15 g carb. (2 g fiber, 1 g sugars), 9 g pro.

NATURALLY LOW-FAT

Fat stays low when you don't add it in the first place—grilled shrimp, shredded fresh cabbage, no added cheese. Then you can pull all that fresh flavor together with just a touch of real sour cream.

Scallops and Pasta with Lemon-Caper Cream Sauce

SERVINGS 6 (1 cup pasta mixture + 2 or 3 scallops each)
CARB. PER SERVING 28 g
START TO FINISH 35 minutes

1$\frac{1}{2}$ lb. fresh or frozen sea scallops
4 oz. dried multigrain or whole grain penne or rotini pasta
3 cups trimmed, coarsely shredded Swiss chard or kale
1 medium zucchini, halved lengthwise and bias-sliced crosswise
Nonstick cooking spray
$\frac{1}{2}$ tsp. salt
$\frac{1}{8}$ tsp. black pepper
2 tsp. olive oil
2 medium leeks, trimmed and thinly sliced
2 cloves garlic, minced
2 cups fat-free milk
2 Tbsp. cornstarch
2 tsp. lemon zest
1$\frac{1}{2}$ tsp. snipped fresh rosemary or thyme or $\frac{1}{2}$ tsp. dried rosemary or thyme, crushed
2 Tbsp. capers, drained

1. Thaw scallops, if frozen. Rinse scallops; pat dry with paper towels. In a large saucepan cook pasta according to package directions, adding chard and zucchini the last 4 minutes of cooking time. Drain; keep warm.
2. Meanwhile, lightly coat an unheated large nonstick skillet with cooking spray. Preheat over medium-high heat. Sprinkle scallops with $\frac{1}{4}$ tsp. of the salt and the pepper. Add scallops to hot skillet; cook 4 to 6 minutes or until scallops are opaque, turning once. Remove scallops from skillet; keep warm.
3. Add oil to hot skillet; reduce heat to medium. Add leeks and garlic; cook 3 to 5 minutes or until tender, stirring to scrape up any browned bits.

4. In a bowl whisk together milk and cornstarch until smooth. Add to leek mixture along with lemon zest, rosemary, and the remaining $\frac{1}{4}$ tsp. salt. Cook and stir until thickened and bubbly. Cook and stir 2 minutes more. Add to pasta mixture, tossing to coat. Top pasta mixture with scallops and capers.

PER SERVING: 247 cal., 3 g total fat (0 g sat. fat), 39 mg chol., 525 mg sodium, 28 g carb. (3 g fiber, 6 g sugars), 26 g pro.

CREAMY WITH LESS FAT

Cream sauces in restaurants are laden with butter and heavy cream. Simmering makes them thicker, so they cling to pasta. A cornstarch-thickened sauce using fat-free milk produces a similar effect without the extra fat and cholesterol you don't need..

Catfish Po'Boy

SERVINGS 4 (1 sandwich + about
1 cup slaw each)
CARB. PER SERVING 27 g
PREP 25 minutes   COOK 4 minutes
per $^{1}/_{2}$-inch thickness

- 4 3-oz. fresh or frozen catfish
  fillets
- 3 cups packaged shredded
  broccoli (broccoli slaw mix)
- 1 medium red sweet pepper,
  cut into thin bite-size strips
- $^{1}/_{4}$ cup thinly sliced red onion
- 2 Tbsp. fat-free mayonnaise
- 1 Tbsp. cider vinegar
- $^{1}/_{4}$ tsp. hot pepper sauce
- 1 tsp. salt-free Cajun seasoning
- $^{1}/_{8}$ tsp. salt
- 2 tsp. canola oil
- 2 whole grain hoagie rolls, split
  and toasted

1. Thaw fish, if frozen. Rinse fish; pat
dry with paper towels. Measure
thickness of fish. In a bowl combine
the next six ingredients (through hot
pepper sauce).
2. Sprinkle fish with Cajun seasoning
and salt. In a large skillet heat oil over
medium-high heat. Cook fish in hot oil
4 to 6 minutes per $^{1}/_{2}$-inch thickness of
fish or until golden brown and fish
flakes easily.
3. Place a fish fillet on each roll half (if
necessary, trim roll tops so they sit flat).
Top with some of the slaw mixture.
Serve with the remaining slaw mixture.

PER SERVING: 258 cal., 9 g total fat
(2 g sat. fat), 48 mg chol., 438 mg sodium,
27 g carb. (3 g fiber, 5 g sugars), 18 g pro.

CUT THE CARBS

You can reduce carbs by up to
20 grams, depending on the
brand of hoagie roll, if you make
this sandwich open-face. Fat
is significantly reduced, too.
A traditional po'boy sandwich
features battered and deep-
fried fish. Our version features
skillet-cooked fish in very little
canola oil.

Green Veggie Fried Rice

SERVINGS 4 (about 1$\frac{1}{4}$ cups each)
CARB. PER SERVING 32 g
START TO FINISH 30 minutes

- 2 eggs
- 1 tsp. soy sauce
- 1 tsp. toasted sesame oil
- 1 Tbsp. canola oil
- 1 clove garlic, minced
- 1 tsp. minced fresh ginger
- 2 cups shredded green cabbage
- $\frac{3}{4}$ cup frozen shelled edamame, thawed
- $\frac{1}{2}$ cup frozen peas, thawed
- 2 cups cooked brown rice, chilled
- 2 Tbsp. soy sauce
- $\frac{1}{4}$ cup sliced green onions
  Crushed red pepper (optional)

1. In a bowl beat egg and 1 tsp. soy sauce. In a wok or large skillet heat sesame oil over medium heat. Add egg mixture; cook and stir gently until set. Remove egg; cool. Cut egg into strips.
2. In the same skillet heat canola oil over medium-high heat. Add garlic and ginger; cook and stir 30 seconds. Add cabbage; cook and stir 2 minutes. Add edamame and peas; cook and stir 2 minutes. Add rice and the 2 Tbsp. soy sauce; cook and stir 2 to 4 minutes or until heated. Add egg mixture and green onions; cook and stir 1 minute. If desired, top with crushed red pepper.

PER SERVING: 251 cal., 9 g total fat (2 g sat. fat), 93 mg chol., 669 mg sodium, 32 g carb. (5 g fiber, 4 g sugars), 11 g pro.

SAVE 11 GRAMS OF FAT

This vegetable fried rice has one-fourth the calories of the vegetable fried rice at a leading Chinese chain restaurant. Using brown rice, fewer eggs, less oil and sauces, and a smaller serving size reduces fat by 11 grams.

Dessert TRANSFORMATIONS

You can eat cake—and pastries, brownies, and cookies, too! Learn how to prepare diabetes-friendly versions of your favorite sweet treats and work them into your daily meal plans. You'll find easy ingredient tweaks to make baked goods more healthful and to dress up reduced-sugar boxed mixes You can even create show-stopping cupcakes by mastering just one recipe.

Tangy Vanilla

Chocolate Caramel

1 Cake +
3 FLAVORS

Start with this delicious made-from-scratch cupcake recipe for a simple and healthful dessert option. Tailor the flavor in three more ways with spices, zest, and frosting change-ups. Give them bake-shop appeal with extra toppings.

Chai Spice

Strawberry-Orange Surprise

1 Cake

Tangy Vanilla Cupcakes

SERVINGS 12 (1 cupcake each)
CARB. PER SERVING 28 g or 23 g
PREP 20 minutes   COOL 5 minutes
BAKE 14 minutes

1½ cups all-purpose flour (tip, *page 228*)
1 tsp. baking powder
¼ tsp. baking soda
¼ tsp. salt
¾ cup buttermilk or sour fat-free milk (tip, *page 228*)
½ cup granulated sugar (tip, *page 228*)
¼ cup canola oil or ⅓ cup 60% to 70% vegetable oil spread, melted
¼ cup refrigerated or frozen egg product, thawed, or 1 egg
1 tsp. vanilla

1 recipe Tangy Chocolate Frosting
1 tsp. unsweetened cocoa powder (optional)

1. Preheat oven to 350°F. Line twelve 2½-inch muffin cups with paper bake cups. Coat paper bake cups with *nonstick cooking spray*.
2. In a bowl combine flour, baking powder, baking soda, and salt. In another bowl whisk together buttermilk, sugar, oil, egg, and vanilla. Add to flour mixture, stirring with a wire whisk just until combined. Spoon batter into prepared muffin cups, filling each two-thirds to three-fourths full.
3. Bake 14 to 16 minutes or until a toothpick inserted in centers comes out clean. Cool in pan 5 minutes. Remove cupcakes; cool on a wire rack.

4. Spread cooled cupcakes with Tangy Chocolate Frosting. (Or using a pastry bag fitted with an open star tip, pipe frosting onto cooled cupcakes.) Store frosted cupcakes in refrigerator. If desired, dust with cocoa powder.
TANGY CHOCOLATE FROSTING In a bowl beat 6 oz. reduced-fat cream cheese (Neufchâtel), softened, on medium until smooth. Beat in ½ cup plain fat-free Greek yogurt and 2 Tbsp. unsweetened cocoa powder. Beat in ½ cup powdered sugar (tip, *page 228*) until smooth (frosting will thin slightly). Cover; chill 4 to 24 hours before spreading or piping on cupcakes.

PER SERVING: 205 cal., 8 g total fat (2 g sat. fat), 11 mg chol., 192 mg sodium, 28 g carb. (0 g fiber, 15 g sugars), 5 g pro.

PER FROSTED CUPCAKE WITH SUBSTITUTE: Same as above, except 193 cal., 23 g carb. (11 g sugars).

227

Flavor **1**

Flavor **2**

Chai Spice Cupcakes

1. Start with the recipe for Tangy Vanilla Cupcakes *(page 227)*. Prepare and bake as directed, except add 2 Tbsp. finely crushed loose-leaf black tea, $1/2$ tsp. ground cinnamon, $1/4$ tsp. each ground ginger and ground cardamom, $1/8$ tsp. ground nutmeg, and dash each ground cloves and black pepper to the flour mixture. Cool completely.

2. Frost cooled cupcakes with White Chocolate-Pecan Whipped Frosting. Store frosted cupcakes in refrigerator. Before serving, sprinkle tops with 2 Tbsp. chopped toasted pecans.

WHITE CHOCOLATE-PECAN WHIPPED FROSTING Place $1/3$ cup (about $1^3/4$ oz.) chopped white baking chocolate (with cocoa butter) in a bowl. Microwave, uncovered, on 50 percent power (medium) 1 to $1^1/2$ minutes or until melted and smooth, stirring once. Stir in 1 Tbsp. fat-free milk; cool about 5 minutes. Fold in $1/4$ cup frozen light whipped dessert topping, thawed, and 2 Tbsp. chopped toasted pecans. Fold in an additional 1 cup dessert topping.

PER FROSTED CUPCAKE: 197 cal., 9 g total fat (2 g sat. fat), 1 mg chol., 145 mg sodium, 27 g carb. (1 g fiber, 13 g sugars), 3 g pro.

PER FROSTED CUPCAKE WITH SUBSTITUTE: Same as above, except 185 cal., 23 g carb. (9 g sugars).

Chocolate Caramel Cupcakes

1. Start with the recipe for Tangy Vanilla Cupcakes *(page 227)*. Prepare and bake as directed, except reduce flour to 1 cup and reduce granulated sugar to $1/4$ cup. Add $1/2$ cup unsweetened cocoa powder and $1/4$ cup packed brown sugar (tip, *left*).

2. Spread cooled cupcakes with Caramel Frosting. Store frosted cupcakes in refrigerator. Before serving, sprinkle frosted cupcakes with crushed sugar-free caramel-flavor or butterscotch-flavor hard candies if desired. Drizzle with $1/4$ cup sugar-free chocolate sauce.

CARAMEL FROSTING In a bowl beat 2 oz. reduced-fat cream cheese (Neufchâtel), softened, on medium until smooth. Beat in $1/4$ cup slightly softened 60% to 70% vegetable oil spread. Beat in $1/4$ cup sugar-free caramel-flavor ice cream topping and $1/4$ tsp. vanilla until smooth. Cover and chill at least 4 hours or up to 24 hours before spreading or piping on cupcakes.

PER FROSTED CUPCAKE: 185 cal., 9 g total fat (2 g sat. fat), 4 mg chol., 197 mg sodium, 24 g carb. (1 g fiber, 10 g sugars), 3 g pro.

PER FROSTED CUPCAKE WITH SUBSTITUTE: Same as above, except 171 cal., 19 g carb. (5 g .sugars).

BAKING SUBSTITUTIONS

Use $1/2$ cup whole wheat pastry flour for $1/2$ cup of the all-purpose flour.

To make $3/4$ cup sour fat-free milk, place 2 tsp. lemon juice or vinegar in a glass measuring cup. Add enough fat-free milk to measure $3/4$ cup total liquid; stir. Let stand 5 minutes before using.

Choose Splenda Sugar Blend to substitute for the granulated sugar. Choose Splenda Brown Sugar Blend to substitute for brown sugar in the Chocolate Caramel cupcakes. Follow package directions to use product amounts equivalent to sugar amounts called for in all recipes. We do not recommend using a sugar substitute for powdered sugar.

Strawberry-Orange Surprise Cupcakes

1. Start with the recipe for Tangy Vanilla Cupcakes *(page 227)*. In a bowl gently stir together $1/3$ cup finely chopped fresh strawberries and 2 Tbsp. low-sugar orange marmalade. Prepare cupcake batter as directed, except add $1/2$ tsp. orange zest to the buttermilk mixture. Spoon half of the batter into the prepared muffin cups.

Spoon strawberry mixture into center of batter in muffin cups. Top with the remaining batter. Bake as directed. To check doneness, insert toothpick just into tops of the cupcakes to avoid strawberry mixture.

2. Spread cooled cupcakes with Orange-Cream Cheese Frosting. Store frosted cupcakes in refrigerator. Before serving, top with cut-up fresh strawberries and/or with orange peel strips if desired.

ORANGE-CREAM CHEESE FROSTING In a bowl beat 4 oz. reduced-fat cream cheese (Neufchâtel), softened, on medium until smooth. Beat in $1/2$ cup plain fat-free Greek yogurt. Stir in $1/3$ cup low-sugar orange marmalade (frosting will thin slightly). Cover and chill at least 4 hours or up to 24 hours before spreading or piping on cupcakes.

PER FROSTED CUPCAKE: 187 cal., 7 g total fat (2 g sat. fat), 8 mg chol., 176 mg sodium, 26 g carb. (1 g fiber, 13 g sugars), 5 g pro.

PER FROSTED CUPCAKE WITH SUBSTITUTE: Same as above, except 174 cal., 22 g carb. (9 g sugars).

Start with a
MIX

Boxed cake and brownie mixes are convenient to use when you are short on time. Doctor them up a bit and your family will never know you started with a box.

Apricot-Ginger Glazed Pumpkin Snack Cake

SERVINGS 16 (1 piece each)
CARB. PER SERVING 32 g
PREP 20 minutes **BAKE** 30 minutes

Nonstick canola oil cooking spray
1 16-oz. pkg. sugar-free yellow cake mix
1 cup canned pumpkin
1 cup water
¾ cup refrigerated or frozen egg product, thawed
3 Tbsp. canola oil
1 tsp. ground cinnamon
¼ tsp. ground nutmeg
¾ cup apricot fruit spread
½ tsp. grated fresh ginger
⅔ cup sliced almonds, toasted

1. Preheat oven to 325°F. Coat a 3-qt. rectangular baking dish with cooking spray. In a bowl combine the next seven ingredients (through nutmeg) according to cake mix package directions. Spread batter in prepared pan.

2. Bake 30 to 35 minutes or until a toothpick inserted near the center comes out clean. Cool completely in pan on a wire rack.

3. In a bowl microwave apricot spread about 1 minute or until heated, stirring once. Stir in ginger; cool slightly. Spread over cooled cake. Sprinkle with almond slices.

TO STORE Prepare as directed through Step 2. Cover cake and store at room temperature up to 2 days or freeze up to 1 month. Thaw if frozen. Before serving, continue with Step 3.

PER SERVING: 175 cal., 7 g total fat (1 g sat. fat), 0 mg chol., 233 mg sodium, 32 g carb. (1 g fiber, 7 g sugars), 3 g pro.

Fresh Berries-Kiwi Ice Box Pies

SERVINGS 20 (1 wedge each)
CARB. PER SERVING 26 g
PREP 20 minutes CHILL at least 1 hour BAKE 20 minutes

Nonstick cooking spray
1 16-oz. pkg. sugar-free yellow cake mix
1 cup quick-cooking rolled oats
1/4 cup canola oil
1/4 cup refrigerated or frozen egg product, thawed
1/4 cup water

1 8-oz. carton light cream cheese spread
2 Tbsp. powdered sugar
1 1/2 tsp. vanilla
1 cup frozen fat-free whipped dessert topping, thawed
1 cup blueberries
1 cup raspberries
2 kiwifruits, peeled and diced

1. Preheat oven to 350°F. Coat two 9-inch pie plates with cooking spray. For crust, in a bowl combine the next five ingredients (through water), using a fork to make a doughy consistency. Lightly press half of the crust mixture into the bottoms and up the sides of prepared plates. Bake 20 to 22 minutes or until golden. Cool crusts completely on a wire rack.

2. Meanwhile, in another bowl beat cream cheese, powdered sugar, and vanilla on medium until fluffy. Gradually fold in dessert topping. Divide cream cheese mixture between the two crusts, spreading evenly. Cover and refrigerate at least 1 hour or until ready to serve. Before serving, top with fruit.

TO STORE Store covered pies in the refrigerator up to 2 days.

PER SERVING: 156 cal., 7 g total fat (2 g sat. fat), 5 mg chol., 228 mg sodium, 26 g carb. (1 g fiber, 3 g sugars), 3 g pro.

Brownie Stick 'Em Ups

SERVINGS 16 (1 brownie each)
CARB. PER SERVING 21 g
PREP 30 minutes **COOL** 1 hour
BAKE 32 minutes

Nonstick cooking spray
1 12.35-oz. pkg. sugar-free brownie mix
1/3 cup canola oil
3 Tbsp. water
1/4 cup refrigerated or frozen egg product, thawed
2 Tbsp. sugar-free caramel-flavor ice cream topping
1 cup frozen fat-free whipped dessert topping
2 Tbsp. miniature semisweet chocolate pieces
16 flat wooden crafts sticks

1. Preheat oven to 325°F. Line an 8-inch square baking pan with foil, extending foil 2 inches over edges of pan. Lightly grease foil.

2. In a bowl combine brownie mix, oil, water, and egg product according to brownie package directions. Spread batter in the prepared pan. Bake about 32 minutes or until a toothpick comes out clean when inserted 2 inches from the edge.

3. Cool completely in pan on a wire rack. Use foil to lift uncut brownies out of pan. Cut into 16 pieces.

4. Meanwhile place the caramel topping in a small bowl. Microwave 12 to 15 seconds to melt slightly. Fold caramel into whipped topping until well blended. Refrigerate until needed.

5. Using a paring knife, cut a small slit in one end of each brownie. Slide a crafts stick about 1 inch into the slit. Spoon about 1 Tbsp. whipped topping mixture over the top and sides of each brownie pop, leaving one side uniced. Sprinkle iced sides with chocolate chips. Serve immediately or refrigerate up to 12 hours.

TO MAKE AHEAD Make make brownies and topping up to 48 hours in advance. Cover and refrigerate them separately.

PER SERVING: 131 cal., 7 g total fat (1 g sat. fat), 0 mg chol., 78 mg sodium, 21 g carb. (2 g fiber, 1 g sugars), 1 g pro.

Strawberry Brownies

SERVINGS 12 (1 brownie each)
CARB. PER SERVING 27 g
PREP 20 minutes   **BAKE** 35 minutes

Nonstick cooking spray
1 12.35-oz. pkg. sugar-free chocolate fudge brownie mix
1/2 cup unsweetened applesauce
1/3 cup chopped pecans
1/4 cup refrigerated or frozen egg product, thawed
3 Tbsp. canola oil
1 cup fresh strawberries, coarsely chopped
1 oz. white, dark, or semisweet chocolate

1. Preheat oven to 350°F. Lightly coat an 8-inch square baking pan with cooking spray. In a bowl combine the next five ingredients (through oil) according to brownie package directions. Spread batter in the prepared pan. Sprinkle the chopped strawberries on top.

2. Bake about 35 minutes or until a toothpick inserted near the center comes out clean. Cool completely on a wire rack.

3. Meanwhile, in a small heavy saucepan melt the chocolate over low heat and drizzle over brownies.

TO STORE Cover and store in the refrigerator up to 3 days.

PER SERVING: 165 cal., 9 g total fat (1 g sat. fat), 1 mg chol., 98 mg sodium, 27 g carb. (4 g fiber, 2 g sugars), 2 g pro.

Peach-Cranberry Coffee Cake

SERVINGS 20 (1 piece each)
CARB. PER SERVING 27 g or 25 g
PREP 25 minutes   BAKE 38 minutes

Nonstick cooking spray
1   16-oz. pkg. sugar-free yellow cake mix
3/4 cup refrigerated or frozen egg product, thawed
1   to 2 tsp. orange zest
1   cup orange juice (tip, *below*)
1/3 cup canola oil
2   cups diced fresh peaches (unpeeled) or frozen, thawed and diced peaches
1/2 cup dried cranberries
1/2 cup wheat bran or wheat germ
1/4 cup sugar*
1/2 cup finely chopped walnuts
1/2 tsp. ground cinnamon

1. Preheat oven to 325°F. Coat two nonstick 9-inch round or square cake pans with cooking spray.

2. In a bowl combine the next five ingredients (through oil) according to cake mix package directions. Divide batter between prepared pans, spreading evenly.

3. Sprinkle peaches and cranberries over batter in pans. Sprinkle with wheat bran. In a bowl combine the remaining ingredients; sprinkle over cakes.

4. Bake 38 to 40 minutes or until a toothpick inserted near the centers comes out clean. Cool in pan on a wire rack. Serve warm or at room temperature.

*SUGAR SUBSTITUTE Choose Splenda Sugar Blend. Follow package directions to use product amount equivalent to 1/4 cup.

TO STORE Cover coffee cake and store at room temperature up to 3 days.

PER SERVING: 162 cal., 8 g total fat (1 g sat. fat), 0 mg chol., 185 mg sodium, 27 g carb. (1 g fiber, 7 g sugars), 2 g pro.

PER SERVING WITH SUBSTITUTE: Same as above, except 158 cal., 25 g carb. (6 g sugars).

TEST KITCHEN TIP

If you want fresh orange juice, you will need 3 to 4 large oranges to squeeze 1 cup juice.

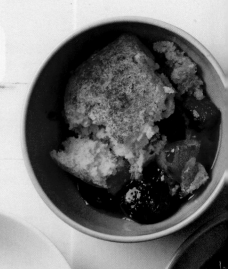

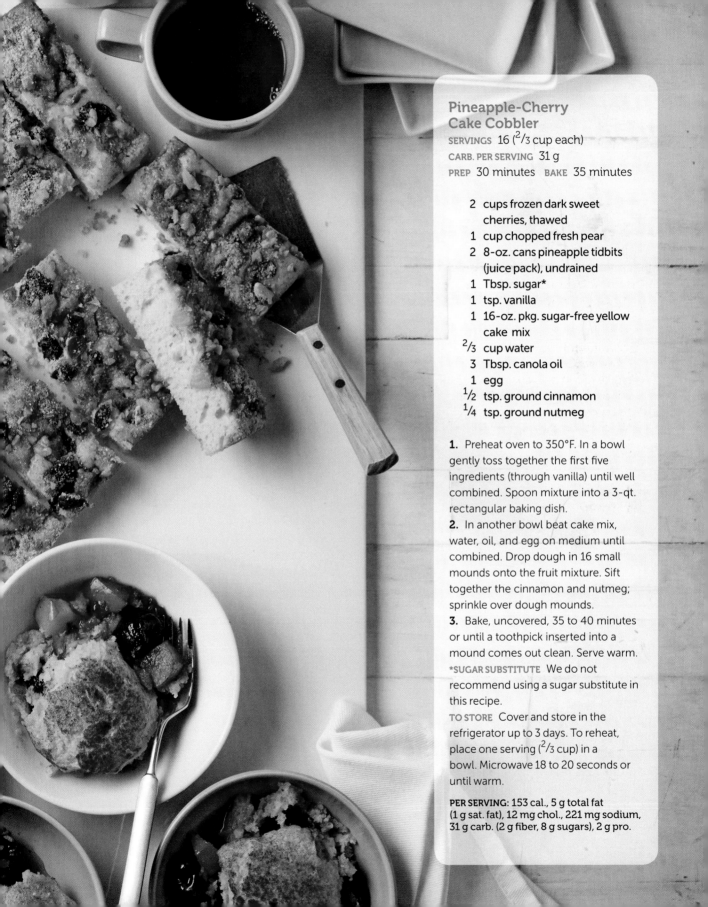

Pineapple-Cherry Cake Cobbler

SERVINGS 16 (^{2}/3 cup each)
CARB. PER SERVING 31 g
PREP 30 minutes   **BAKE** 35 minutes

2	cups frozen dark sweet cherries, thawed
1	cup chopped fresh pear
2	8-oz. cans pineapple tidbits (juice pack), undrained
1	Tbsp. sugar*
1	tsp. vanilla
1	16-oz. pkg. sugar-free yellow cake mix
^{2}/3	cup water
3	Tbsp. canola oil
1	egg
^{1}/2	tsp. ground cinnamon
^{1}/4	tsp. ground nutmeg

1. Preheat oven to 350°F. In a bowl gently toss together the first five ingredients (through vanilla) until well combined. Spoon mixture into a 3-qt. rectangular baking dish.

2. In another bowl beat cake mix, water, oil, and egg on medium until combined. Drop dough in 16 small mounds onto the fruit mixture. Sift together the cinnamon and nutmeg; sprinkle over dough mounds.

3. Bake, uncovered, 35 to 40 minutes or until a toothpick inserted into a mound comes out clean. Serve warm.

*SUGAR SUBSTITUTE We do not recommend using a sugar substitute in this recipe.

TO STORE Cover and store in the refrigerator up to 3 days. To reheat, place one serving (^{2}/3 cup) in a bowl. Microwave 18 to 20 seconds or until warm.

PER SERVING: 153 cal., 5 g total fat (1 g sat. fat), 12 mg chol., 221 mg sodium, 31 g carb. (2 g fiber, 8 g sugars), 2 g pro.

Revamping
SWEET TREATS

You deserve dessert! Replace a few high-fat or carb-laden ingredients in recipes and satisfy your sweet tooth without the guilt.

Blue Raspberry Phyllo Wedges

SERVINGS 12 (1 wedge each)
CARB. PER SERVING 17 g or 15 g
PREP 30 minutes   BAKE 15 minutes

    1 lemon
    8 tsp. granulated sugar*
 1½ tsp. cornstarch
    1 cup fresh raspberries
    1 cup fresh blueberries
       Nonstick cooking spray
  12 14×9-inch sheets phyllo dough,
       thawed
       Nonstick cooking spray
    2 tsp. powdered sugar*

1. Preheat oven to 375°F. Remove ½ tsp. zest and squeeze 1 tsp. juice from lemon. In a small saucepan combine lemon zest, granulated sugar, and cornstarch. Stir in the lemon juice, raspberries, and blueberries. Cook and stir over medium heat until thickened and bubbly. Cook and stir 2 minutes more; cool.

2. Line a large baking sheet with parchment paper or foil. (If using foil, lightly coat with cooking spray.) Lay one phyllo sheet flat on a work surface; coat lightly with cooking spray. (Keep remaining phyllo sheets covered with plastic wrap while assembling wedges.) Top with a second phyllo sheet; coat with cooking spray. Repeat with a third phyllo sheet and cooking spray.

3. Cut the phyllo stack lengthwise into three strips. Place about 1 Tbsp. of the fruit mixture 2 inches from the end of one strip. Diagonally fold the end of the pastry over the filling to make a triangle. Continue folding like a flag to completely enclose the filling and use the entire phyllo strip. Place, seam side down, on the prepared baking sheet. Repeat filling and folding remaining two pastry strips. Repeat with the remaining phyllo sheets and filling, using three phyllo sheets per stack, to make 12 wedges total. Lightly coat tops of wedges with cooking spray.

4. Bake about 15 minutes or until golden brown. Remove; cool slightly on a wire rack. Dust with powdered sugar before serving.

*SUGAR SUBSTITUTES Choose Splenda Sugar Blend. Follow package directions to use product amount equivalent to ⅓ cup granulated sugar. We do not recommend using a sugar substitute for the powdered sugar.

PER SERVING: 85 cal., 1 g total fat (0 g sat. fat), 0 mg chol., 92 mg sodium, 17 g carb. (1 g fiber, 5 g sugars), 2 g pro.

PER SERVING WITH SUBSTITUTE: 81 cal., 15 g carb. (3 g sugars).

THE REVAMP

Instead of traditional fat-filled pastry, use thin **phyllo dough** and coat with **nonstick cooking spray** rather than brushing with butter. Fruit filling adds fiber and vitamins.

237

Chai Carrot Cake with Walnuts

SERVINGS **16** (1 piece each)
CARB. PER SERVING **33 g or 26 g**
PREP **45 minutes**   BAKE **25 minutes**
CHILL **1 hour**

- 2 spiced chai tea bags
- 1½ cups all-purpose flour
- ⅓ cup whole wheat pastry flour or whole wheat flour
- 3 Tbsp. flaxseed meal
- 2 tsp. baking powder
- ½ tsp. baking soda
- ¼ tsp. salt
- 2½ cups finely shredded carrots
- 1 cup refrigerated or frozen egg product, thawed, or 4 eggs, lightly beaten
- ½ cup granulated sugar*
- ½ cup packed brown sugar*
- ½ cup unsweetened applesauce
- ⅓ cup canola oil
- 1 recipe Spicy Cream Cheese Frosting**
- ⅓ cup coarsely chopped walnuts, toasted

1. Preheat oven to 350°F. Grease two 8- or 9-inch round cake pans; line bottoms of the pans with waxed paper. Grease waxed paper; lightly flour pans. Cut tea bags open and pour tea mixture into a spice grinder or mortar; grind to a fine powder.
2. In a bowl stir together ground tea mixture and the next six ingredients (through salt). In another bowl combine the next six ingredients (through oil). Add egg mixture all at once to flour mixture. Stir until combined. Divide batter between prepared pans, spreading evenly.
3. Bake 25 to 30 minutes for 8-inch pans, 20 to 25 minutes for 9-inch pans, or until a toothpick inserted near centers comes out clean. Cool layers in pans 10 minutes. Remove layers from pans; cool on wire racks.
4. Prepare Spicy Cream Cheese Frosting.** Place one cooled cake layer on a serving plate. Top with half of the frosting. Place the second cake layer on another plate; spread with remaining frosting. Chill layers 1 hour. Place second layer on top of layer on the serving plate. Sprinkle with walnuts.

SPICY CREAM CHEESE FROSTING In a small saucepan sprinkle 1 tsp. unflavored gelatin over 2 Tbsp. cold water. Let stand 5 minutes. Stir over medium-low heat until gelatin is dissolved. Remove from heat; stir in ¼ cup honey. Transfer to a bowl. Beat on high 5 to 7 minutes or until mixture lightens and expands to about 1¼ cups. In another bowl beat 4 oz. reduced-fat cream cheese (Neufchâtel), softened, on medium 30 seconds. Gradually beat in ½ cup light sour cream until smooth. Beat in ½ tsp. vanilla and ⅛ tsp. each ground cardamom, ground nutmeg, and ground cinnamon. Fold in about one-fourth of the honey mixture to lighten. Fold in remaining honey mixture.

*SUGAR SUBSTITUTES Choose Splenda Sugar Blend for the granulated sugar. Choose Splenda Brown Sugar Blend for the brown sugar. Follow package directions to use product amounts equivalent to ½ cup each granulated and brown sugars.
**TIP Don't prepare the frosting until you are ready to frost the cake.

PER SERVING: 227 cal., 9 g total fat (2 g sat. fat), 7 mg chol., 209 mg sodium, 33 g carb. (2 g fiber, 19 g sugars), 5 g pro.

PER SERVING WITH SUBSTITUTES: Same as above, except 206 cal., 207 mg sodium, 26 g carb. (12 g sugars).

THE REVAMP

Reduce fat by using **applesauce** for some of the vegetable oil and **egg product** for whole eggs. Increase fiber with **flaxseed meal** and **whole wheat pastry flour**. Reduce calories and sugars by frosting only the middle and top of the cake, not the sides.

Maple-Date Cookies with Cinnamon-Espresso Frosting

SERVINGS 28 (1 cookie each)
CARB. PER SERVING 23 g or 21 g
PREP 30 minutes   BAKE 8 minutes

- $^1/_2$ cup butter, softened
- $^1/_2$ cup packed brown sugar*
- $^1/_2$ tsp. baking soda
-    Dash salt
- $^1/_3$ cup pure maple syrup
- 2 Tbsp. refrigerated or frozen egg product, thawed
- $^1/_2$ tsp. vanilla
- $1^2/_3$ cups all-purpose flour
- $^1/_3$ cup whole wheat pastry flour
- $^1/_3$ cup finely chopped unsweetened pitted dates
- 1 recipe Cinnamon-Espresso Frosting

1. Preheat oven to 350°F. Lightly grease a cookie sheet. In a bowl beat butter on medium to high 30 seconds. Add sugar, baking soda, and salt. Beat until combined, scraping bowl occasionally. Add maple syrup, egg product, and vanilla; beat until combined. Beat in flours. Stir in dates.

2. Drop dough by teaspoons 2 inches apart onto prepared cookie sheet; flatten slightly. Bake 8 to 10 minutes or until edges are light brown. Remove; cool on wire racks. Spread Cinnamon-Espresso Frosting on cooled cookies.

CINNAMON-ESPRESSO FROSTING In a bowl stir together 2 tsp. hot water and 1 tsp. instant espresso coffee powder. Add $^1/_4$ cup butter, cut up and softened; 1 cup powdered sugar;* and $^1/_4$ tsp. ground cinnamon. Beat with a mixer until smooth. Beat in 1 cup additional powdered sugar. Add additional water, $^1/_2$ tsp. at a time, as needed to reach spreading consistency.

*SUGAR SUBSTITUTES Choose Splenda Brown Sugar Blend. Follow package directions to use product amount equivalent to $^1/_2$ cup brown sugar. We do not recommend using a sugar substitute for powdered sugar in the frosting.

PER SERVING: 141 cal., 5 g total fat (3 g sat. fat), 13 mg chol., 73 mg sodium, 23 g carb. (1 g fiber, 16 g sugars), 1 g pro.

PER SERVING WITH SUBSTITUTE: Same as above, except 135 cal., 21 g carb. (14 g sugars).

THE REVAMP

Maple syrup and **dates** give sweetness without processed sugars. Reduce fat and cholesterol with **egg product** instead of whole eggs. **Whole wheat pastry flour** adds fiber.

Chocolate Chip Oatmeal Bars

SERVINGS 24 (1 bar each)
CARB. PER SERVING 20 g or 12 g
PREP 20 minutes   STAND 20 minutes
BAKE 18 minutes

$1/4$ cup water
$1^{1}/2$ tsp. ground chia seeds*
1   cup regular rolled oats
1   cup white whole wheat flour
$1/2$ tsp. salt
$1/2$ tsp. baking powder
$1/2$ tsp. baking soda
$1/4$ cup butter, softened
$3/4$ cup packed brown sugar**
$1/3$ cup granulated sugar**
$1/4$ cup refrigerated or frozen
     egg product, thawed, or 1 egg,
     lightly beaten
1   tsp. vanilla
1   cup semisweet chocolate pieces

1. Preheat oven to 350°F. Line a 13×9-inch baking pan with foil-lined parchment pan-lining paper. In a bowl combine the water and ground chia seeds; let stand 20 minutes.
2. Meanwhile, place $1/2$ cup of the oats in a food processor. Cover and process until finely ground. Add the next four ingredients (through baking soda). Cover and process until combined.
3. In a bowl beat butter and sugars on medium until mixture starts to cling to the sides of the bowl. Beat in egg product, vanilla, and chia mixture until combined. Add the remaining $1/2$ cup oats and the flour mixture, beating on low to medium until combined. Stir in chocolate pieces (dough will be stiff). Spread dough in the prepared pan.
4. Bake 18 to 20 minutes or until edges are golden. Cool in pan on a wire rack. Cut into 24 bars.
*TIP If you have whole chia seeds, grind them using a spice grinder or a mortar and pestle.

**SUGAR SUBSTITUTES Choose Splenda Brown Sugar Blend for the brown sugar. Choose Splenda Sugar Blend for the granulated sugar. Follow package directions to use product amounts equivalent to $3/4$ cup brown sugar and $1/3$ cup granulated sugar.

PER SERVING: 121 cal., 4 g total fat (3 g sat. fat), 5 mg chol., 108 mg sodium, 20 g carb. (1 g fiber, 14 g sugars), 2 g pro.

PER SERVING WITH SUBSTITUTE: Same as above, except 91 cal., 106 mg sodium, 12 g carb. (6 g sugars).

THE REVAMP

Reduce fat and cholesterol by replacing whole eggs with **chia seeds** mixed with water and **egg product**. **White whole wheat flour** has more nutrients and fiber than all-purpose flour.

Raspberry Cheesecake Swirl Brownies

SERVINGS 12 (1 brownie each)
CARB. PER SERVING 28 g
PREP 25 minutes BAKE 50 minutes
CHILL 2 hours

Nonstick cooking spray
½ cup all-purpose flour
½ cup sugar*
½ cup unsweetened cocoa powder
¼ tsp. kosher salt
¼ tsp. baking soda
½ cup plain fat-free Greek yogurt
1 egg
3 Tbsp. fat-free milk
1 tsp. vanilla
1 8-oz. pkg. reduced-fat cream cheese (Neufchâtel), softened
1 cup plain fat-free Greek yogurt
2 eggs
½ cup sugar*
1 tsp. vanilla
½ cup sugar-free red raspberry preserves

1. Preheat oven to 350°F. Coat an 8-inch square baking pan with cooking spray.
2. For brownie layer, in a bowl stir together the next five ingredients (through baking soda). In another bowl whisk together the next four ingredients (through vanilla). Gently fold yogurt mixture into flour mixture just until combined. Spread in the prepared pan.
3. For cheesecake layer, in a bowl whisk together the next five ingredients (through vanilla) until well mixed. Pour over brownie layer in prepared pan.
4. Drop spoonfuls of raspberry preserves over the cheesecake layer. Using a knife or thin metal spatula, swirl preserves into cheesecake layer.
5. Bake 30 minutes. Reduce heat to 325°F. Bake about 20 minutes more or until cheesecake layer is set (center of cheesecake layer should not jiggle). Cool in pan on a wire rack. Cover and chill at least 2 hours before serving. Cut into 12 brownies.

*SUGAR SUBSTITUTE We do not recommend using a sugar substitute for this recipe.

PER SERVING: 183 cal., 6 g total fat (3 g sat. fat), 60 mg chol., 179 mg sodium, 28 g carb. (1 g fiber, 19 g sugars), 7 g pro.

Dessert Transformations

THE REVAMP

Use **fat-free dairy products** (yogurt, cream cheese, and milk) to reduce fat to allow for a generous serving.

Hazelnut Crusted Mascarpone Cheesecake

SERVINGS 16 (1 wedge each)
CARB. PER SERVING 17 g or 12 g
PREP 35 minutes   BAKE 1 hour
COOL 45 minutes + $1^{1}/_{2}$ hours
CHILL 4 hours

- 1 cup finely crushed low-fat graham crackers
- $^{1}/_{4}$ cup coarsely ground toasted hazelnuts*
- $^{1}/_{4}$ tsp. ground allspice
- $^{1}/_{3}$ cup light butter, melted
- 2 8-oz. pkg. fat-free cream cheese, softened
- 1 8-oz. pkg. mascarpone cheese, softened
- $^{2}/_{3}$ cup sugar**
- 3 Tbsp. fat-free milk
- $1^{1}/_{2}$ tsp. vanilla
- 3 egg whites, lightly beaten
- 1 oz. bittersweet or dark chocolate, melted (optional)

1. Preheat oven to 325°F. For crust, in a bowl combine crackers, hazelnuts, and allspice. Stir in butter. Press crumb mixture onto bottom and about 1 inch up sides of an 8-inch springform pan.

2. For filling, in a bowl beat cream cheese on medium until smooth. Beat in the next four ingredients (through vanilla). Add egg whites. Beat on low just until combined (do not overbeat).

3. Pour filling into crust-lined pan. Place on a shallow baking pan. Bake 60 to 70 minutes or until center appears nearly set when gently shaken.

4. Cool in pan on a wire rack 15 minutes. Loosen crust from sides of pan; cool 30 minutes more. Remove sides of pan; cool completely. Cover; chill at least 4 hours before serving.

5. If desired, drizzle cooled cheesecake with melted chocolate and top with *fresh raspberries*.

*TIP To toast hazelnuts, spread nuts in a shallow baking pan. Bake in a 350°F oven 8 to 10 minutes or until toasted, stirring once or twice. Cool slightly. Transfer hazelnuts to a dry kitchen towel. Rub hazelnuts with the towel to remove the papery skins.

**SUGAR SUBSTITUTE Choose Splenda Sugar Blend. Follow package directions to use product amount equivalent to $^{2}/_{3}$ cup sugar. Decrease baking time to 50 to 60 minutes.

PER SERVING: 178 cal., 10 g total fat (5 g sat. fat), 27 mg chol., 278 mg sodium, 17 g carb. (1 g fiber, 11 g sugars), 6 g pro.

PER SERVING WITH SUBSTITUTE: Same as above, except 166 cal., 12 g carb. (7 g sugars).

THE REVAMP

Substitute healthful **nuts** for some of the crackers in the crust. Reduce fat by using **low-fat graham crackers, fat-free cream cheese, light butter, egg whites,** and **fat-free milk.**

Black Tie Cake

SERVINGS 12 (1 wedge each)
CARB. PER SERVING 27 g or 21 g
PREP 25 minutes BAKE 20 minutes
COOL 15 minutes

3/4 cup fat-free milk
1/3 cup unsweetened cocoa
     powder
  2 oz. unsweetened chocolate,
     chopped
     Nonstick cooking spray
2/3 cup all-purpose flour
1/2 cup sugar*
1/2 tsp. baking powder
1/4 tsp. baking soda
1/8 tsp. salt
  3 egg whites, room temperature
1/4 cup sugar*
  1 recipe White Chocolate Mousse
1/2 oz. semisweet chocolate,
     melted
  1 recipe Chocolate-Covered
     Strawberries (optional)

1. In a small saucepan combine milk and cocoa powder. Heat over medium heat, whisking constantly, until mixture just comes to boiling. Remove from heat. Whisk in unsweetened chocolate until smooth. Cool to room temperature.

2. Preheat oven to 350°F. Lightly coat an 8-inch springform pan with cooking spray. In a bowl stir together the next five ingredients (through salt). Stir cooled chocolate mixture into flour mixture until well combined (batter will be thick).

3. Beat egg whites on medium until soft peaks form (tips curl). Gradually add the 1/4 cup sugar, 1 Tbsp. at a time, beating on high until stiff peaks form (tips stand straight). Gently fold one-third of the beaten egg whites into the chocolate mixture to lighten. Fold in the remaining beaten egg whites just until combined. Spread batter in the prepared baking pan.

4. Bake 20 to 25 minutes or until top springs back when lightly touched. Cool in pan 15 minutes. Remove side of pan; cool on a wire rack.

5. Spread White Chocolate Mousse over cooled cake. Drizzle with melted semisweet chocolate; let stand until set. If desired, arrange Chocolate-Covered Strawberries around edge of cake. Chill until ready to serve.

WHITE CHOCOLATE MOUSSE In a small saucepan combine 2 oz. white baking chocolate with cocoa butter, chopped; 1/4 cup light tub-style cream cheese; and 1 Tbsp. fat-free milk. Cook and stir over low heat until melted and smooth. Remove from heat. Stir in 1/4 cup frozen light whipped dessert topping, thawed, until smooth. Transfer to a bowl; cool for 5 minutes. Fold in 1 1/4 cups additional dessert topping. Chill 1 hour before frosting cake.

CHOCOLATE-COVERED STRAWBERRIES Microwave 1 1/2 oz. chopped semisweet chocolate on 50% power (medium) 1 minute; stir. Microwave on 50% power 30 to 60 seconds more or until melted and smooth, stirring once or twice. Dip 12 small fresh strawberries, tops on, halfway into the melted chocolate. Spread chocolate to a thin layer on the strawberries and scrape off any excess. Place on a baking sheet lined with waxed paper. Let stand until chocolate is set.

*SUGAR SUBSTITUTE Choose Splenda Sugar Blend. Follow package directions to use product amounts equivalent to 1/2 cup and 1/4 cup sugar.

PER SERVING: 171 cal., 6 g total fat (4 g sat. fat), 4 mg chol., 113 mg sodium, 27 g carb. (2 g fiber, 17 g sugars), 4 g pro.

PER SERVING WITH SUBSTITUTE: Same as above, except 152 cal., 21 g carb. (11 g sugars).

THE REVAMP

Control portions by making a single-layer cake. Cut back on fat with **fat-free milk, egg whites** instead of whole eggs, **light cream cheese,** and **light whipped topping.**

Test Kitchen

See how we calculate nutrition information to help you count calories, carbs, and serving sizes.

⟨ High-Standards Testing

This seal assures you every recipe in *Diabetic Living® Healthy Makeovers for Diabetes™* has been tested in the Better Homes and Gardens® Test Kitchen. This means each recipe is practical, reliable, and meets our high standards of taste appeal.

Inside Our Recipes

Precise serving sizes (listed below each recipe title) help you to manage portions. Test Kitchen tips and sugar substitutes are listed after recipe directions. Kitchen basics such as ice, salt, black pepper, and nonstick cooking spray often are not listed in the ingredients list; they are italicized in the directions.

Ingredients
• Tub-style vegetable oil spread refers to 60% to 70% vegetable oil product.
• Lean ground beef refers to 95% or leaner.

Nutrition Information

Nutrition facts per serving are noted with each recipe. Ingredients listed as optional are not included in the nutrition analysis. When ingredient choices appear, we use the first one to calculate the nutrition analysis.

Key to Abbreviations

cal. = calories
sat. fat = saturated fat
chol. = cholesterol

carb. = carbohydrate
pro. = protein

RECIPE INDEX

METRIC INFORMATION

product differences ────────○

Most of the ingredients called for in the recipes in this book are available in most countries. However, some are known by different names. Here are some common American ingredients and their possible counterparts:

○ Sugar (white) is granulated, fine granulated, or castor sugar.

○ Powdered sugar is icing sugar.

○ All-purpose flour is enriched, bleached or unbleached white household flour. When self-rising flour is used in place of all-purpose flour in a recipe that calls for leavening, omit the leavening agent (baking soda or baking powder) and salt.

○ Light-color corn syrup is golden syrup.

○ Cornstarch is cornflour.

○ Baking soda is bicarbonate of soda.

○ Vanilla or vanilla extract is vanilla essence.

○ Green, red, or yellow sweet peppers are capsicums or bell peppers.

○ Golden raisins are sultanas.

volume & weight ────────○

The United States traditionally uses cup measures for liquid and solid ingredients. The chart below shows the approximate imperial and metric equivalents. If you are accustomed to weighing solid ingredients, the following approximate equivalents will be helpful.

○ 1 cup butter, castor sugar, or rice = 8 ounces = ½ pound = 250 grams

○ 1 cup flour = 4 ounces = ¼ pound = 125 grams

○ 1 cup icing sugar = 5 ounces = 150 grams

○ Canadian and U.S. volume for a cup measure is 8 fluid ounces (237 ml), but the standard metric equivalent is 250 ml.

○ 1 British imperial cup is 10 fluid ounces.

○ In Australia, 1 tablespoon equals 20 ml, and there are 4 teaspoons in the Australian tablespoon.

○ Spoon measures are used for smaller amounts of ingredients. Although the size of the tablespoon varies slightly in different countries, for practical purposes and for recipes in this book, a straight substitution is all that's necessary. Measurements made using cups or spoons always should be level unless stated otherwise.

Common Weight Range Replacements

Imperial / U.S.	Metric
½ ounce	15 g
1 ounce	25 g or 30 g
4 ounces (¼ pound)	115 g or 125 g
8 ounces (½ pound)	225 g or 250 g
16 ounces (1 pound)	450 g or 500 g
1¼ pounds	625 g
1½ pounds	750 g
2 pounds or 2¼ pounds	1,000 g or 1 Kg

Oven Temperature Equivalents

Fahrenheit Setting		Gas Setting
300°F	150°C	Gas Mark 2 (very low)
325°F	160°C	Gas Mark 3 (low)
350°F	180°C	Gas Mark 4 (moderate)
375°F	190°C	Gas Mark 5 (moderate)
400°F	200°C	Gas Mark 6 (hot)
425°F	220°C	Gas Mark 7 (hot)
450°F	230°C	Gas Mark 8 (very hot)
475°F	240°C	Gas Mark 9 (very hot)
500°F	260°C	Gas Mark 10 (extremely hot)
Broil	Broil	Grill

Electric and gas ovens may be calibrated using celsius. However, for an electric oven, increase celsius setting 10 to 20 degrees when cooking above 160°C. For convection or forced air ovens (gas or electric), lower the temperature setting 25°F/10°C when cooking at all heat levels.

Baking Pan Sizes

Imperial / U.S.	Metric
9x1½-inch round cake pan	22- or 23x4-cm (1.5 L)
9x1½-inch pie plate	22- or 23x4-cm (1 L)
8x8x2-inch square cake pan	20x5-cm (2 L)
9x9x2-inch square cake pan	22- or 23x4.5-cm (2.5 L)
11x7x1½-inch baking pan	28x17x4-cm (2 L)
2-quart rectangular baking pan	30x19x4.5-cm (3 L)
13x9x2-inch baking pan	34x22x4.5-cm (3.5 L)
15x10x1-inch jelly roll pan	40x25x2-cm
9x5x3-inch loaf pan	23x13x8-cm (2 L)
2-quart casserole	2 L

U.S. / Standard Metric Equivalents

⅛ teaspoon = 0.5 ml	
¼ teaspoon = 1 ml	
½ teaspoon = 2 ml	
1 teaspoon = 5 ml	
1 tablespoon = 15 ml	
2 tablespoons = 25 ml	
¼ cup = 2 fluid ounces = 50 ml	
⅓ cup = 3 fluid ounces = 75 ml	
½ cup = 4 fluid ounces = 125 ml	
⅔ cup = 5 fluid ounces = 150 ml	
¾ cup = 6 fluid ounces = 175 ml	
1 cup = 8 fluid ounces = 250 ml	
2 cups = 1 pint = 500 ml	
1 quart = 1 litre	